Microsoft®
Windows® Server 2003

SAMS

201 W. 103rd Street
Indianapolis, IN 46290

Don Jones and Mark Rouse

DELTA GUIDE

Microsoft® Windows® Server 2003 Delta Guide

Copyright © 2003 by Sams Publishing

All rights reserved. No part of this book shall be reproduced, stored in a retrieval system, or transmitted by any means, electronic, mechanical, photocopying, recording, or otherwise, without written permission from the publisher. No patent liability is assumed with respect to the use of the information contained herein. Although every precaution has been taken in the preparation of this book, the publisher and authors assume no responsibility for errors or omissions. Nor is any liability assumed for damages resulting from the use of the information contained herein.

International Standard Book Number: 0-7897-2849-4

Library of Congress Catalog Card Number: 2002113851

Printed in the United States of America

First Printing: March 2003

06 05 04 03   4 3 2

Trademarks

All terms mentioned in this book that are known to be trademarks or service marks have been appropriately capitalized. Sams Publishing cannot attest to the accuracy of this information. Use of a term in this book should not be regarded as affecting the validity of any trademark or service mark.

Windows is a registered trademark of Microsoft Corporation.

Microsoft is a registered trademark of Microsoft Corporation.

Warning and Disclaimer

Every effort has been made to make this book as complete and as accurate as possible, but no warranty or fitness is implied. The information provided is on an "as is" basis. The authors and the publisher shall have neither liability nor responsibility to any person or entity with respect to any loss or damages arising from the information contained in this book.

Associate Publisher
Michael Stephens

Series Editor
Don Jones

Acquisitions Editor
Loretta Yates

Development Editor
Laura Norman

Managing Editor
Charlotte Clapp

Project Editor
Tonya Simpson

Production Editor
Megan Wade

Indexer
Ken Johnson

Proofreader
Carla Lewis

Technical Editor
Peter Bruzzese

Team Coordinator
Cindy Teeters

Interior Designer
Anne Jones

Cover Designer
Gary Adair

Page Layout
Kelly Maish

About the Authors

Don Jones is a founding partner of BrainCore.Net, one of the world's leading companies dedicated to technical certification and assessment technologies and development. Don is the author of nearly a dozen computer books. He has more than two decades of experience with computers, ranging from his first Commodore PET computer to more than eight years as a network engineer, architect, and consultant. Don is a regular contributor to industry technical publications; is a contributing editor for *MCP Magazine*; and can be found speaking at some of the world's leading technical conferences, including MCP TechMentor. Don can be reached through the BrainCore.Net Web site at www.braincore.net.

Mark Rouse (MCSE, MCDBA, MCSA, MCT, Compaq ASE) is a trainer and senior consultant for a Microsoft Certified Solution Provider and Certified Technical Education Center. As a former systems administrator, Mark has more than 10 years experience with designing and implementing network solutions. Mark has contributed to a number of technical publications and has been involved with the development of MCP exams as a Subject Matter Expert for Microsoft.

Dedication

This book is dedicated to Kelly Wilcox (not to mention the Beatles, Uranus, the Odyssey One, Freddy, Commodore, Star Trek, and Atari). Thanks for your friendship and imagination.—Don

To Elizabeth, who makes everything worthwhile.—Mark

Acknowledgments

No book is written by one or two people; a huge number of folks worked behind the scenes to make this a possibility. The authors would like to thank Loretta Yates, the acquisitions editor at Sams who championed this book and this brand-new series. We'd also like to thank our development editor, Laura Norman, and our production editor, Megan Wade, who helped ensure this book was well-organized, informative, and readable. It's sometimes difficult to realize how important these editors are to a book's production, and these folks have put an incredible amount of effort into this new series. We'd also like to thank our technical editor, J. Peter Bruzzese, for taking the time to make sure we were as accurate as possible when writing about a product that wasn't itself completely finished. And finally, we'd like to thank everyone at our literary agency, Studio B, especially Neil Salkind, for all the hard work that went into making both this book and this series a reality.

Don would like to offer special thanks to Chris, for putting up with yet another lengthy writing project, and to my business partners at BrainCore.Net, Jeremy Moskowitz and Derek Melber. You guys were great at understanding my need to meet my deadlines, even if that made the company's business a little bit harder to accomplish on time. I'd also like to thank my coauthor, Mark Rouse, who did a fantastic job at balancing a job, a family, and a life to get his portion of the book done accurately, and as well-written as I've ever seen. I'd like to thank my good friend Mike Danseglio at Microsoft, who was always able to offer an explanation when something in the product didn't quite make sense at first. Finally, I'd like to offer thanks to two product groups at Microsoft: The Windows product group, of course, for continuing to produce great software that meets their customers' needs, and the product group that produced my Microsoft Office keyboard, which has now survived through an unprecedented six books.

Mark would especially like to thank his wife, Mary, for her encouragement and understanding. Thank you for enduring the long hours when it must have seemed like I disappeared. I would like to extend special thanks to our acquisitions editor, Loretta Yates, for her patience and flexibility. I would also like to thank my coauthor Don Jones for getting me involved in this project and constantly challenging me to extend my limits.

Contents at a Glance

    Introduction **1**

1 Introduction to the Windows Server 2003 Family **3**

2 Installation and Deployment **15**

3 Interface Changes **31**

4 Security **45**

5 Active Directory **65**

6 Group Policy Changes **81**

7 Internet Information Services **101**

8 Network Services **125**

9 Web Development **145**

10 Networking, Remote Access, and Communications **159**

11 Terminal Services **179**

12 Clustering **199**

13 Management **215**

14 Maintenance **231**

15 64-bit Windows **253**

    Index **263**

Contents

Introduction 1
  Who Should Read This Book 1
  How to Use This Book 2

1 Introduction to the Windows Server 2003 Family 3
  Microsoft's Newest Operating System 3
  Windows Server 2003 Family 4
  Selecting an Edition 5
    Windows Server 2003, Standard Edition 6
    Windows Server 2003, Enterprise Edition 7
    Windows Server 2003, Datacenter Edition 8
    Windows Server 2003, Web Edition 10
  Product Activation and Volume Licensing 11
    How Windows Server 2003 Is Licensed 11
    Microsoft Licensing Programs 11
    Activating Windows 13

2 Installation and Deployment 15
  What's New 15
  Installation Changes 16
    Attended Installations 16
    Emergency Management Services Installation 20
    Unattended Installations 20
    Image Downloads 23
    Windows Product Activation 23
  Server RIS 26
    Installing RIS 26
    Configuring RIS 27
  Upgrading from Prior Versions 27
    Supported Upgrade Paths 28
    Mass Upgrades 30

3 Interface Changes 31
  What's New 31
  User Interface Themes 32

Compressed Folders **32**
    NTFS Folder Compression **32**
    Compressed (Zipped) Folders Feature **33**
CD Burning **34**
Remote Desktop and Remote Assistance **37**
    Remote Desktop **37**
    Remote Assistance **37**
Other Interface Changes **40**
    The Desktop **40**
    The Start Menu **41**

4 Security 45
What's New **45**
Microsoft's New Security Philosophy **46**
Security Tools **47**
    Security Configuration Manager **48**
    Security Templates, Configuration, and Analysis **48**
    Hfnetchk.exe **56**
Encrypting Data **56**
Common Security Holes **57**
    DNS **58**
    Dynamic Host Configuration Protocol **58**
    Network Monitor **59**
    Internet Information System **61**
Developing a Security Strategy **62**
    Auditing **62**
    Security Maintenance **63**

5 Active Directory 65
What's New **65**
Active Directory Functional Levels **66**
Tools and Utilities **68**
Administration **69**
    Administrative Tool Enhancements **69**
    Saved Queries **70**

       Resultant Set of Policy   70
       Domain and Domain Controller Rename   73
  Architecture   74
       Partitioning   74
       Schema Deactivation   74
       Replication Improvements   75
  Security   76
  Operations   77
       Active Directory Application Mode   77
       Updating Logon Times   78
       Remote Office Logons   78
       Replication from Media   78

6   Group Policy Changes   81
  What's New   81
  General Group Policy Changes   82
       WMI Filtering   82
       Cross-Forest Support   83
       Software Deployment   84
  Group Policy Management User Interface   86
       Group Policy Object Editor   86
       Resultant Set of Policy   87
       Group Policy Management Console   92
  New Group Policies   93
       New Computer Configuration Policy Sections   94
       New User Configuration Policies Sections   98

7   Internet Information Services   101
  What's New   101
  IIS: Not Installed by Default   103
  Architecture and Memory Management   104
       Putting It All Together   105
       Worker Process Isolation   106
       Backward Compatibility   107

Administrative Changes   108
   Configuring Server and Web Site Options   108
   Configuring Application Pools   109
   Configuring Web Services Extensions   112
   Web-Based Administration   114
Security Enhancements   117
Migrating from IIS 5 to 6   118
Metabase and Management Enhancements   119
The POP3 and SMTP Services   120

8 Network Services   125
What's New   125
WINS, DHCP, and DNS   126
   WINS   126
   DHCP   128
   DNS   129
Fax Sharing   132
   Faxing the Windows 2000 Way   132
   Faxing the Windows Server 2003 Way   133
File Sharing   135
Distributed File System   137
   New DFS Features   138
Network Attached Storage and Storage Area Network Management   139
   Too Many Acronyms   139
   Windows Server 2003 Improvements for NAS and SAN   140
Encrypting File System   141
   EFS Implementation   141
   Storing Encrypted Files Remotely   141
WebDAV and Remote Sharing   142

9 Web Development   145
What's New   145
The .NET Framework   146
   Managing the Assembly Cache   150
   Managing Configured Assemblies   151

      Managing the Runtime Security Policy   **152**
      Managing Remoting Services   **154**
      Managing Individual Applications   **154**
  Web Services Support   **154**
  Other Development Platform Enhancements   **156**

10 Networking, Remote Access, and Communications   **159**
  What's New   **159**
  IPv6 Overview   **160**
      IPv6 Tutorial   **161**
      IPv6 in Windows Server 2003   **163**
  IPSec Improvements   **164**
      New Tools   **166**
  Universal Plug and Play Support   **168**
  New Networking Services   **169**
  RRAS Enhancements   **170**
  Other Networking and Communications Improvements   **174**
      Network Location Awareness   **175**
      New Group Policies   **175**
      Native Support for PPPoE   **175**
      Network Bridging   **175**
      IEEE-1394 (FireWire) Support   **175**
      Automatic Network Configuration   **176**
      A New Netstat Tool   **176**
      Native Support for xDSL   **177**
      Wireless Improvements   **177**
      Missing Protocols   **177**

11 Terminal Services   **179**
  What's New   **179**
  Terminal Services Overview   **180**
  Remote Desktop for Administration   **180**
      Windows 2000 Remote Administration Mode   **181**
      Windows Server 2003 Terminal Services Modes   **181**
      New Client(s)   **183**
      New Administration   **186**

      Remote Desktop Protocol 5.1   **190**
          Local Resource Redirection   **190**
          Is RDP Ready for Prime Time?   **192**
      Security Enhancements   **193**
      Terminal Server Session Directory   **194**
          The Problem with Clustering Terminal Servers   **194**
          The Solution   **195**
          Terminal Server IP Address Redirection   **197**

12 Clustering **199**

      What's New   **199**
      Clustering Terminology   **200**
      Cluster Service   **201**
          Cluster Service Concepts   **202**
          Creating a New Cluster   **203**
          Cluster Administrator   **204**
      Network Load Balancing   **207**
          NLB Concepts   **207**
          Creating a New NLB Cluster   **208**
          Configuring NLB Port Rules and Affinity   **211**
          Using NLB Manager   **212**
      Clusterable Services   **213**

13 Management **215**

      What's New   **215**
      General Management Changes   **216**
          Security Templates   **216**
          Software Restrictions   **218**
          Software Deployment   **220**
      Headless Servers   **220**
          Headless Hardware   **221**
          Headless Software   **223**
      New Command-Line Tools   **225**
          WMI Command-Line Tool   **225**
          Other New Command-Line Tools   **227**

14 Maintenance 231
What's New 231
Hotfix and Service Packs Management 232
- *Software Update Services* 233
- *Managing and Monitoring Updates* 242
- *Inventorying Updates* 243

Administrative Scripting 246
Backup and Restore 249
Automated System Recovery 250
- *ASR Backup* 251
- *ASR Restore* 251

15 64-bit Windows 253
What's New 253
64-bit Overview 254
64-bit Architecture 255
- *Partition Management* 255
- *Boot Architecture* 257

32-bit Windows Compatibility 258
- *Software Compatibility* 258
- *Hardware Compatibility* 259

Significant Differences 259

Index 263

Foreword

Windows Server 2003 will be the fifth version of Windows NT—as the operating system used to be called—that I've had to learn to use. Looking back to the first version I used, Windows NT Advanced Server 3.1, I can see that the product has come a long way! In fact, there are almost no similarities between the new version and its ancient ancestor. But looking back to the most recent version, Windows 2000 Server, reveals a less drastic evolution. Sure, there's a lot of new functionality, and some menu options have changed, and so forth, but there's still a lot that's shared between Windows Server 2003 and Windows 2000 Server.

That commonality has always been something that has bugged me when I set out to learn a new version of Windows, or any other product. Bookstore shelves are always full of books promising to teach me the new version in a few days or purporting to be the most complete reference available on the new product. That's great, but all those books assume I know nothing about Windows, which isn't the case: I know plenty about the previous version. What I've always wanted is a book that will just tell me what's new in the latest version of Windows, allowing me to build on my skills with the prior version, rather than requiring me to start from scratch. I often speak at technical conferences, and the most popular sessions I do are "What's New" lectures that cover the differences in a product. My audience is usually quite familiar with the prior version of the product and just wants to know what has changed and how it will affect them. Why can't there be a book that does the same thing?

That's what this book—and indeed, this entire series—is all about. Instead of picking up another $50 book that assumes you know nothing, this relatively slim volume builds on your Windows 2000 Server knowledge and helps you become an expert on Windows Server 2003. Everything in this book is focused on helping you learn what's new in Windows Server 2003, how it will affect you and your environment, and how you can leverage new capabilities to make your job easier and your network more efficient and productive. This book doesn't teach you the basics of TCP/IP, and you won't have to wade through a discussion on how the Microsoft Management Console works: You're assumed to know all that based on your work with Windows 2000 Server.

On the other hand, this book isn't just a list of features, either. Any Microsoft sales drone can provide you with such a list, if that's all you need. This book is designed to show you how new features operate, how to design them into your network, and how to work around any new weaknesses or incomplete features that might have cropped up. In short, this book is your shortcut to Windows Server 2003, and it will save you the time of starting from scratch, like I've always had to do when a new version of Windows has come out.

So, what if you're not already a Windows 2000 guru? Maybe you've used Windows 2000 Server a lot, but you've never bothered to play with Certificate Services, or perhaps you've only glanced at Internet Information Services (IIS). Don't worry because this book doesn't leave you out in the cold. Plenty of additional material exists in the form of online sidebars and is referenced within the text of this book. These online sidebars provide background information to help bring you up to speed, so that the information in this book is still helpful. Practically speaking, then, this book is ideal for anyone with a year or more of experience with Windows 2000 Server. If there's a particular topic, such as IIS or Certificate Services, that you're a little behind on, those online sidebars will give you all the information you need to use this book effectively. We'll also keep the Web site updated with additional online information, errata, and other material, as necessary—so be sure to check it out!

Future titles in this series will have the same mission, acting as your shortcut for products such as Exchange Server, SQL Server, and a variety of others. All these products will have new versions coming out soon, and if you're already using the current version, this series will offer the shortcut you're looking for. Some of these books will be written by authors you already know, whereas others will be written by new authors that share my vision for this series. Throughout each book, I'll be making sure that we're not wasting your time with old information and that each title helps you learn the new version of that particular product as quickly as possible. If you have a suggestion for a title that would make your life easier, feel free to contact me through my Web site at www.braincore.net.

So, what are you waiting for? Dive in and start becoming a Windows Server 2003 expert!

Don Jones

Series Editor and founding partner of BrainCore.Net, LLC

We Want to Hear from You!

As the reader of this book, *you* are our most important critic and commentator. We value your opinion and want to know what we're doing right, what we could do better, what areas you'd like to see us publish in, and any other words of wisdom you're willing to pass our way.

As an associate publisher for Sams, I welcome your comments. You can email or write me directly to let me know what you did or didn't like about this book—as well as what we can do to make our books better.

Please note that I cannot help you with technical problems related to the *topic* of this book. We do have a User Services group, however, where I will forward specific technical questions related to the book.

When you write, please be sure to include this book's title and author as well as your name, email address, and phone number. I will carefully review your comments and share them with the author and editors who worked on the book.

Email: feedback@samspublishing.com

Mail: Michael Stephens
Sams Publishing
201 West 103rd Street
Indianapolis, IN 46290 USA

For more information about this book or another Sams title, visit our Web site at www.samspublishing.com. Type the ISBN (excluding hyphens) or the title of a book in the Search field to find the page you're looking for.

INTRODUCTION

Who Should Read This Book

If you've never used a prior version of Windows Server, stop right here: This book probably isn't for you. We won't be covering the basic concepts for technologies such as TCP/IP, nor will we be providing detailed tutorials on installing Windows, or any other basic topics. This book was designed with the experienced Windows 2000 Server (or Windows NT Server) administrator in mind. We've written every word to leverage your experience with Windows 2000 Server, and we'll be making many comparisons between Windows 2000 Server and Windows Server 2003. Our goal is to simply "add on" to your knowledge, helping you understand the differences between Windows 2000 Server and Windows Server 2003 and how to take advantage of those differences.

If you've used Windows 2000 Server but don't consider yourself an expert, this book is still for you. We've provided ample background information in the form of online sidebars, which we'll reference from within the text. These sidebars provide all the information you need to understand advanced topics such as Certificate Services, while keeping the main body of the text focused firmly on what's new in Windows Server. Windows NT administrators should find the sidebars especially useful because they'll help bridge the gap between Windows NT and Windows Server 2003.

How to Use This Book

Each chapter of this book focuses on a specific area of Windows Server 2003: Internet Information Services, security, Active Directory, and so forth. Use the Table of Contents to flip right to the section you need to learn first, or just start with Chapter 1, "Introduction to the Windows Server 2003 Family," and read the book straight through to learn all there is to know about what's new in Windows Server 2003.

Throughout the book, you'll find a number of special elements designed to increase your understanding of this new product:

Note | These notes are designed to call your attention to information that's particularly important. We'll use these notes to highlight often-overlooked facts, interesting features, and other important information.

Caution | We'll use these cautions to alert you to potentially damaging actions and to give you some advice for avoiding a potential disaster. We'll also use these cautions to highlight places where the product doesn't work quite like you think it might, so that you can avoid any unpleasant surprises that can damage your network or cause a security vulnerability.

Tip | Tips will provide extra real-world information that will help you use Windows Server more effectively. These tips generally come from our experience with the product, and they're our way of passing on hard-earned lessons and saving you time.

These elements will refer you to additional online sidebars for background information or more in-depth coverage of basic concepts and other topics. We'll refer to the online material by an ID number, such as **A010101**. Visit www.samspublishing.com and enter this book's ISBN number (no hyphens or parentheses) in the Search field; then click the book's cover image to access the book details page. Click the Web Resources link in the More Information section, and locate the article's ID number.

➤ We'll use cross-references to refer you to relevant material elsewhere in this book. For example, to begin reading this book, **see** Chapter 1, **p. 3**.

We'll also use some special typefaces in this book to highlight particular pieces of information. We'll *italicize* new terms when we define them, so that you can more easily locate those terms later if you need to remember exactly what they mean. Whenever we tell you to type something, we'll list it in a bold, monospaced font: Type **ipconfig** at a command-line prompt. We'll also boldface user interface elements when we refer to them, such as asking you to select **Open** from the **File** menu, or to click the **OK** button on a dialog box.

1

INTRODUCTION TO THE WINDOWS SERVER 2003 FAMILY

In This Chapter

- Selecting the appropriate Windows Server 2003 edition, **page 5**.
- Finding a licensing program that fits your needs, **page 11**.
- Activating Windows Server 2003, **page 13**.

Microsoft's Newest Operating System

Windows Server 2003 is the latest in Microsoft's line of server operating systems and is based on the Windows NT and Windows 2000 platforms. Version-wise, Windows Server 2003 is roughly equivalent to Windows XP. In fact, both Windows Server 2003 and Windows XP were originally code-named Whistler; Microsoft released the desktop operating system first as Windows XP and spent some additional time refining the server-specific features included only in Windows Server 2003.

> **Note** If you're familiar with Windows XP, many of Windows Server 2003's new features (such as CD burning) will be familiar to you because they were first included in Windows XP. For performance reasons, however, Windows Server 2003 lacks Windows XP's new user interface design, so the two seem much more different than they really are.

One of the biggest questions on your mind is probably, "How different is Windows Server 2003 from Windows 2000 Server?" After all, Windows 2000 was a major change from the previous version—Windows NT Server 4.0. Windows Server 2003 is definitely a major change over Windows 2000 in terms of functionality, but it isn't as big a change as Windows 2000 was when it was first introduced. Instead, Windows Server 2003 builds on Windows 2000's features with several improvements. What makes Windows Server 2003 such a major change is that it builds on almost every one of Windows 2000's features; all those relatively minor changes add up to a major new operating system.

Windows Server 2003 also introduces an entirely new edition of the operating system: Windows Server 2003, Web Edition. The addition of Web Edition to the product line changes the way administrators must architect new servers, especially in a Web services or Web server environment. Windows Server 2003 also includes Microsoft's first 64-bit server operating system editions, providing additional architectural flexibility for administrators in high-demand, enterprise environments.

Windows Server 2003 Family

The Windows Server 2003 family consist of four distinct products:

- **Windows Server 2003, Standard Edition**—The basic edition, replacing Windows 2000 Server.
- **Windows Server 2003, Enterprise Edition**—The upscale edition with additional processor and memory support, clustering, and so forth. This edition replaced Windows 2000 Advanced Server.
- **Windows Server 2003, Datacenter Edition**—Replaced Windows 2000 Datacenter Server as the top-end version of Windows.
- **Windows Server 2003, Web Edition**—An entirely new edition, intended to compete with low-priced (and free) Web server operating systems such as Linux.

Although you can think of these editions in a tier, with Windows Server 2003, Web Edition at the bottom and Windows Server 2003, Datacenter Edition at the top, that's not really how Microsoft positions the products. True, Web Edition has less functionality than Datacenter Edition, but that's because Web Edition is designed for an entirely different purpose. Experienced Windows administrators often classify the server editions as "use the standard edition unless you need clustering, then use the advanced edition." Datacenter isn't usually considered by most administrators (for reasons we'll discuss later in this chapter), and Web

Edition, of course, is an entirely new thing to deal with. Unfortunately, the "use standard unless you need clustering" doesn't really leverage the various editions' advantages very well, especially with Windows Server 2003, where the editions have definite advantages in different scenarios. So, as a Windows Server 2003 administrator, it is important that you choose the right edition of the product to meet your organization's needs.

Selecting an Edition

So, which edition is right for your needs? Standard, Enterprise, Datacenter, or Web? Deciding can be difficult because each offers specific advantages for specific applications. In the next four sections, you'll be introduced to the exact feature set provided by each edition and be provided with some recommendations for how each one can be best utilized.

> **Note** To help make this book easier to read, we'll use "Windows Server 2003" to refer to the entire family of server operating systems. We'll use shortened names of specific editions, such as "Web Edition," "Standard Edition," and so forth, to refer to those individual editions. Whenever we're making a comparison to a prior version of Windows, we'll use the full product name, such as "Windows Server 2003, Standard Edition," to help distinguish between the different versions and editions.

If you're installing new servers, selecting the right edition of Windows Server 2003 is all you need to do, and most server manufacturers will be able to sell you a server with the correct version preinstalled. However, you'll probably be upgrading a fair number of servers from previous editions of Windows, so you'll need to play close attention to edition features and compatibility to select the appropriate version for your upgrades.

> To compare Windows Server 2003 editions to previous editions of Windows or to review the differences between Windows NT and Windows 2000 editions, visit www.samspublishing.com and enter this book's ISBN number (no hyphens or parentheses) in the Search field; then click the book's cover image to access the book details page. Click the Web Resources link in the More Information section, and locate article ID# **A010101**.

The information in the next four sections applies only to 32-bit versions of Windows Server 2003; 64-bit versions, written for Intel's Itanium processor family, have slightly different capabilities and limitations. Note that not all editions of Windows Server 2003 are available for the Itanium family.

> ➤ For more details on the 64-bit editions of Windows Server 2003 and how they differ from their 32-bit counterparts, **see** "Significant Differences," **p. 259**.

Windows Server 2003, Standard Edition

Standard Edition is the basic edition of Windows Server 2003 and is the one you'll likely use the most. It's suited to the broadest range of applications, particularly file serving, print serving, and low-demand application serving. Standard Edition supports a maximum of 4GB of server RAM, 4TB of disk space, and up to four processors.

Standard Edition supports the entire basic set of Windows Server 2003 features. It can act as a domain controller, public key infrastructure (PKI) server, and so forth. It does not offer clustering capabilities, aside from Network Load Balancing (NLB), which is included with all editions of Windows Server 2003.

> For information on NLB and its capabilities, **see** "Network Load Balancing," **p. 207**.

Standard Edition cannot host Microsoft Metadirectory Services (MMS), a technology used to integrate multiple directory services, such as Active Directory, Novell Directory Services (NDS), and so forth. Standard Edition also lacks support for advanced scalability features, including the capability to add memory to a server while it's running, non-uniform memory access, and so on. Standard Edition does, however, include Terminal Services, but it does not support the Terminal Server Session Directory—a feature that allows users to easily reconnect a disconnected Terminal Services session hosted by a farm of Terminal Services computers.

Where is Standard Edition best used? In a broad variety of applications:

- **As a file server**—However, for critical files, you might want to use a server cluster capable of failover to ensure the constant availability of those files. Standard Edition doesn't support clustering.
- **As a print server**—As with files, mission-critical printing might be better hosted on a server cluster that supports failover, and Standard Server doesn't offer that option.
- **As an application server for applications such as Exchange Server or SQL Server**—However, environments with heavy application server usage, or environments that rely heavily on the services of these applications, might be better off on a cluster (for reliability) and Windows Server 2003, Enterprise Edition (for better memory support).
- **As a Web server**—However, Windows Server 2003, Web Edition might offer a less expensive alternative, particularly if your Web servers are typical in their feature requirements and don't need to be a domain controller or play another role that Web Edition doesn't support.
- **As a domain controller**—This is an ideal role for Standard Edition in any situation; although you can host domain controllers on clusters, the distributive nature of Active Directory makes doing so redundant, so Standard Edition offers all the features you need.

- **As a network services server**—For example, as a domain name service (DNS) or Dynamic Host Configuration Protocol (DHCP) server. Generally, these functions are not hosted on a cluster, making Standard Edition the perfect platform.

Standard Edition is especially ideal as an all-purpose platform for smaller environments, where advanced features like clustering or large memory support aren't required.

Windows Server 2003, Enterprise Edition

Windows Server 2003, Enterprise Edition fills many of the same roles as Standard Edition and adds features primarily geared toward improving reliability and scalability. Enterprise Edition supports a maximum of eight processors, which is double Standard Edition's capability. Enterprise Edition also supports Address Windows Extensions (AWE), providing an extra gigabyte of memory to applications by reserving only 1GB for Windows, rather than Standard Edition's 2GB/2GB split between the operating system and applications.

Enterprise Edition also supports Windows Clustering, allowing you to build failover clusters with two nodes. The Cluster Service allows you to create clustered file shares and clustered printers and supports clustered applications, such as SQL Server Enterprise Edition and Exchange Server Enterprise Edition. The Cluster Service even enables you to cluster applications that aren't specifically designed for clustering, provided they meet certain criteria spelled out in the Windows online documentation.

Enterprise Edition can also host Microsoft Metadirectory Services (MMS), allowing large organizations to integrate multiple heterogeneous directories.

Enterprise Edition ups the ante for scalability and reliability, as well. Enterprise Edition is available in a 64-bit edition for Intel's Itanium family of 64-bit processors. With the proper server hardware support, Enterprise Edition also supports *hot-add memory*, which is the capability to add server memory while the server is running, and non-uniform memory access (NUMA). NUMA is a fairly new concept in the Windows world and occurs only in servers that are built with multiple separate processor busses. Each bus has its own memory, which is accessible at very high speeds to processors on that bus. When processors must access memory on other busses, however, access is slower. This disparity between memory access times is referred to as *NUMA*. High-end servers will be built with this multiple-bus architecture to provide faster memory access times.

Finally, Enterprise Edition supports the Terminal Server Session Directory, which makes working with large Terminal Services server farms more intuitive for users.

➤ For more information on the Terminal Server Session Directory, **see** "Terminal Server Session Directory," **p. 194**.

Enterprise Edition is an ideal platform for high-demand, mission-critical applications, including

- Mission-critical shared files
- Mission-critical printer access
- High-demand or mission-critical applications such as SQL Server or Exchange Server
- Any applications that can benefit from the 3GB memory space supported by Enterprise Edition

Windows Server 2003, Datacenter Edition

Datacenter Edition builds on the feature set offered by Enterprise Edition and eliminates a few features that aren't considered appropriate for a large enterprise data center. For example, Datacenter does not support the Internet Connection Firewall or Internet Connection Sharing, two features designed to make Windows an Internet gateway for network clients. Both features are, however, supported by Standard Edition and Enterprise Edition.

Datacenter Edition adds support for up to 64GB of server RAM and up to 32-way processor support. These features require a specialized Hardware Abstraction Layer (HAL), which is provided by the server hardware manufacturer. Datacenter Edition's Cluster Service supports eight-way clusters, enabling you to build more complex failover clusters for mission-critical applications.

Although Datacenter Edition does provide a "bigger and better" product over Enterprise Edition and Standard Edition, that's not really the point of Datacenter Edition. The real point of Datacenter Edition is much more important and is almost philosophical in nature: You can only buy Datacenter in conjunction with an approved server, directly from an approved server vendor. To receive product support for Datacenter Edition, you must contact the server vendor, not Microsoft, and you cannot make any hardware changes to the server without prior approval from the server vendor.

This philosophy is at the heart of Microsoft's Datacenter program, which is designed to provide you with a server that can remain up and running 99.999% of the time—the magical "five nines" reliability number that enterprises demand. In case you're wondering, that's slightly less than nine hours of downtime per year.

| Tip | That nine hours of downtime applies only to unplanned downtime; downtime due to scheduled maintenance is separate. Keep in mind that the use of high-availability features such as clustering can reduce or eliminate the downtime required to install service packs, hot fixes, and so forth. |

Everything about the Datacenter program is focused on reliability:

- All hardware included in a Datacenter-approved server must meet rigid Microsoft standards and pass a battery of compatibility and reliability tests.
- All device drivers must be certified and digitally signed by Microsoft.
- Customers cannot make any unauthorized changes to the server hardware. This includes every aspect of the hardware. For example, if you purchase a quad-processor Datacenter system, you can't upgrade it to eight processors unless that's also a certified, supported configuration from your vendor.

As we mentioned earlier, Datacenter Edition is sold only through server vendors and is sold preinstalled only on certified server hardware. You'll find that the hardware on which Datacenter Edition is offered is usually the highest of the high end: multiprocessor computers with copious amounts of RAM, redundant network adapters and power supplies, and so forth. Datacenter Edition computers are almost always clustered for higher availability and generally run an enterprise's most mission-critical applications.

Microsoft takes more care with updates for Datacenter Edition, too. Operating system service packs and hot fixes for Datacenter Edition generally lag behind such releases for other editions of Windows Server 2003 because Microsoft and its server vendor partners rigorously test all fixes for the operating system to ensure nothing will interfere with Datacenter Edition's 99.999% reliability record.

Likely applications for Datacenter Edition include any high-volume, mission-critical use, such as the following:

- Massive file and print servers
- Large, non-partitionable databases
- Consolidated servers that each assume the functionality of multiple lesser servers
- Other enterprise applications that simply cannot be unavailable

Tip — You can add some of Datacenter's reliability to Standard Edition, Web Edtion, and Enterprise Edition by following some of the practices the Datacenter program enforces: using only Microsoft-signed device drivers, using only Microsoft-tested hardware, and so on.

Expect to pay for Datacenter Edition's reliability. Although Microsoft doesn't publish pricing for Datacenter Edition are established by the server vendors who resell the operating system—the operating system itself, not to mention the high-end server hardware on which it runs, commands a premium price. If you're interested in finding out exactly how much, contact your local Hewlett-Packard or IBM sales representative. Tell him you're interested in purchasing a Datacenter Edition computer and watch his ears perk up! In fact, the sheer expense of Datacenter Edition and the associated server hardware makes it the least-deployed version of Windows. Many administrators might go their entire career without working on a Datacenter Edition, even in fairly large enterprises.

Windows Server 2003, Web Edition

In recent years, Microsoft has taken a pummeling in the Web server business. At one time, IIS and Windows NT Server 4.0 was the most popular commercial Web server platform; today, Windows 2000 Server and Windows Server 2003 are fighting against a wave of free and inexpensive versions of the Linux operating system and Apache Web server software. Microsoft argues that such servers don't come with the support that a multi-billion dollar company like Microsoft can provide; fans of Linux/Apache solutions say, "Who cares?" As a result, Microsoft has worked hard to provide a lower-cost version of Windows that's optimized to be a high-speed Web server. Although lower-cost certainly doesn't beat free, it does help close the gap and make potential buyers look at the additional features IIS offers, as well as the support Microsoft can provide. Microsoft's lower-cost Web server solution is Windows Server 2003, Web Edition.

Windows Server 2003, Web Edition's lower price doesn't mean you're getting a free lunch, though. For example, Web Edition lacks the other Windows Server 2003 editions' Enterprise UDDI (Universal Data Definition Interface) services, which is an industry-standard way of publishing and locating information about XML Web services. And, even though Web Edition can be a member of an Active Directory domain, it can't be a domain controller. Web Edition also lacks support for Microsoft Clustering, although it does include the NLB software that's appropriate for creating Web farms.

Web Edition lacks some of the communication features of the other editions, including the Internet Authentication Service (IAS), network bridging, Internet Connection Sharing, and the Internet Connection Firewall. Web Edition cannot host MMS. Unlike all other editions of Windows Server 2003, Web Edition does not support removable storage management, Fax Services, Remote Installation Services, Windows Media Services, or Services for Macintosh—all features that are useful on a network but are not specifically useful for a Web server. Although Web Edition does include Terminal Services' Remote Desktop for Administration, allowing you to remotely control your Web Edition computers, Web Edition doesn't support any other uses of the Terminal Services technologies.

Web Edition also lacks the scalability and reliability features of Enterprise Edition and Datacenter Edition, including a 64-bit edition, hot add memory, and NUMA support. Web Edition's scalability and reliability derives entirely from the inherently reliable and scalable nature of Web farms, which you can build using the included NLB software.

Web Edition's potential applications? Just one: as a Web server, either in the Internet or on your company's intranet. With more and more applications being implemented on Web servers, though, Web Edition's lack of breadth can hardly be considered a limitation. And if you're accustomed to paying a couple thousand bucks for the basic edition of Windows to run your Web servers, Web Edition's sub-$1,000 list price should be a welcome change.

Product Activation and Volume Licensing

Of course, no version of Windows is totally free. Pinning down exactly how much Windows costs can be difficult, at best. Of course, you can always pay the regular list price, which Microsoft includes on its Web site. But practically nobody pays that much; Microsoft offers a variety of volume licensing programs and other discount programs that can significantly reduce your outlay for server operating system software. Microsoft has also carried product activation into Windows Server 2003 to help reduce software piracy and illegal use of its products. We'll discuss both licensing and product activation in the next three sections.

How Windows Server 2003 Is Licensed

No matter how you purchase Windows Server 2003, or how much you pay, you'll still be buying licenses for the operating system. Microsoft server operating systems actually require two licenses: A *server license* allows you to actually run the operating system on a single server computer; a *client access license (CAL)* allows a single user to connect to the server and utilize its services.

Windows Server 2003—and indeed, pretty much every preceding version of Windows—recognizes two types of client licensing. The first is per-seat licensing, in which you buy one CAL for each client computer in your organization. The second is per-client licensing, in which you buy one CAL for each connection that will be made between a particular server and a client. This is the same type of licensing that both Windows 2000 Server and Windows NT Server 4.0 use.

Tip | Depending on where you purchased your client operating systems, you might be set for CALs. Some editions of Windows XP Professional and Windows 2000 Professional include server CALs.

Microsoft Licensing Programs

Microsoft's three programs are each targeted at different sizes of businesses with different needs and different budgets. Two basic programs apply to Windows Server 2003: Open License and Select License. Other custom licensing programs can be negotiated by larger companies that deal directly with Microsoft.

Open License programs are designed to be easy for businesses to take advantage of. Your initial purchase size sets your discount level for the program, and your program agreement lasts for two years. Additional licenses can be ordered in any quantity at your fixed discount level, and you can buy those licenses on the open market.

Microsoft offers two licensing subprograms under the Open License name: Open Business and Open Volume. The Open Business program allows businesses to place an initial order for at least five Microsoft products and establishes a fixed discount level. Businesses can then purchase additional licenses one at a time at their discount level for the duration of the program agreement. Open Volume is similar to Open Business, but it allows higher discount levels. Your discount level is determined for each of three product categories: applications, systems (including Windows Server 2003), and servers. Your initial purchase quantity in each category must meet a predefined minimum to qualify for the program. Initial purchases larger than the minimum do not result in a higher discount level. Both Open Business and Open Volume agreements last for two years.

> **Note** Microsoft offers additional open license programs for government agencies, academic organizations, and 501(c)(3) nonprofit organizations. For more details, visit www.Microsoft.com/licensing.

Open Business is the most straightforward program because you must buy only five products from any category to qualify. Open Volume is more complex because each Microsoft product is assigned a point value. To qualify for the Open Volume program, you have to purchase at least 500 points worth of products from the servers, systems, or applications category. For example, Windows Server 2003 is worth 15 points, whereas a Windows Server 2003 CAL is worth only 1 point. You must purchase at least 500 points worth of product from at least one category, and you receive an Open Volume agreement only for the categories for which you qualify.

One catch with both Open License programs is that they don't include actual product. When you purchase a license, it shows up under your account on Microsoft's eOpen Web site. The Web site allows you to track the licenses you've purchased, which ones have Software Assurance associated with them, and so forth (more on Software Assurance later in this chapter). What you don't get when you purchase an Open License is a CD, manual, or other physical product. So, how do you get the physical stuff? Microsoft offers a special fulfillment channel, which enables you to purchase the media and manuals for a nominal fulfillment and shipping fee.

Select License agreements are for larger companies that have at least 250 computers and the capability to roughly forecast future purchases. Enrollment in the Select program requires a larger initial purchase than an Open Volume agreement, although your eligibility and discount levels are determined by using the same three product categories and the same product point values. Select agreements last for three years; to qualify for the program, you must agree to purchase at least 1,500 points worth of products from any one category within that three-year timeframe. If you agree to purchase more product within your three-year agreement term, you'll get a higher discount level:

- Level A runs from 1,500 to 11,999 points.
- Level B runs from 12,000 to 29,999 points.

- Level C runs from 30,000 to 74,999 points.
- Level D runs from 75,000 points and up.

When your Select agreement expires, you can renew it for one or three years, at your option. Unlike Open Volume agreements, which allow you to purchase licenses from a large reseller channel, Select agreements and licenses must be purchased through a more exclusive channel, called the Microsoft Authorized Large Account Resellers (LARs) channel. After you're in the Select program, obtaining the actual product is easier than with the Open Volume program: You're shipped a fulfillment kit containing compact discs or DVDs for every product in the categories covered by your agreement. As products are updated, Microsoft ships you updated discs automatically.

> **Tip** Another benefit of the Select program is the ability to pay for your agreed-upon licenses over the term of the agreement, instead of up front, if you're purchasing Software Assurance with your licenses.

Where most companies get into trouble with the Select program is in the point forecasting. Most companies err on the side of caution, selecting a lower point commitment for their term. If you agree to purchase 11,999 points worth of product, and wind up buying 30,000, you'll still get only the level A discount level.

> To learn more about how these licensing programs apply specifically to Windows Server 2003, visit www.samspublishing.com and enter this book's ISBN number (no hyphens or parentheses) in the Search field; then click the book's cover image to access the book details page. Click the Web Resources link in the More Information section, and locate article ID# **A010102**.

When you start to calculate the prices for the licenses you need, don't forget to factor in Software Assurance, Microsoft's new proactive software upgrading program. In the past, Microsoft usually licensed its software outright and offered special upgrade pricing for users of previous versions. Now, Microsoft won't offer upgrade pricing any longer. Instead, you essentially buy your upgrades in advance through Software Assurance.

Software Assurance costs about 25% extra per year. So, for two years of Software Assurance, your licensing costs will increase by 50%. So long as Software Assurance is in effect, you'll receive all product upgrades at no additional charge. Without Software Assurance, you'll still receive service packs and other mid-version fixes, but you won't receive any major new versions of the product. If you want them, you'll have to pay full price.

Activating Windows

To help combat illegal use of its software, Microsoft has begun implementing product activation in many of its products, including Windows Server 2003. When you install Windows Server 2003 from *retail media*—the CD-ROM you buy in a store or from another retailer—you

Chapter 1 Introduction to the Windows Server 2003 Family

type in a unique product ID during the setup process. This product ID is generally printed on the back of the CD jewel case. After the installation is complete, Windows Server 2003 contacts Microsoft over the Internet (there's a phone-in option if you're not connected) and registers your product ID. From that point, your product ID is permanently tied to your server's hardware configuration. You can reinstall and reactivate Windows as many times as you want on that particular hardware; if you try to use the same product ID to install Windows on a different server, the activation process will fail.

Activation can present a few problems. Normally, Windows adapts to changes in your hardware configuration and remains activated, provided those changes are few in number and occur over a period of time. If several things—for example, BIOS serial number, memory, hard drive, and CPU type—all change at once, Windows deactivates itself, believing that it has been cloned onto a different computer and is no longer legal. If that happens, you'll have to call the Microsoft Product Activation Center and plead your case for a new activation key.

If you've received your Windows Server 2003 CDs through a volume channel, such as a Microsoft Select License fulfillment package, you won't have a product ID. Instead, you'll have a *volume license key*, which enables you to install Windows on any number of machines without having to go through product activation. Of course, you can legally install Windows only as many times as your license allows, but there's no product activation feature to act as a watchdog for you.

Caution | Don't confuse product IDs and volume license keys. You can't use a product ID with volume license CDs, and you can't use volume license keys with retail CDs. If you have both types of media in your organization, be sure to keep track of which ID numbers go with which CDs.

If you'll be installing Windows Server 2003 on a large number of computers, it pays to acquire a volume license agreement with Microsoft and get volume license media from which to install. That way you won't have to fuss with product activation after every installation. Volume license media makes using automated deployment methods, such as Remote Installation Services (RIS), easier because product activation isn't a factor.

➤ For more information on RIS, **see** "Server RIS," **p. 26**.

2

INSTALLATION AND DEPLOYMENT

In This Chapter

- Automating Windows Server 2003 Installations, **page 20**.
- Product Activation, **page 23**.
- Remote OS Deployments, **page 26**.
- Upgrading from Previous Versions **page 28**.

What's New

Much of installing and deploying Windows Server 2003 is the same as in Windows 2000. As you will see in this chapter, some changes have occurred, primarily in the way of improvements and extensions to the previous methodologies. Improvements have also been made in the creation of unattended setup files and extensions to RIS to include support for deploying more operating systems, including the Windows Server 2003 server platforms. A new feature that affects installation and deployments, Windows Product Activation, is also discussed, including the differences between deploying with retail and volume product license keys. Finally, we will take a look at what's involved in upgrading to Windows Server 2003, such as supported upgrade paths, deployment methodologies, and considerations for mass upgrades.

Installation Changes

The installation process for Windows Server 2003 is basically the same as in Windows 2000. You can perform network installations or CD-based installations, including booting from CD. Similar to the previous version, the setup process has several phases. There is a DOS-style initial phase for configuring and formatting drives and selecting the installation location. This is followed by a graphical (GUI) phase in which system hardware is detected; licensing is configured, including entering the license key; the computer name and administrator password are specified; network settings and regional options are configured; and the computer can be joined to a domain. All this is basically the same as in previous versions—the differences in the installation process are in the available options and what you can configure.

Attended Installations

Just like in previous versions, you can perform an installation from the Windows CD or from source files across the network. We'll start with a walk-through of a CD-based install, specifically booting from CD, and then take a look at network-based installations. As we walk through the installation process, you'll note how similar it is to Windows 2000.

CD-Based Install of Windows Server 2003

To start installing Windows Server 2003 on a new system, simply insert the Windows Server 2003 CD and turn on the system. If the system is configured to boot from CD and there are no configured disk partitions, the setup program launches automatically and begins installing Windows Server 2003. If disk partitions are configured, it displays the following prompt: Press Any Key to Boot from CD. You then must press a key to launch the setup program. If you don't have a bootable CD-ROM drive, you can boot to a DOS floppy disk with CD-ROM drivers and launch setup by running winnt.exe from the i386 directory of the Windows CD. Alternatively, if you have a previous installation of Windows on your system, you can perform an upgrade or fresh installation by running winnt32.exe, which is also in the i386 directory. We will look at upgrading from previously installed operating systems later in this chapter.

When booting from the Windows Server 2003 CD, the initial phase looks exactly like Windows 2000. You get the familiar blue Windows Setup screen, as shown in Figure 2.1.

If you need to install device drivers for your disk array, press **F6** when prompted at the bottom of the screen, just like Windows 2000. After it detects initial hardware devices and loads the setup application, you are prompted to set up Windows, repair a previous windows installation, or quit.

> **Disaster Recovery**
>
> Selecting Repair during the setup launches the recovery console. The recovery console, first introduced in Windows 2000, essentially provides a minimal DOS-style console where you can set the startup state of services (automatic, manual, disabled), manage drive partitions, copy files, and perform other diagnostic and repair functions.

Another setup option for disaster recovery is to press F2 when prompted when Setup first starts. This launches Automated System Recovery (ASR), which is a replacement for the Emergency Repair process. The Emergency Repair process in previous versions scans system and Registry files and attempts to repair any corruptions or differences based on a previously created Emergency Repair Disk. It really only ever works if you have missing or corrupted system files. The Automated System Recovery process is really an automated full system restore. Prior to performing ASR, you need to create an ASR disk. The ASR disk is created when performing an ASR backup using the Windows backup utility and contains the information necessary to restore the backup.

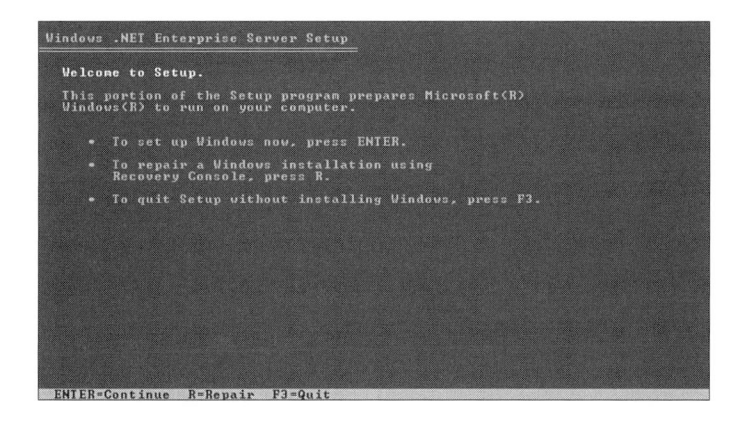

Figure 2.1 Windows Server Setup starts off looking exactly like previous versions of Windows NT and Windows 2000.

Assuming you choose to continue with the installation of Windows, the license agreement is displayed and you must press **F8** to agree to the terms and continue. Next, you are given the opportunity to create/delete partitions and select the installation drive. When booting from CD, you can do just about anything to the drive partitions. You can create new partitions and delete any or all of the existing partitions. After you have the drives partitioned the way you want, select a partition on which to install Windows Server 2003. Next, setup detects whether there is an existing version of Windows on the partition you chose. If there is, you are prompted to upgrade it or erase it and start fresh. Next, you are prompted on what to do to the existing file system. You can format with NTFS, format with FAT, or leave it unchanged, just like Windows 2000. However, as shown in Figure 2.2, if previous partitions exist, you now have the option to perform quick formats with NTFS or FAT to save time.

The default is to format the partition using the NTFS file system. The system then formats the drive (if that's what you chose). It checks the integrity of the drive and then copies the Windows files. After the file copy is complete, setup reboots and the GUI phase starts.

Note | The default installation directory for Windows Server 2003 is Windows, not WINNT like in Windows 2000 and Windows NT 4.0.

18   Chapter 2   Installation and Deployment

Figure 2.2   New choices for formatting existing partitions using NTFS or FAT.

After the reboot following the DOS phase, Setup enters the GUI phase. The first option you have during the GUI phase of the installation is to configure Regional and Language options. Next is personalizing the installation by entering your name and company name. You are then prompted to enter the product license key and to select the licensing mode—per server or per seat. This is followed by the configuration of the computer name and administrator password. One new feature is an insecure password warning: If you enter an insecure password, as shown in Figure 2.3, Setup pops up with a message warning that your password is too simple and suggests criteria for a stronger password.

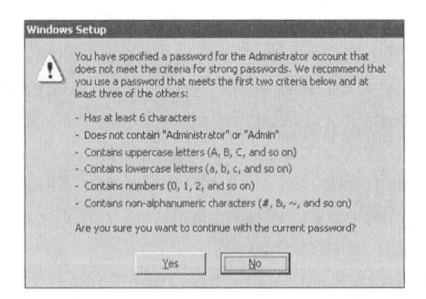

Figure 2.3   Setup detects whether the password you entered is insecure and prompts you to enter a stronger one.

The next step is entering the date, time, and time zone. Setup then detects any network components (such as network cards) that might be installed and prompts you to configure them. If you have multiple cards, you can configure the settings independently for each card. You have the option to configure with Typical Settings (Client for Microsoft Networks, File and Print Sharing for Microsoft Networks, TCP/IP configured to use DHCP) or Custom Settings.

Selecting Custom Settings enables you to specify static IP addresses or add/remove services and protocols. Next is the option to join a domain or specify a workgroup. After that, Setup finishes copying files and configuring the system, reboots, and starts Windows Server 2003. The first time you log on, the Manage Your Server Wizard starts and enables you to configure your server for its custom role, as shown in Figure 2.4.

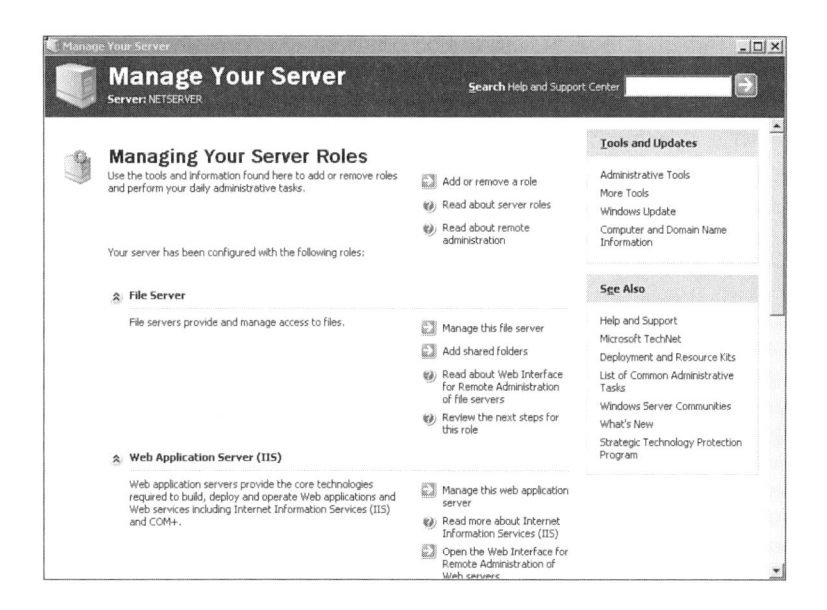

Figure 2.4 The Manage Your Server Wizard starts automatically after installation and enables the configuration of the server for its particular role.

You might have noticed that, unlike Windows 2000, there is no opportunity in the installation process to specify which server components and services (DNS, WINS, DHCP, RIS, IIS, and so on) to install. Installation and configuration of server components are performed after the OS is installed, unless you specify otherwise in an unattended installation script. You build those scripts the same way that you did in Windows 2000; for more details, search Windows Server 2003's online Help and Support Center for "unattended installation". We'll also touch on unattended installs later in this chapter.

Network-Based Installations

Installing Windows Server 2003 from the network is basically the same as installing from CD—there is just an extra initial phase for copying the setup files prior to the DOS-based setup phase. It is also the same as in Windows 2000; you simply map a drive to the network location containing the Windows Server 2003 CD files and run `winnt.exe` or `winnt32.exe` from the `i386` directory. The main difference between running Setup using `winnt.exe` or `winnt32.exe` (either across the network or from CD) and running it by booting from CD is the restrictions on what you can do when partitioning drives in the DOS phase. When installing from the network, the files for the Setup program itself must be downloaded to the local system. Consequently, the partition containing those files cannot be deleted during the drive partition phase of setup.

> **Note** The choice of whether to run `winnt.exe` or `winnt32.exe` is dependent on the existing operating system. `winnt32.exe` is sometimes referred to as the *upgrade setup* because it can be run from previous Windows operating systems. If you have Windows NT or Windows 2000 installed, you can run `winnt32.exe` to upgrade the OS. If you don't have an existing operating system (in other words, you boot from a DOS boot disk), you must run `winnt.exe`.

After Setup gets past the drive configuration step, the rest of the setup process for a network-based install is identical to a CD-based install.

Emergency Management Services Installation

A new feature of Windows Server is Emergency Management Services. This new feature is available on systems that have special hardware that supports firmware console redirection and have a Serial Port Console Redirection (SRPC) table. Essentially, Emergency Management Services provides out-of-band access to your servers. It is a sort of text-mode console into the server even when the operating system is down. This gives you access to do anything on the server, short of physically removing and installing hardware.

As such, it provides an additional option for installing Windows Server 2003. For example, you could perform remote installations of Windows Server 2003. After the console is redirected, you can insert the Windows Server 2003 CD, boot the system, and run through an install. Unfortunately, because of the way Emergency Management Services works, you won't be able to see the GUI phase of setup. Consequently, when Setup reaches the end of the DOS phase, it prompts to automatically configure the GUI portion. Selecting this option enables you to proceed with the GUI installation; however, you won't have any choice in what it installs. It installs with the default options, but at least it gets the OS installed. One way to overcome this drawback is by using an automated install using an unattended answer file.

Unattended Installations

For the most part, unattended installations are the same as in Windows 2000: They can be launched from the network or CD using `winnt.exe` or `winnt32.exe`. Windows Server 2003, however, supports the use of an unattended installation file and an optional uniqueness database file to specify the answers to setup questions.

> **Tip** The documentation for the unattended installation files is now `ref.chm` instead of `unattend.doc` in the deploy.cab file. You can access the contents of `deploy.cab` (or any `.cab` file) by using WinZIP or a similar shareware application.

Because new and different features and components are available in Windows Server 2003, the main differences from Windows 2000 are in the answer files themselves and the methods for creating them.

> **Tip** The Windows Setup program is hard-coded to look at the floppy drive for a file called `winnt.sif`. If the file exists and is in the proper format, it reads it and performs an automated setup based on the answers in the file.

Setup Manager Wizard

The Setup Manager Wizard, which is used to create the answer files, has been improved to ease the creation of automated installation files. It walks through all the questions asked during setup, allowing you to specify the answers. It then creates the appropriate unattended installation file(s) based on your answers. The Setup Manager Wizard can be installed by extracting `setupmgr.exe` from `deploy.cab` in the Support\Tools directory of the Windows Server 2003 CD (Windows 2000 also requires an additional file, `setupmgx.dll`). The Setup Manager Wizard on the Windows Server 2003 CD can be used for creating answer files for all Windows XP and Windows 2003 editions, except Data Center. To create answer files for Windows 2000, use the Windows 2000 Setup Manager Wizard.

The main improvement in the Setup Manager Wizard is the interface. Rather than a screen-by-screen prompt for each question and answer, all the main options are on one screen, as shown in Figure 2.5.

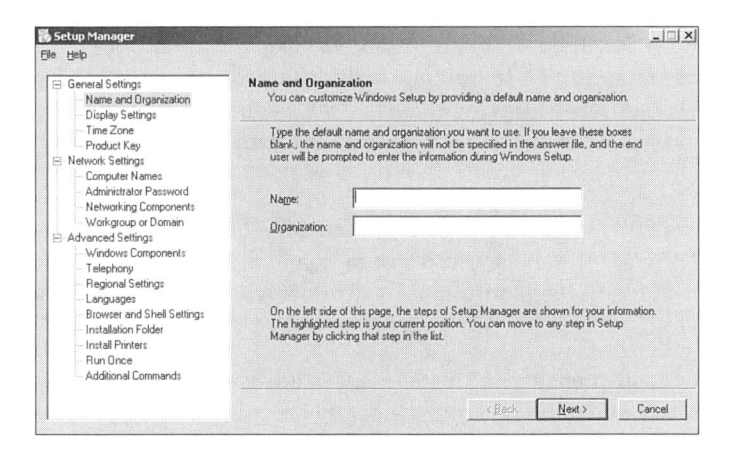

Figure 2.5 The new consolidated Setup Manager Wizard options screen streamlines the setup process.

The Windows Server 2003 Setup Manager Wizard also includes a number of additional options. First, in Windows 2000, the Setup Manager Wizard does not prompt for the product license key, so you have to manually edit the answer files or get prompted for the license key during setup. In the Windows Server 2003 Setup Manager Wizard, you can specify the product license key to use.

> **Tip** The Setup Manager Wizard has one quirk. If you click Next to advance between each of the configuration options, when you get to the Product Key the cursor is in the second to last field, not the first one. More than once I've started filling in the product key only to have it entered in the wrong fields. Very annoying.

Another problem with the Windows 2000 wizard is specifying the local administrator password. If you enter it in the wizard, it is stored in the answer file in clear text. Obviously, anyone who has access to the file would then know the local administrator password, which is a potential security risk. In the Windows Server 2003 Setup Manager Wizard, not only can you specify the local administrator password, but you also have the option to encrypt it in the answer file. This eliminates the potential security risk of the local administrator password being stored in clear text.

> **Note** One annoying thing about encrypting the password is that the option is available only for the local administrator account. There is no option to encrypt the password for the account used to join the domain. The domain account is potentially a more security sensitive account, so it's odd that Microsoft does not provide a mechanism to encrypt it.

Two additional options the Windows Server 2003 Setup Manager Wizard prompts for that the Windows 2000 one does not are Windows Components and Additional Commands. Windows Components enables you to specify the installed Windows Components, such as World Wide Web Service, SMTP Service, Remote Installation Service, Terminal Server, and so on. Additional Commands enables you to automatically run programs after the unattended setup completes while the computer is starting up. This can be used to further customize the installation by installing programs or setting configuration settings—anything that can be executed without requiring a user to be logged on.

Just like the Windows 2000 version, the Setup Manager Wizard in Windows Server 2003 creates the answer file, the udf file, if any, and a sample batch file based on the answers provided. You can then use these files as is to automate your deployments or further customize with a text editor.

> For an explanation of unattended installations in Windows 2000, visit http://www.samspublishing.com/ and enter this book's ISBN number (no hyphens or parenthesis) in the Search field; then click the book cover image to access the book details page. Click the Web Resources link in the More Information section, and locate article ID# **A010202**.

Image Downloads

Yet another method for deploying Windows Server 2003 is by using third-party imaging software. The process is largely the same as in Windows NT 4.0 and Windows 2000. A reference machine is prepared with all software installed and configured the way you like it. The `sysprep.exe` utility is then run to remove all machine-specific information, such as SID, computer name, and so on. This generic installation is then copied to a network share using third-party imaging software, which makes an exact bit-by-bit copy of the hard drives on the system. The image is stored on a server and later downloaded to one or more target machines. When the target machine boots up from the deployed image, a mini-setup wizard starts asking for all the machine-specific information removed by sysprep, such as the computer name, license key, and the like. When it's done, a brand-new system is up and running with a hardware and software installation identical to the original.

Windows Server 2003 supports deployment via imaging, just like previous versions. What's new is the `sysprep.exe` file that is used to strip out the computer-specific information.

A nice feature of the new sysprep is that it is more forgiving of different hardware. A switch (`-bmsd`) can be used to generate a list of available mass storage devices for `sysprep.inf`. You can then specify any additional mass storage devices that the mini-setup wizard should attempt to detect.

Tip | Running `sysprep /?` displays a list of the available switches.

Additionally, a new Factory Mode is available. If sysprep is run with the `-factory` switch, when the system reboots and you log on, it comes up into Factory Mode, as shown in Figure 2.6, instead of running the mini-setup wizard. When in this mode you can perform other operations, such as installing software or drivers, which helps to minimize the number of base images you need to store. You can store a few images sysprepped to boot to factory mode; then when it comes time to deploy, you can download the image to a target machine and load the software and drivers for the particular machine type. Finally, you can select the reseal option to run sysprep again to clean up, and the system will be ready to be imaged again to be deployed en masse.

Windows Product Activation

Windows Server 2003 has a new anti-piracy feature for ensuring software licensing compliance—Windows Product Activation. When Windows is installed, you are prompted to enter a license key, which forms the basis for your product ID.

Note | If you're using a Volume License copy of Windows Server 2003, such as one obtained through the Microsoft Select program, you must enter a volume license key instead of a license key. When using a volume license key with a volume license copy of Windows Server 2003, you don't have to perform product activation. This issue is examined in more detail in the next section.

24 Chapter 2 Installation and Deployment

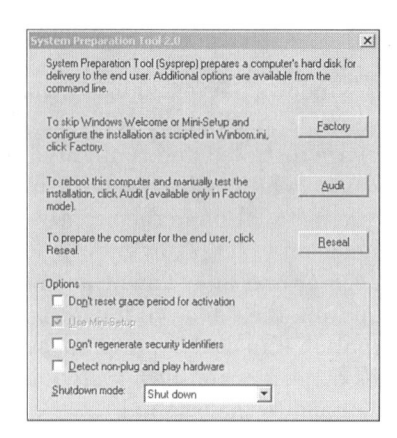

Figure 2.6 The new system preparation Factory Mode provides a means to install additional applications or drivers.

When activating Windows Server 2003, a hash is created from the existing hardware in your machine. This hardware hash is then used to uniquely identify your machine and is sent to Microsoft, along with your product ID, when you activate Windows Server 2003. This associates the product ID to your specific hardware, thus ensuring that the product license key cannot be used on other hardware.

Tip | You can see your product ID by looking at system properties (right-click **My Computer** and select **Properties**). The product ID is the 20-digit code in the Registered To section.

Once installed, you have a limited time (30 days) before you have to "activate" the installation. If the Windows Server 2003 is not activated within the grace period, it ceases to function. A reminder pops up in the Notification Area until you activate it. Clicking the reminder balloon brings up the Activate Windows screen shown in Figure 2.7.

As you can see, a couple of different methods are available for activating Windows. You can activate it immediately by selecting **Yes, Let's Activate Windows Over the Internet Now**. Alternatively, you can call Microsoft to obtain an Activation Key and manually enter it. If you call Microsoft, you need to provide the installation ID for your system (a 54-character numeric string). You will then be given a corresponding 42-character string that you must enter—talk about tedious! Obviously, activating over the Internet is much easier, provided you have an Internet connection.

After you have activated Windows, if you attempt to install Windows Server 2003 on a different machine using the same product license key, Windows Activation fails. Because you are using the same product license key, you will have the same product ID; however, because it is a different machine, you will have a different hardware hash. When this information is sent to

Microsoft during Windows Activation, the hardware hash won't match and the activation request will be rejected. Upgrading the hardware in an existing machine can potentially cause Windows Activation to fail. If too much hardware is upgraded, the hardware hash could be different. Obviously, valid reasons exist for using the same license on different hardware, such as replacing the existing machine with a newer one. You can still use the product license key in these situations, but you must call Microsoft to obtain an Activation Key and then use that key to manually activate Windows.

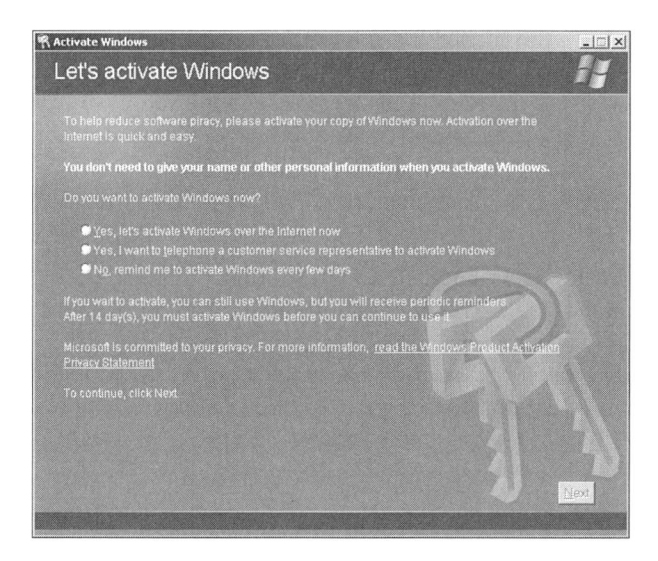

Figure 2.7 Windows Product Activation is required only when using a retail version of Windows Server 2003.

Retail Versus Volume Product Keys

The process outlined previously is required for any retail or original equipment manufacturer (OEM) version of Windows Server 2003. The product license keys obtained in retail copies of Windows Server 2003 require activation.

What about volume licenses? Must you activate every installation of Windows Server 2003? For large organizations, this could be particularly troublesome because large corporations usually purchase Microsoft licenses in bulk via one of the volume licensing programs such as Select or Open license. These programs generally have a single license key for each platform that is used for installation of all the machines for the respective platform. What are these organizations to do? Must they call Microsoft and manually key in the Activation Key for every installation after the first? Of course not—that would be ridiculous and the industry would revolt.

If an organization purchases a Select or Enterprise license agreement, it obtains a special installation CD that has a setup program coded to automatically enter the Select program license key. This special license key does not require activation. If you use this Select CD, you aren't prompted to enter a product license key during setup and you also don't have to activate Windows after installation.

Other license programs, such as the Open license agreement, allow you to purchase a single physical copy with a single product license key, but you are allowed to install it on multiple machines because you have purchased (on paper) the appropriate server licenses. In these cases, a single product license key is used for hundreds, even thousands, of installations. With these license programs, a special volume license key is obtained from Microsoft that bypasses the Windows Activation, thus machines installed with these keys do not require activation.

Server RIS

As with the other deployment methods, Remote Installation Services (RIS) in Windows Server 2003 is similar to Windows 2000. The major difference is the platforms supported for RIS installations. When Windows 2000 was released, it supported only RIS installations of Windows 2000 Professional. Hot fixes and service packs eventually added support for Windows 2000 server and Windows XP. Windows Server 2003 RIS supports the installation of all versions of Windows 2000, Windows XP, and Windows Server 2003, except Windows 2000 Data Center and Windows Server 2003 Data Center, of course.

> Note   Although you can deploy all versions of Windows Server 2003 with RIS, the 64-bit version of Windows Server 2003, Enterprise Edition can be deployed only using CD-based images; all the others can be deployed with either CD-based or RIPrep images.

> For a brief overview of RIS in Windows 2000, visit http://www.samspublishing.com/ and enter this book's ISBN number (no hyphens or parenthesis) in the Search field; then click the book cover image to access the book details page. Click the Web Resources link in the More Information section, and locate article ID# **A010201**.

Installing RIS

Remote Installation Services in Windows Server 2003 is installed the same as it is in Windows 2000—by installing the Remote Installation Service Windows Component in Add or Remove Programs. Just like in Windows 2000, installing the Windows component only installs the service components. However, installing the service in Windows Server does not require a reboot like Windows 2000 does. RIS still needs to be configured separately before it can be used. Unlike Windows 2000, the configuration of RIS is much more straightforward and easier to find. In Windows 2000, you must find the risetup.exe file to launch the configuration program. In Windows Server 2003, however, a shortcut to risetup.exe (Remote Installation

Services Setup Properties) is placed on the Administrative Tools menu. Running this shortcut creates the initial CD-based image and configures RIS to respond to client requests.

Configuring RIS

Remote Installation Services properties are configured in the same place as they were in Windows 2000—on the Remote Install tab of the Computer object of the RIS server in Active Directory Users and Computers. A new Verify Server button appears on the Remote Install tab that can be useful in troubleshooting a RIS installation. Clicking this button launches the Check Server Wizard that runs diagnostics to determine whether any problems exist with the Remote Installation Services installation on the specified computer. It can also restart the RIS services and attempt to authorize the RIS server as a DHCP server in Active Directory. These same diagnostics can be performed by running the Remote Installation Services Setup Properties. After RIS has been configured, this wizard has a new option labeled Check This Remote Installation for Errors. Selecting this option runs the RIS server diagnostics.

Another new button on the Remote Install tab is the Show Clients button. This button runs an Active Directory query to display all the RIS installed clients associated with the specified RIS server. This enables you to see how many clients each server is managing, which helps in load balancing your RIS deployments.

Note | The Verify Server and Show Clients buttons are also available with Service Pack 3 for Windows 2000.

Furthermore, the client RIS experience can be managed with the same group policies as Windows 2000. The RIS group policy settings determine the options available to the user and the amount of interaction during the setup process, whether the user can restart a previously failed setup, whether he sees the RIS maintenance and troubleshooting tools, how much he can interact with the installation, whether it is fully automated, whether he is prompted for anything, and whether he can customize and change anything.

➤ For more information on Group Policies, **see** "New Group Policies," **p. 93**.

Upgrading from Prior Versions

As mentioned previously, existing operating systems can be upgraded by running `winnt32.exe`. This launches the setup wizard, where you are given the choice to perform an upgrade or a fresh install. Next, you are prompted to accept the license agreement and then enter the license key. The next step is something new in Windows Server 2003: You are prompted to connect to the Internet to update the setup files, as shown in Figure 2.8. This downloads the latest setup files and drivers, as well as updates the compatibility database.

Chapter 2 Installation and Deployment

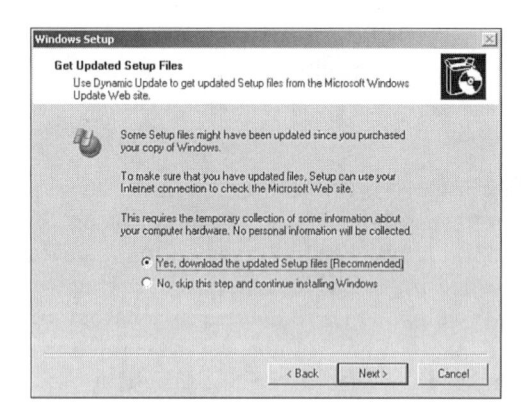

Figure 2.8 Windows Setup can use dynamic update to check for critical product updates prior to installing Windows Server 2003.

Setup then scans your system and compares it to the compatibility database in an attempt to detect any known hardware or software incompatibilities. Before performing any upgrade, you should always verify that the current hardware and software are compatible with the new OS.

> **Tip** You can run the compatibility check without actually installing Windows Server 2003 by running `winnt32.exe /checkupgradeonly`, just like in Windows 2000. The compatibility check is also available as a download from www.Microsoft.com/windowsserver2003, and the downloadable version is kept updated. The version on the Windows Server 2003 CD can be expected to be out of date a few months after it's released.

After the compatibility scan, a report is displayed showing any detected incompatibilities and suggestions on how to correct them, as shown in Figure 2.9.

Provided there are no critical incompatibilities, Setup then copies the setup files from the source location (CD or network) to the system and reboots. The rest of the setup process is virtually identical to a fresh install. It proceeds with the DOS phase of setup and then the GUI phase. The only difference is that, if you chose to upgrade the existing system instead of a fresh install, you aren't prompted for anything because it uses the same configuration settings as the previously installed operating system.

Supported Upgrade Paths

One of the things restricting your choice of whether to do an upgrade or a full install is the supported upgrade paths. The following are the supported upgrade paths for Windows Server 2003, Standard Edition:

- Windows NT Server 4.0 with Service Pack 5 or later
- Windows NT Server 4.0 Terminal Server Edition with Service Pack 5 or later
- Windows 2000 Server

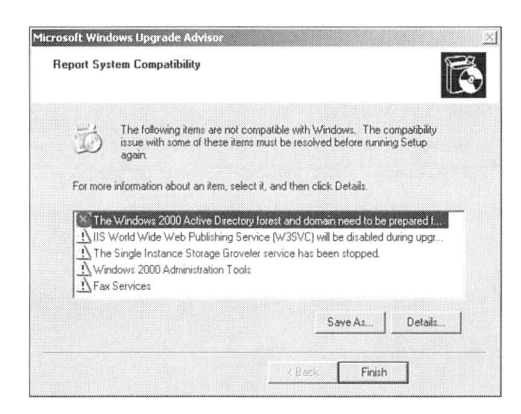

Figure 2.9 The Windows Compatibility Report displays any applications or drivers that might not be compatible with Windows Server 2003.

The supported upgrade paths to Windows Server 2003, Enterprise Edition are

- Windows NT Server 4.0 with Service Pack 5 or later
- Windows NT Server 4.0 Terminal Server Edition with Service Pack 5 or later
- Windows NT Server 4.0 Enterprise Edition with Service Pack 5 or later
- Windows 2000 Server
- Windows 2000 Advanced Server
- Windows Server 2003, Standard Edition

The supported upgrade paths can be summed up in a single statement: Any Windows NT 4.0 (with SP5) or Windows 2000 server platform can be upgraded to the same platform or better, but downgrades are allowed.

Operating systems prior to Windows NT 4.0, such as Windows NT 3.51, require an upgrade to one of the previously mentioned operating systems first; then you can upgrade to Windows Server 2003 (or reinstall from scratch, of course).

> **Note** Upgrading to the Standard Server version of Windows Server 2003 is supported only on systems with one or two processors. If you have more than that, such as three or four processors, you must select Windows Server 2003, Enterprise Edition. Also, you cannot upgrade to Windows Server 2003, Standard Edition from Windows NT 4.0 Server Enterprise Edition or Windows 2000 Advanced Server.

The easiest upgrade to Windows Server 2003 is from Windows 2000 as the underlying technology, and much of the processes is basically the same.

Although the upgrade from Windows 2000 is the smoothest, special care needs to be taken when upgrading domain controllers. Before you can upgrade Windows 2000 domain controllers or install new Windows Server 2003 domain controllers into an existing Windows 2000 domain, the Active Directory schema must be extended to support the new Windows Server 2003 domain controllers. This schema extension is performed by first running adprep /forestprep, allowing it to replicate, and then performing adprpep /domainprep. Does this mean you have to raise the domain functional level to Windows 2000 Native or Windows Server 2003? No. You can still have "down-level" domain controllers. Windows Server 2003 maintains compatibility at the lower functional levels with Windows NT 4 domain controllers and Windows 2000 domain controllers.

> For more information about Active Directory, **see** "Active Directory Functional Levels," **p. 66**.

Whenever possible, I recommend a fresh install over an upgrade to ensure that no legacy files or Registry settings are left lying around that could potentially cause problems. You also have the opportunity to reconfigure the underlying hardware, such as hard drive partitions, and even reformat the drives to start clean. The choice of whether to upgrade is usually a matter of logistics and what is possible. Usually, it comes down to how difficult it would be to reinstall the existing applications. An upgrade maintains the installed applications and Registry settings, whereas a fresh install obviously does not. Sometimes taking a server down and doing a complete reinstall is simply not feasible. For example, you might have an application whose configuration settings are not completely documented. That, of course, never happens, right? All the configuration settings of every application on every server throughout the entire organization are all completely documented, right? Okay, maybe not. In those cases you might be forced to upgrade.

Mass Upgrades

For mass deployments of fresh installations of Windows Server 2003, the same methods are available as Windows 2000: RIS, automated installations, or third-party imaging applications. However, to perform mass upgrades of existing systems, your only option is to automate the upgrade by using answer files. You can create an unattended installation file that upgrades the existing OS; the trick is kicking off the upgrade and specifying the answer file. If you have some type of software distribution infrastructure then you can use that to deploy the upgrade package. Alternatively, you can use group policy to deploy the upgrade package.

As you have seen in this chapter, deploying Windows Server 2003 is very similar to deploying Windows 2000. It should be because it is based on the same technology. However, although the basic processes and techniques are the same, a few improvements and additions have been included that could help smooth your deployments.

3

INTERFACE CHANGES

In This Chapter

- A cool new look, without all the fluff, **page 32**.
- Save disk space, **page 32**.
- Create your own CDs, **page 34**.
- Getting Support, **page 37**.

What's New

This chapter touches on some of the new interface changes and features in Windows Server 2003. Just as Windows NT Server 4.0 shares a user interface with Windows 95 and Windows NT Workstation 4.0 and just as Windows 2000 Server shares an interface with Windows 2000 Professional, the Windows Server 2003 interface is the same as Windows XP. All the features in this chapter were first introduced in Windows XP; Windows Server 2003 now brings features such as new visual themes, compressed folders, CD burning, and the remote desktop/remote assistance technologies to the server platform. If you are already familiar with Windows XP, you might want to briefly skim this chapter. Most of these features provide enhanced functionality previously available only through third-party products. Overall, these features provide a more pleasant look and feel and enhance the overall user experience.

User Interface Themes

The first difference in the user experience provided by Windows Server 2003 is in the themes available for the user desktop. What is a theme? A *theme* is a collection of user environment configuration settings (wallpaper, desktop icons, menu styles, sounds, and so on) used to give a cohesive desktop appearance. It is a collection of all the individual settings you could manually change yourself, but it puts all these setting in one place. All the settings have the same "theme," making it much easier to give your desktop a complete overhaul, yet maintain a consistent appearance. Windows Server 2003, however, doesn't really have any themes. For the longest time, administrators have been admonished not to run resource-intensive desktops and screensavers, such as OpenGL (those are the fancy screensavers like Pipes that use up a lot of processor power). Many times the administrators' response was, "If we're not supposed to use it, why is it an option?" Well, now it's not—at least not by default. Although Windows Server 2003 supports themes, only one theme is actually included in the product, Windows Classic. Also, only three screensavers are included (Blank, Marquee, and Windows)—none of which are resource intensive. There are, however, a few new desktop wallpapers—the same visually stimulating wallpapers available in Windows XP.

Although only one theme is included with Windows Server 2003, it does have a new method for making it easier to obtain and install your own themes. It has an option to connect to Microsoft's Web site to download themes online. However, the only currently available themes on Microsoft's site are those included with Microsoft Plus! for Windows XP.

Compressed Folders

The next new feature we'll look at is compressing files and folders. This provides the utilitarian function of saving disk space by reducing the amount of physical disk space occupied by files. Windows NT has always had a mechanism for saving disk space by compressing files: the NTFS file compression attribute feature. With Windows Server 2003, Microsoft introduces another method for compressing files—compressed (zipped) folders. This section discusses the two mechanisms and how they differ.

NTFS Folder Compression

NTFS file and folder compression is implemented as a file-level attribute. A check box in the properties of a volume, folder, or file designates it as compressed. If enabled, the operating system handles the compressing and uncompressing of the file without any user intervention. Whenever a file or folder with the compressed attribute enabled is opened, the operating system automatically uncompresses it. When the file is saved, the OS automatically compresses it again, completely transparent to the user. However, all this compressing and uncompressing of files adds extra processing overhead because the OS has to constantly uncompress and re-compress files whenever they're opened and closed. The benefits of freeing up disk space and ease of use for the user must be balanced against the extra processing load when determining whether to use NTFS compression. Another drawback to NTFS compression is that, because it is a file system attribute, it is compressed only on the file system. The implication of this is that, if you access the file across the network, it is first uncompressed by the operating system and then sent across the network in an uncompressed format. Thus, no network bandwidth improvement occurs because the file is sent across the network as if it were never compressed. In actuality, degradation in the file transfer occurs because of the extra processing to uncompress the file. Yet another drawback to NTFS compression is that it is incompatible with the Encrypting File System (EFS) NTFS attribute introduced in Windows 2000. You can enable either the file compression attribute or the file encryption attribute, but not both.

> For more information about EFS, **see** "Encrypting File System," **p. 141**.

Note | To compress a file, you need at least as much disk space available as the uncompressed file size. For example, if you attempt to copy a 100MB file to a compressed location with 80MB free, even if the file can be compressed to 50MB, you will be unable to copy the file because it must be copied first and then compressed.

Compressed (Zipped) Folders Feature

Windows Server 2003 still has the NTFS file compression attribute, just like previous versions do. However, it now has the new Compressed Folders feature. This feature is more akin to third-party compression utilities such as WinZip or its earlier cousin PKZIP. As shown in Figure 3.1, Compressed Folders is implemented as a pop-up menu option. Just select the files or folders you want to compress, right-click, select **Send To**, and then select **Compressed (Zipped) Folder**.

This creates a separate (Zip) file containing all the files and folders you selected. You can use this new feature to individually compress files and folders for archival purposes. Unlike NTFS file compression, though, user intervention is required to compress and uncompress the files with this method. It really creates compressed copies of the file(s), whereas NTFS compression compresses the original file. Additionally, because it is a utility doing the compression and not a file-level attribute, you can compress any file or folder—even those on FAT partitions. The true benefit is the ability to take the Zip archive that is created and move it elsewhere, such as across the network. This gives you the capability to transport the files in a compressed format. You can then use this to minimize your network traffic when copying the archive to another location or make it small enough to fit on some other archival media, such as CD-ROM, Zip, or floppy disk, for transport elsewhere. These are just a couple examples of the uses of compressed files. Another common use is to compress multiple files and wrap them up in a single package, which is particularly useful for emailing large documents or pictures to friends or support personnel.

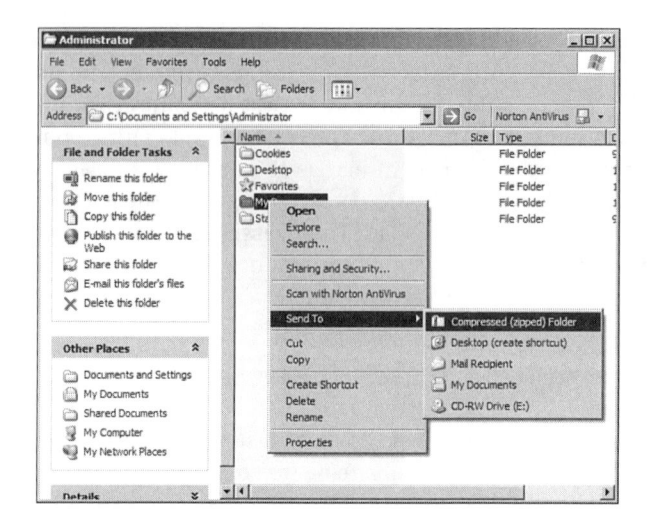

Figure 3.1 Right-click a file or folder to create a Zip file with the new Compressed Folders feature.

Tip | In addition to being able to create and read your own Zip files, the Compressed Folders feature enables you to extract Zip archives, even those created with other Zip applications.

Note | The Compressed Folders feature is not available on 64-bit versions of Windows Server 2003.

For a comparison of the Compressed Folders feature and third-party compression utilities such as WinZip, visit www.samspublishing.com and enter this book's ISBN number (no hyphens or parenthesis) in the Search field; then click the book cover image to access the book details page. Click the Web Resources link in the More Information section, and locate article ID# **A010301**.

CD Burning

Windows XP and now Windows Server 2003 provide built-in support for CD burners. Not only do they recognize CD drives and have a built-in database of CD-R and CD-RW drivers, but they also provide built-in methods for writing to the CD drives.

Windows Server 2003 has drag-and-drop support for burning CDs, which means you can create data CDs simply by dragging the files to the drive letter of your CD burner. A balloon pops up in the Notification Area (formerly know as the system tray) to let you know you have files waiting to be written to the CD. Clicking the balloon brings up the view of the CD drive, as shown in Figure 3.2.

CD Burning **35**

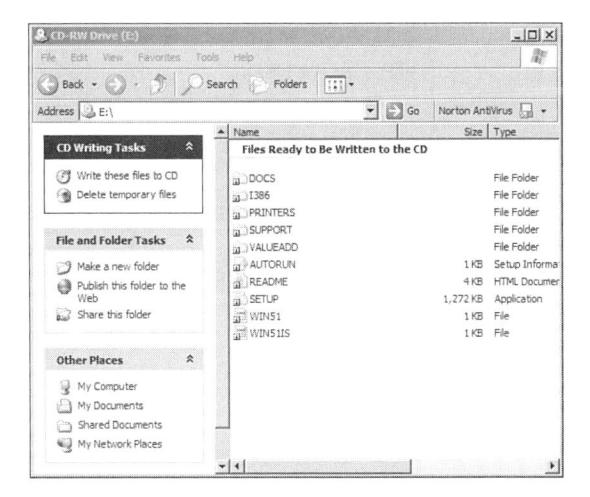

Figure 3.2 Create a data CD by dragging files to the CD burner.

You can add and remove files to this list. To remove all pending files, click **Delete Temporary Files** under the CD Writing Tasks section. When you've arranged all your files and are ready to burn the files to CD, simply click **Write These Files to CD** under CD Writing Tasks on the left. This launches the CD Writing Wizard, which allows you to choose a CD label to name your CD and then physically writes the files to a blank CD in your CD-R or CD-RW drive. As you can see in Figure 3.3, when the wizard is finished writing the files, you can choose to make another copy of the CD. Also, notice that the CD burning software was developed under license from Roxio, Inc., the makers of CD Creator.

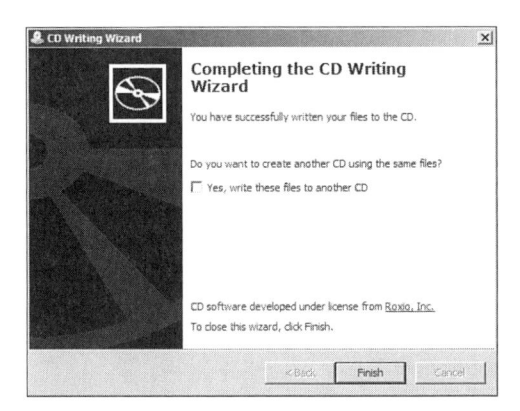

Figure 3.3 Choosing to make another copy on this screen saves time because the initial preparation is already done.

36   **Chapter 3**   Interface Changes

For a comparison of the CD burning feature and third-party utilities such as Nero Burning ROM and CD Creator, visit www.samspublishing.com and enter this book's ISBN number (no hyphens or parenthesis) in the Search field; then click the book cover image to access the book details page. Click the Web Resources link in the More Information section, and locate article ID# **A010302**.

Another method for burning CDs is to simply select the files and right-click, which brings up a pop-up menu. As shown in Figure 3.4, if you move the mouse over Send To, the menu extends and you can select CD-RW Drive(E:), where CD-RW Drive(E:) is the name and drive letter of your CD-R or CD-RW drive. This brings up the view of the files temporarily copied to CD as before, allowing you to add and remove files and then launch the CD Writing Wizard as before, when you are ready to create the CD.

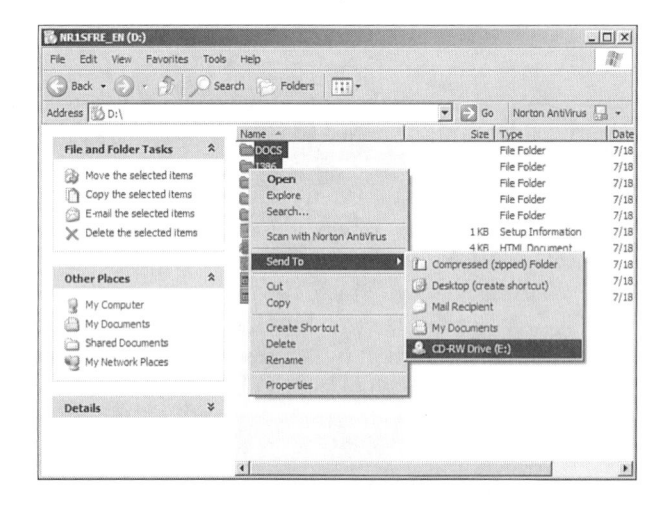

Figure 3.4   Right-click to choose to send files to the CD burner.

Tip   When a blank CD is inserted in the CD-R or CD-RW drive, it automatically gives you the choice to start creating a CD (provided autorun is enabled).

In addition to being able to create your own data CDs, built-in support is available for creating audio CDs. You can use Windows Media Player to create your own audio CDs by doing the following:

1. Open Windows Media Player.
2. Create a new playlist.
3. Open and select MP3 files to add to your playlist, rearranging them as necessary.
4. Click **Copy to CD or Device**.

5. Select your playlist, and perform any last-minute reorganizations as necessary.
6. Click the **Copy Music** button in the upper-right corner.

In most cases, I wouldn't recommend using your servers for creating music CDs, unless you have a server dedicated to the task, because the overhead impacts other processes, but it's there if you need it.

Remote Desktop and Remote Assistance

Other new features introduced by Windows XP that are now incorporated in Windows Server 2003 include two features for remotely controlling users' workstations: Remote Desktop and Remote Assistance. Both Remote Desktop and Remote Assistance use the Remote Desktop Protocol (RDP) for communicating between local and remote systems.

Remote Desktop

The term *Remote Desktop* is somewhat deceptive and can be confusing. There are actually two components to Remote Desktop—the client-side component (Remote Desktop Connection) and the server-side component (Remote Desktop for Administration). These two pieces are just a rename of the previous Terminal Services client and Terminal Services server from previous versions of Windows.

> For more information about Remote Desktop, **see** "Remote Desktop for Administration," **p. 180**.

The main point here is that with Remote Desktop for Administration enabled, you can remotely connect to your Windows Server 2003 (or Windows XP) machines by using the Remote Desktop Connection (or any other Terminal Services client) and obtain a graphical interface as if you were physically at the server. This can be done whether anyone is at the server or not.

Remote Assistance

Remote Assistance is similar to Remote Desktop, but it is designed primarily for helping someone who is physically at the box. As such, it has some significant differences. First, and probably most important, Remote Assistance is totally user (client-side) driven. The sessions are initiated by the user, and the decision to allow someone to remotely take control is determined by the user. Second, to protect the user, Remote Assistance imposes time restrictions on the length of the remote control session.

Just like Remote Desktop, Remote Assistance needs to be enabled before it can be used. Remote Assistance is enabled from the Remote tab of System properties. Simply select **Turn on Remote Assistance and Allow Invitations to be Sent from This Computer**.

Remote Assistance is part of the Help and Support Center. To access it, select **Help and Support** from the Start menu. In the Help and Support Center, click **Support**. Next, select **Get Remote Assistance**. To initiate the Remote Assistance process, the user must select **Invite Someone to Help You**. The following are three methods by which a user can send the invitation:

- **Instant message**—Uses Windows Messenger to send the invitation to the helper. Unlike Windows XP, Windows Messenger is not installed by default on Windows Server 2003. To send an invitation via Windows Messenger, Internet access is required.
- **Email**—Sends the invitation to the helper via email. The user fills in the address of the helper and sends the email. When the helper receives the email, she simply clicks the link to open a session. To send by email, some type of email application (such as Outlook or Outlook Express) needs to be installed. Outlook Express is installed by default.
- **File**—This method specifies a file location to save the invitation file. The file location must be accessible to both the user (to create the invitation) and the helper (to open and use it).

No matter which method is used to create the invitation, the user also specifies the duration (in hours) of how long the invitation is good. The invitation is then used by the helper to connect to the user's machine. After the interval for the invitation expires, it is no longer good for accessing the machine. Further protection of the invitation can be provided by specifying a password. Of course, the password must be communicated to the helper somehow so she can open the invitation. The process works like this:

1. The user configures and sends an invitation to the helper.
2. The helper receives the invitation and clicks the URL or opens the file to respond.
3. As shown in Figure 3.5, the user is prompted to allow the helper to connect.

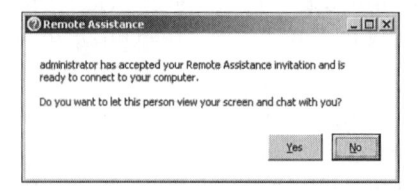

Figure 3.5 This dialog box shows the helper attempting to connect to a Remote Assistance session.

4. After the user accepts, the helper can see the user's desktop and send and receive chat messages, as shown in Figure 3.6.

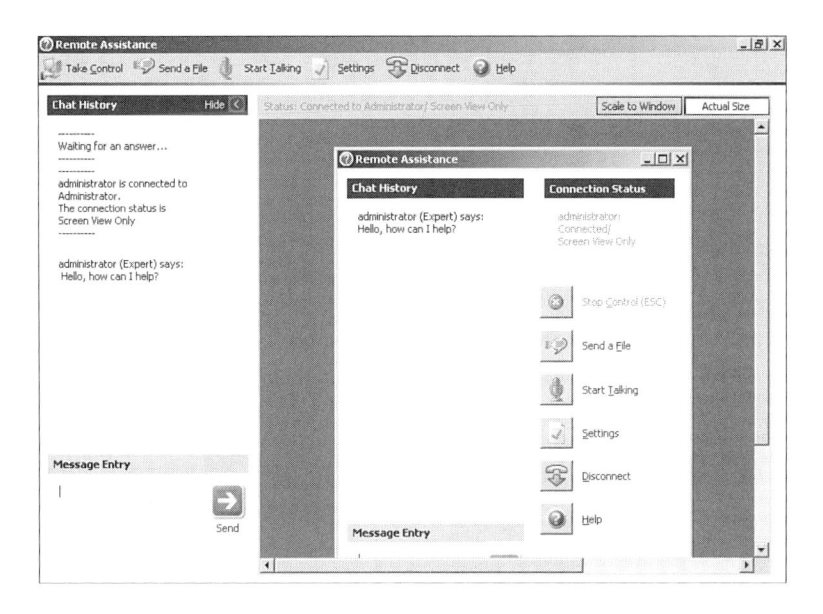

Figure 3.6 A Remote Assistance session has been initiated.

5. Once connected, the user and helper can exchange files, but it is still user driven. If the helper initiates sending a file, the user must accept it and designate where to store it.
6. The helper can request to take control of the user's desktop (see Figure 3.7).

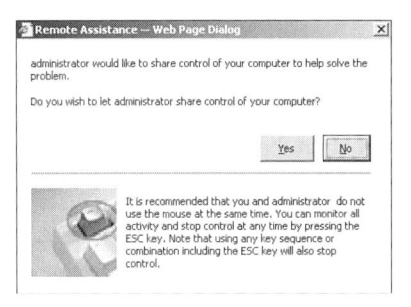

Figure 3.7 The helper can only request to take control.

7. If desired, the user can allow the helper to take control. This then gives the helper access to the user's desktop, but the user can still see what the helper is doing.

Consistent with giving the user full power over the remote control session, the user can cancel the remote control session at any time simply by pressing the Esc key. It's sort of a fail-safe to give the user a warm fuzzy. If the helper starts doing something the user doesn't like, the user can just press Esc.

> **Note** A group policy enables helpers to solicit users for remote assistance. This just enables the helper to prompt the user; the user still initiates the session, and it is still totally user driven.

Quite frankly, the Remote Assistance model is designed more for end user desktops. As such, it will probably be used more in Windows XP than in Windows Server 2003. Chances are the user and the help desk support personnel will be running Windows XP instead of Windows Server 2003. You wouldn't ordinarily have anyone logged and sitting at the server console to send and respond to Remote Assistance messages. Remote Desktop for Administration is the more viable remote control console for the server platform because it enables administrators to connect to the server without anyone being there, just like the former Terminal Services.

Other Interface Changes

Traditionally, Microsoft has increasingly added new features to enhance the desktop user's experience, and Windows Server 2003 is no exception. A number of new display settings and effects are available for customizing the look and feel of the desktop in Windows Server 2003. Historically, settings that enhance the user experience have had the potential to degrade performance and as such are not appropriate on a server platform. In Windows Server 2003, although these settings exist, a lot of them are either disabled by default or can be disabled relatively easily. For example, the default desktop is blank—there is no flashy background wallpaper, just the standard blue Windows desktop.

The Desktop

One of the first things you will probably notice when you log on to Windows Server 2003 is that there is nothing on the desktop (except the Recycle Bin). Where did everything go? All the icons formerly on the desktop have been moved to the Start menu, although you can adjust the display settings to put some of them back on the desktop.

In addition, several settings are available for enhancing the behavior of menus and windows that can unnecessarily impact performance, such as animating windows when maximizing and minimizing, fading menus into view, and so on.

Fortunately for the server platform where minimizing such performance degradations is of concern, a single location is provided to modify these settings based on their impact to server performance. On the Advanced tab of the System control panel applet is a Performance section. Clicking the Settings button brings up the Performance Options window shown in Figure 3.8.

As you can see, you have the option to manually enable or disable each of the various display settings, or you can choose a single radio button to optimize for performance.

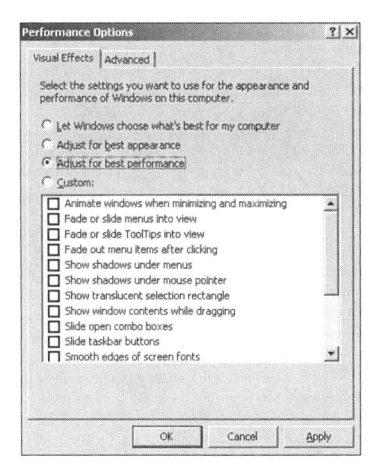

Figure 3.8 Customize the desktop appearance to optimize performance.

The Start Menu

At first glance, it looks like the entire Start menu has been rearranged. In actuality, as you can see in Figure 3.9, the Start menu has been broken down into the following sections:

- **Pinned Programs**—This section allows you to "pin" shortcuts for easy access right off the Start menu. By default, it contains shortcuts for the Manage Your Server Wizard and Windows Explorer. You can also add the special desktop shortcuts for Internet or email applications, such as Internet Explorer or Outlook, or any other shortcuts you want.
- **Recently Used Programs**—This section is similar to the former Documents section, except it contains a list of all recently used programs, such as Command Prompt, Active Directory Users and Computers, and the like, as shown in Figure 3.9. You can specify how many recently used items will appear by modifying the Start menu properties.
- **All Programs Menu**—This section contains the items that were formerly on the Programs menu, including Windows Update and any installed programs, as well as user-added shortcuts at the root of the Start menu.
- **Standard Folders**—This section contains the items that were formerly on the desktop, such as My Computer, My Documents, My Network Places, and My Recent Documents, if enabled. By default, only My Computer is displayed.
- **Control Panel**—This section contains the Control Panel applet, Administrative Tools, Printers and Faxes, and potentially other control panel items (such as Network Connections and so on).
- **Default Utilities**—This section contains most of the former Start menu items, including Run, Search, and Help (now called the Help and Support).

42 Chapter 3 Interface Changes

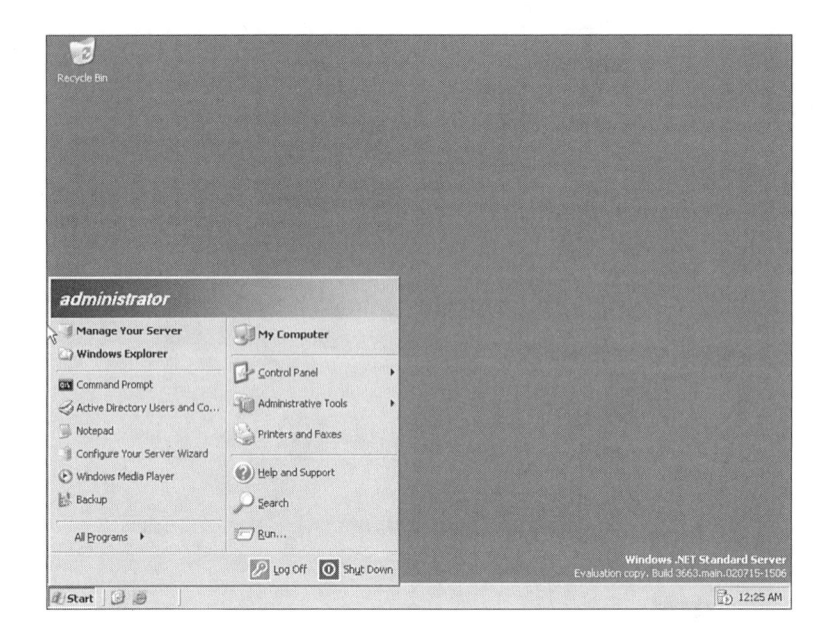

Figure 3.9 The new Start menu.

These sections can be modified by customizing the Start menu and Taskbar properties. Follow these steps:

1. Right-click anywhere on the taskbar or Start menu, and select **Properties**.
2. Select the **Start Menu** tab; then click the **Customize** button next to the Start Menu radio button.
3. On the General tab of the Customize Start Menu screen, you can modify the number of programs that appear in the Recently Used Programs section as well as select the Internet and email application to display in the Pinned Programs section.
4. Select the **Advanced** tab, where you can choose which items to display in each of the other sections—for example, whether to show Administrative Tools and Network Connections. You can also specify to display recently opened documents, such as the former Documents Start Menu item. One final setting on this tab is the option labeled Highlight Newly Installed Programs (or not). This setting causes a balloon to pop up over the Start menu notifying you when a new application has been installed. The pop-up balloon can be somewhat annoying, but it also highlights the new application in a different color on the Start menu, making it easier to find.

Note | You can only add your own shortcuts to the Pinned Programs and All Programs Menu sections; the other sections of the Start menu do not allow the creation of shortcuts.

As you have seen in this chapter, several user interface and functionality improvements have been made in the Windows Server 2003 shell. Most of these improvements were first introduced in the corresponding client platform, Windows XP. As such, many of them, such as Remote Assistance, are more appropriate for the client platform. However, they do provide a potentially richer user experience, even for the bleary-eyed administrator still logged on to the server at 3 a.m. Some of them, such as compressed folders, provide utilitarian functionality previously available only through third-party add-ons. One nice thing about all these new features is that they are not being forced down your throat. You can enable or disable most of these settings and customize your environment the way you like. If you don't like the minimal functionality provided by compressed folders and CD burning, you can still purchase the third-party solutions.

4

SECURITY

In This Chapter

- Understanding Microsoft's security philosophy, **page 46**.
- Using security tools, **page 47**.
- Encrypting data, **page 56**.
- Developing a security strategy, **page 62**.

What's New

Security was a major focus area for Microsoft during the development of Windows Server 2003. In fact, Microsoft created its new Trustworthy Computing initiative during the development of Windows Server 2003 and actually suspended Windows Server 2003's development for two months to focus exclusively on security issues.

As a result, Windows Server 2003 is perhaps the most secure out-of-the-box version of Windows to date. However, that does not mean you can simply install Windows Server 2003 and have a completely secure server. Security is always a trade-off between security and functionality, and you need to configure your servers to strike the appropriate balance for your environment. Windows Server 2003 does make it easier to secure your environment with a variety of security-specific tools, data encryption, and so forth.

Another major security problem Microsoft has tried to deal with over the years is secure code. Viruses, malicious scripts, and other forms of unsecure code have plagued Microsoft operating systems for years. With the release of the .NET Framework, Microsoft has created the first software development environment that incorporates security from the ground up. As software developers move to the .NET Framework for corporate application development, you as a Windows administrator will have more control over the code that executes in your environment, allowing you to prevent malicious code from affecting the productivity of your users.

Microsoft's New Security Philosophy

In mid-2002, an unprecedented series of major security flaws were uncovered in Windows 2000, Internet Explorer 6.0, and IIS 5.0, which are some of Microsoft's most strategically important products. The resulting media backlash resulted in a now-famous "trustworthy computing" internal memo from Bill Gates to all Microsoft employees. The gist of the memo was this: Stop programming and take a look at what you're doing from a security perspective. For two months, production on all Microsoft products stopped, and Microsoft programmers and other employees attended a series of classes designed to highlight common programming practices that often result in security flaws. The programmers also reviewed the code for their products, including Windows Server 2003, with an eye toward removing those unsecure programming practices. The result, according to Microsoft, is that a huge number of security flaws were removed from Windows Server 2003 (and other products) before it was released to manufacturing.

Other practices changed, too. For example, Microsoft products usually go through a beta cycle and then a release candidate (RC) cycle. During the RC phase, new features aren't supposed to be added to the product and major changes aren't supposed to be made. The RC phase is normally designed to catch and fix bugs; any feature that has bugs that can't be fixed is dropped from the product and rolled to the next version's development. For Windows Server 2003, however, the door was left open for security-related changes throughout the product's lifecycle and even into the RC phase. Normally prohibited changes, such as changes to the product's user interface, were allowed if they had a security implication. The message was clear: Deadlines could be missed and features could change if doing so was necessary to prevent security problems in the product.

The new security philosophy resulted in several important changes. For example, IIS has been a major area for security vulnerabilities, due primarily to the fact that IIS is installed by default on all Windows 2000 Server computers. Windows Server 2003 improves its own security by not installing IIS by default and, when IIS is installed by an administrator, using a default configuration that disables many of IIS's more commonly exploited features, such as dynamic Web pages.

> **Caution** The biggest security mistake is complacency. Despite Microsoft's new philosophy and attention to security, Windows Server 2003 has undiscovered security vulnerabilities. Maintaining a secure environment requires constant vigilance, an aggressive program of applying security updates to all computers, and an inherently secure network design. In other words, you should expect a good portion of your time as an administrator to be spent on security and security-related tasks. Don't rely on Microsoft to do your security work for you; investigate potential security holes in your infrastructure and develop ways to protect them.

A major portion of Microsoft's new security philosophy can be reflected in the default configurations for its products. In the past, Microsoft's goal was to provide a default configuration that offered maximum functionality. Now, Microsoft's goal is to provide a more secure default configuration, even at the expense of advanced functionality and features. In other words, Microsoft is willing to provide features that aren't turned on by default and require an administrator to manually enable those features and implicitly acknowledge the features' security implications.

This new philosophy puts a lot more of the security burden on you, the Windows administrator. Before you change any default settings or install any additional components, think about what they'll do to the security of your network. Research settings and components to discover their potential weaknesses and find out how hackers might exploit them to attack your network.

Security Tools

Windows Server 2003 doesn't introduce a lot in the way of new security tools. It does, however, introduce some minor improvements in its tools and includes many helpful tools that are available as add-ons for Windows 2000. For this one section of the book, we're going to veer slightly off our regular course. In general, we're not using this book to explain things that exist in Windows 2000; instead we're saving space to cover just what's new and changed in Windows Server 2003. However, Microsoft's user surveys—and our personal experience— indicates that most administrators have never used many of Windows 2000's security tools. For that reason, we're going to approach the major tools from scratch, showing you how they work and explaining their effects on Windows Server 2003's overall security picture. If you're already familiar with these tools, feel free to skim through the next few sections looking for the bits that have changed.

> **Note** Security isn't a standalone item in Windows Server 2003; it's incorporated throughout the operating system. We've provided a handy list of cross-references at the end of this chapter that direct you to other security-related topics in this book, including Active Directory and IIS.

Security Configuration Manager

You'll see that the Windows Server 2003 documentation refers to the Security Configuration Manager toolset. The phrase itself is a bit misleading because there's no one tool actually named "Security Configuration Manager." Instead, Windows Server 2003 includes a group of related tools—Security Templates, Security Configuration and Analysis, and so forth—that provide security-specific functionality. Windows Server 2003's primary security tools include

- **Security Templates, and Security Configuration and Analysis**—These two MMC snap-ins, which are discussed in the next section, make applying consistent security settings across your organization easier.
- **Security Settings extension to Group Policy**—This tool makes editing the security information on a domain, a site, or an organizational unit (OU) within Active Directory easy.
- **Local Security Policy**—This MMC snap-in edits the security configuration of a local computer, including its password policy and other security settings. A similar snap-in on domain controllers enables you to edit these security properties for an entire domain.
- `Secedit.exe`—This command-line tool applies or analyzes security templates. Its nongraphical interface makes it ideal for use in batch files.

Windows Server 2003 includes another tool we especially like, called Hfnetchk.exe (which stands for HotFix NETwork CHecKer). Hfnetchk.exe is designed to analyze Windows computers and let you know whether they're missing any recent security updates. We cover this tool later in this chapter, in the section "Hfnetchk.exe."

Security Templates, Configuration, and Analysis

Configuring Windows Server 2003's security features requires a lot of attention to detail. One of the biggest problems, therefore, is in consistently applying a detailed security configuration across an enterprise. After all, manually configuring a company's computers is time-consuming, not to mention error-prone. To help consistently apply complex security configurations, Windows 2000 introduced the concept of security templates, and Windows Server 2003 makes great use of templates to enable consistent enterprise-wide security.

The idea behind a *security template* is straightforward: Bundle a bunch of security settings into a single file, and then apply that file to multiple computers. In effect, the template is like a security checklist, forcing computers to configure themselves according to a standard you've created. The best—and worst—part about security templates is that they are *cumulative*, which means they can build on one another. For example, you might apply template A to configure your company's baseline security settings and then apply template B to configure department-specific security settings that build on the company's baseline. This flexibility makes it easier to manage enterprise security with a relatively small number of templates, but it can also make troubleshooting configuration problems a real nightmare because you have to figure out which templates apply each setting.

> **Tip** When you're using security templates, the easiest way to stay out of trouble is to thoroughly document what each template does. That way, you'll be able to easily determine what the end result of several templates will be, and you'll avoid time-consuming backtracking when you have to troubleshoot problems.

To make things easier, Windows Server 2003 offers two MMC snap-ins dedicated to security templates: The Security Templates snap-in and the Security Configuration and Analysis snap-in. Windows Server 2003 doesn't come with a preconfigured console for the snap-ins, so you must open the MMC and add them yourself. We like to add both snap-ins to the same console because they're so closely related. Figure 4.1 shows them in use.

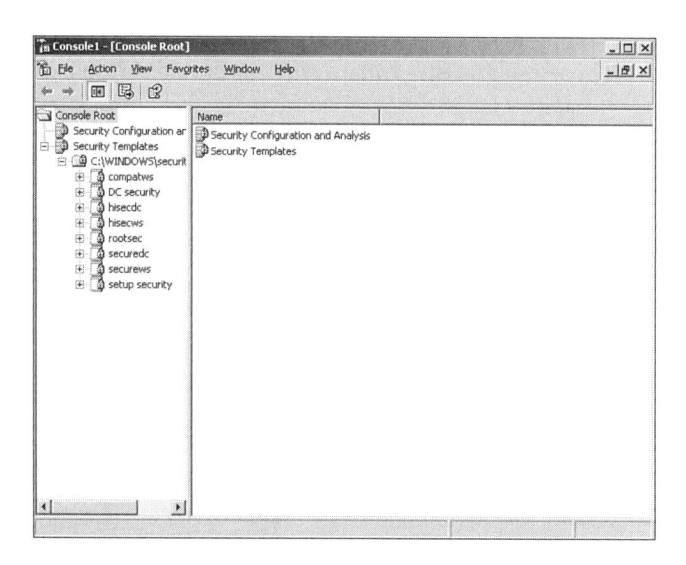

Figure 4.1 Save your custom console for easier use in the future.

Security Templates Snap-in

The Security Templates snap-in is the best place to start. The snap-in starts with a list of the templates that are included with Windows Server 2003:

- **Compatws**—Designed to lower specific file system and Registry permissions to enable some older Windows applications to run properly.
- **DC security**—Designed to be applied to domain controllers, it provides a higher level of security.

- **Hisecdc**—An even more secure configuration for domain controllers, it requires network encryption from clients.
- **Hisecws**—A highly secure configuration that enables IPSec encryption with secure servers. This template can be applied to workstations and member servers in a domain.
- **Securedc**—A slightly less-secure template than Hisecdc, intended for use on domain controllers.
- **Securews**—A slightly less-secure template than Hisecws, intended for use on workstations and member servers.

We don't recommend trying to memorize what these templates do. Instead, consult the Windows Server 2003 documentation for details. You should know, however, that each template configures settings in seven areas:

- **Account Policies**—These policies include password policies, account lockout policies, and Kerberos protocol policies.
- **Local Policies**—These include auditing, user rights, and miscellaneous security options.
- **Event Log**—These policies configure the size and retention behavior for the built-in application, security, and system event logs.
- **Restricted Groups**—These policies define the membership of key user groups, such as the local Administrators group.
- **System Services**—These define the status of services, enabling an administrator to centrally control which services are permitted to run on company computers.
- **Registry**—These policies define security on system Registry keys.
- **File System**—These policies define NT File System (NTFS) security permissions for the entire file system.

> For a quick refresher on NTFS file permissions, visit www.samspublishing.com and enter this book's ISBN number (no hyphens or parenthesis) in the Search field; then click the book cover image to access the book details page. Click the Web Resources link in the More Information section, and locate article ID# **A010401**.
>
> If you've skipped Windows 2000 and are coming straight from Windows NT, you'll find this article especially helpful because it explains how Windows Server 2003 and Windows 2000 NTFS permissions differ from NT.

As you can see, the list of things you can configure within a security template is quite comprehensive. You can even modify the settings in any of the built-in templates (although we recommend you make a backup copy first, in case you want to revert to the original settings later). Simply double-click any setting to open a dialog box that enables you to change it. Figure 4.2 shows the result of a change to the Hisecws template. Notice how the setting for the Alerter service has been changed to Disabled.

Security Tools   **51**

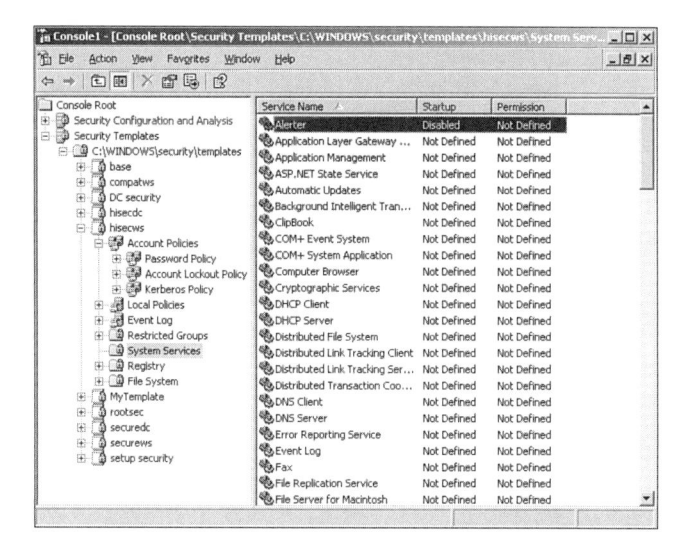

Figure 4.2   To save your changes, right-click the template name and select **Save** from the pop-up menu.

Figure 4.2 also illustrates an important security template concept: *Definition*. Notice in the figure that all services except Alerter are set to Not Defined**.** This setting means the template doesn't actually contain a setting and that applying the template to a computer will not change that particular setting on the computer. If you see something configured as Not Defined in a security template, you know that the template will have no effect on that setting when the template is applied.

If you don't want to start with one of the default templates, you can create your own from scratch. Simply right-click a templates folder, such as `C:\WINDOWS\security\templates` and select **New Template** from the pop-up menu. You'll be asked to provide a name and location for your new template, and then you'll be able to modify its settings, as shown in Figure 4.3. All new templates start out with all their settings undefined, allowing you to customize the template to contain exactly the security settings you want.

After you've created the templates you need, you can deploy them. We'll discuss that next.

Security Configuration and Analysis

Working with templates can be difficult. Although you can use the Security Templates snap-in to see what's in a template, knowing what effect the template will have on a computer is sometimes difficult. The Security Configuration and Analysis (SCA) snap-in is designed to do just that: Show you what effect any given template will have.

Chapter 4 Security

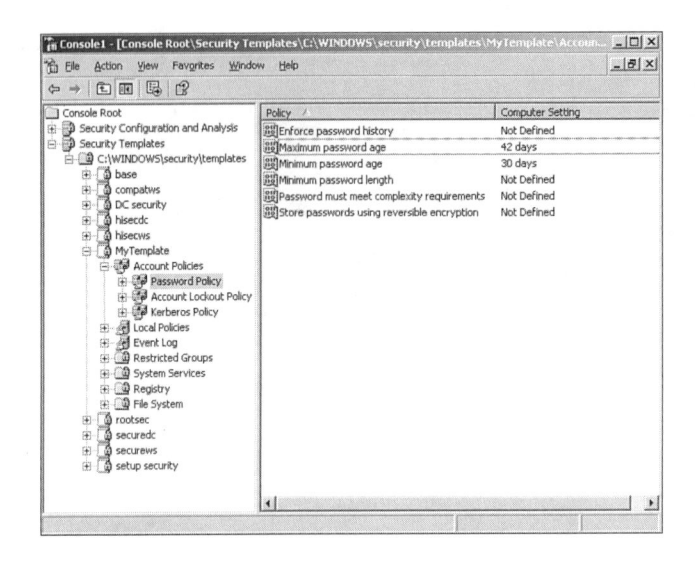

Figure 4.3 Creating your own templates provides maximum security flexibility.

The SCA works with a security database and can create, open, and manage multiple databases so that you can manage different security configurations. A *security database* contains all the settings you want to apply to a computer. SCA includes an import function, so you can import security templates into the database. Figure 4.4 shows the import dialog box, which has a check box in the lower-left corner labeled Clear This Database Before Importing. When this check box is cleared, the import process adds a new security template to the database, layering it on top of whatever's already in there—exactly how security templates work when applied to a computer. When you select the check box, however, the import process first clears the database, starting with a clean configuration. Select the check box when you're ready to begin working with a new database or if you want to wipe out the work you've done so far and start over.

For example, suppose you start with a blank database and import a security template named Template1. Then, you import a second template, named Template2, and you leave the check box cleared. The database will now contain all the settings in both Template1 and Template2. If the two templates contain any conflicting settings, the ones in Template2 will be effective. If, on the other hand, you had selected the check box when importing Template2, the database would contain only the settings in Template2. Everything from Template1 would have been cleared out prior to the import.

After you've imported one or more security templates into a database, you can *analyze* the database against the computer. The analyze process compares the settings in the database to the active configuration of the current computer, without actually applying those settings. The result, shown in Figure 4.5, enables you to easily see exactly what effect the database's settings will have. Figure 4.6 shows additional analysis details. Notice how SCA uses icons to highlight settings in the database that don't match the computer's current configuration. Were you to actually apply the template to the computer, those settings would be changed. Settings that aren't defined in the database, or settings that are defined in the template and currently configured on the computer, aren't called out with a special icon.

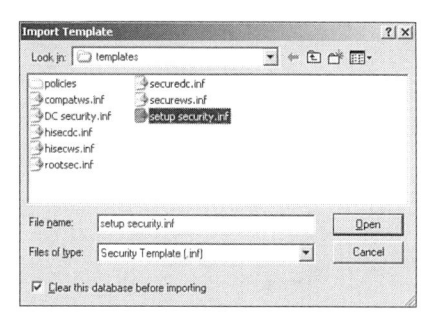

Figure 4.4 You can import multiple security templates into a single security database.

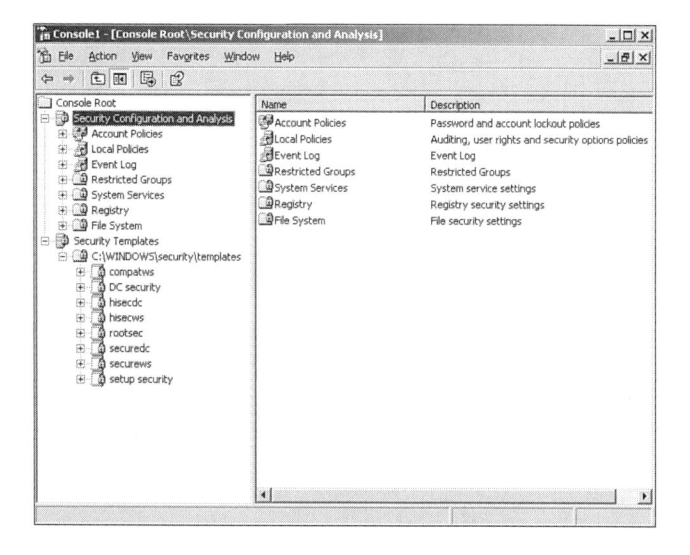

Figure 4.5 Analyzing lets you easily see the effect that one or more security templates will have on a standard computer configuration.

You can also make changes to the security database manually, without the use of a template. The process is similar to modifying a security template: Simply double-click the setting you want to change. Different types of settings present different dialog boxes. For example,

54   **Chapter 4**   Security

Figure 4.7 shows what a file security setting looks like, whereas Figure 4.8 shows a password policy setting. You can remove a setting from the database by clearing the check box that defines the policy in the security database.

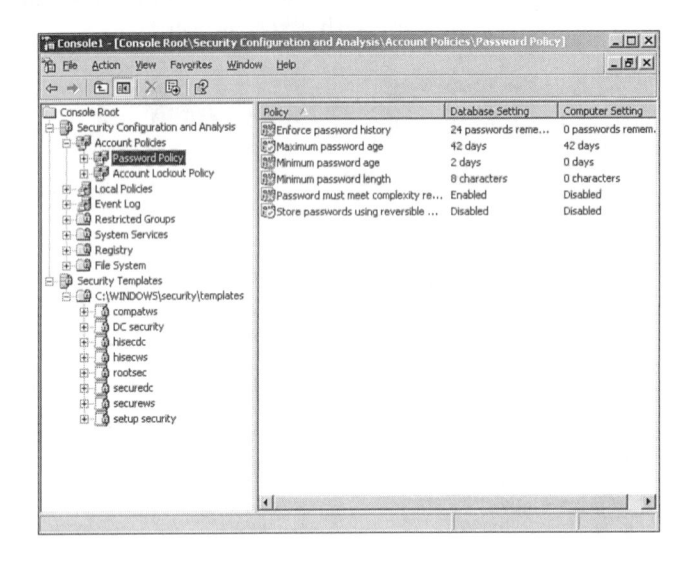

Figure 4.6   Special icons call your attention to differences between the security database and the current configuration.

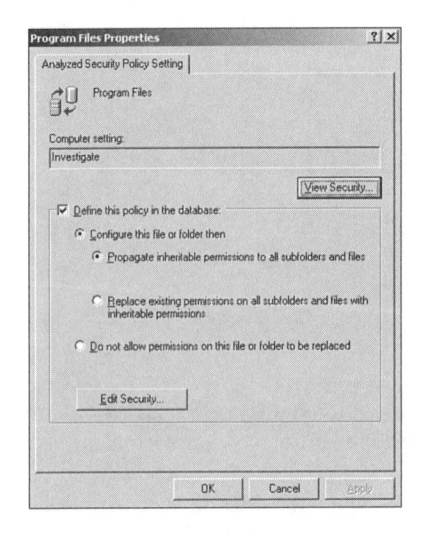

Figure 4.7   Use a security database to specify file permissions.

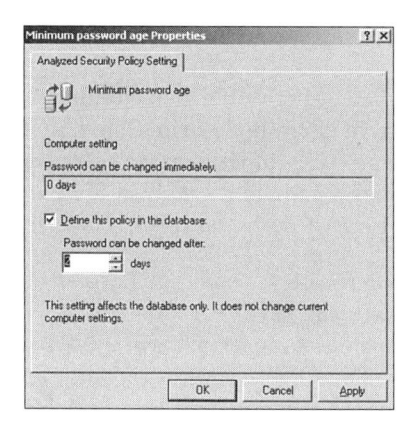

Figure 4.8 Use a security database to specify a password policy setting.

After you've configured your security database exactly the way you want it—either by importing the desired security templates or by manually configuring the database—you have two options for deploying the settings. The easiest is to simply apply the database directly to the computer by right-clicking the **SCA** snap-in and selecting **Configure** from the pop-up menu. Doing so applies the current database to the local computer's active configuration, making the two match. You can also export the database into a security template, which is a bit easier to deploy automatically throughout your enterprise.

Tip | Windows Server 2003 also includes Secedit.exe, a command-line tool introduced in Windows 2000. Secedit.exe can be used to import security templates into a database, analyze databases, and configure the local computer. One way to deploy security settings is to deploy a preconfigured security database and use Secedit.exe—perhaps in a batch file—to apply that database to the local computer.

Perhaps the easiest way to deploy security settings in an Active Directory domain is by using Group Policy. With Group Policy, you can create a new Group Policy object (GPO); import a security template (either one of the included templates or one you created); and link the GPO to a site, an OU, or a domain. All computers contained in that site, OU, or domain will receive the new security settings within an hour or so. Keep in mind that the standard order of group policy application applies: Site policies first, followed by domain policies, and then OUs.

Caution | Not all Windows operating systems support the same security features. Windows 2000 and Windows XP offer slightly different features, so you probably should maintain individual security templates for each operating system. Applying a security template intended for one operating system to a different version can potentially have devastating effects, so be sure to test your templates and apply them only where appropriate.

Hfnetchk.exe

Hfnetchk.exe is a free download from Microsoft's Web site (www.Microsoft.com/download). Hfnetchk was actually developed by an outside firm, Shavlik (www.shavlik.com), and licensed to Microsoft; you can purchase a more fully functional version directly from Shavlik. The commercial version of the tool includes a complete graphical user interface; Microsoft's free version is strictly a command-line tool. Both of them, however, work similarly.

> **Note** Hfnetchk is documented in Microsoft Knowledge Base article Q303215 (http://support.Microsoft.com/default.aspx?scid=kb;en-us;Q303215). You can learn more about the commercial version at http://www.shavlik.com.

Hfnetchk is driven by an XML-based security database, which the tool can download directly from Microsoft. This database describes the latest security updates (formerly known as *security hotfixes*) available from Microsoft, including service packs. The database also describes the specific changes each security update makes to the operating system, especially to files and Registry keys. These descriptions enable Hfnetchk to analyze your computer and determine exactly which security updates have, or have not, been correctly applied. Hfnetchk produces a comprehensive report that tells you exactly which updates you should obtain and apply. Most importantly, it can run across a network, analyzing remote computers to which you have administrative permissions.

Hfnetchk is a useful tool to have in your security arsenal, and it's a tool you should run on a regular basis, especially against security-critical servers such as firewalls and domain controllers. Keep in mind, however, that Hfnetchk is primarily a *reactive* tool, which means it can alert you only to existing security problems. An enterprise-wide deployment of a more proactive solution, such as Software Update Services (SUS), can ensure that your computers always have the latest security updates applied. You can then use Hfnetchk in more of an auditing role to ensure that SUS is working properly and that security updates are, in fact, being applied as intended.

Encrypting Data

Similar to Windows 2000, Windows Server 2003 supports the Microsoft Encrypting File System (EFS), which enables users and administrators to encrypt files using Windows strong built-in encryption capabilities. *Encryption* provides an extra level of security over file permissions: Even if the server is compromised and someone gains access to encrypted files, he won't be able to use the files without the appropriate decryption key.

Windows Server 2003 takes EFS one step further than Windows 2000, however, incorporating multiple-user access (a feature already present in Windows XP). Under Windows 2000, only the user who encrypted a file, or a designated recovery agent, can decrypt a file; in Windows Server 2003, users and administrators can designate other users to have decryption capabilities. To access the new feature, right-click any encrypted file and select **Properties** from the pop-up menu. Then, select **Advanced** in the Properties dialog box and click **Details** next to the check box that enables encryption. You'll see a dialog box similar to the one in Figure 4.9, in which you can manage the users who can access the file.

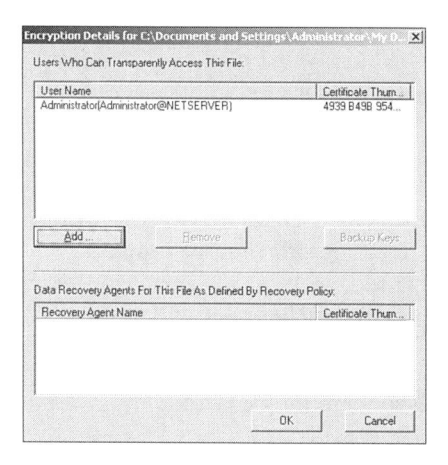

Figure 4.9 Adding multiple users is great for departments that need to protect files while still providing access for multiple users.

Note | Keep in mind that EFS doesn't encrypt folders. You can designate a folder for encryption, but that simply tells Windows to individually encrypt each file within the folder. As a result, you can't assign multiple decryption users on a folder; you have to make the assignment on the files themselves. You can, however, highlight multiple files in Explorer and change their properties all at once.

Windows Server 2003 also provides complete support for encrypting network data via the IPSec network security protocol, Secure Sockets Layer (SSL) encryption for HTTP and other protocols, and so forth. For more information on these security options, see the cross-reference list at the end of this chapter.

Common Security Holes

Have you thought about how the network services in your environment might be used against you and how Windows Server 2003's components offer features to protect your network? A good *security administrator*—a role that is increasingly recognized as a standalone job task within larger environments—has to be constantly paranoid. Even the most seemingly innocent and beneficial network services can be used against you. The next few sections cover some examples to get your paranoid juices flowing. Windows Server 2003 provides options to secure almost all the services against common security attacks, but you'll have to take it upon yourself to implement more secure configurations. Although Windows Server 2003 is more secure out of the box than any previous version of Windows, some security configurations require a trade-off in functionality, so they're not always included in the defaults.

DNS

DNS is your network's phone book, providing a means for computers to resolve easy-to-remember computer names to more functionally useful IP addresses. Windows Server 2003 provides a Dynamic DNS (DDNS) service, which accepts dynamic DNS record registrations from computers that have dynamic IP addresses. DDNS ensures that all computers can be accurately listed in the DNS database. DDNS, however, provides a potential security flaw: If an intruder can insert a bogus DNS record, she can redirect legitimate traffic to a different computer. For example, if an intruder were able to replace the IP addresses of a domain controller, she could easily gain access to authentication traffic and potentially user passwords.

Fortunately, the worst-case scenarios are pretty hard to imagine. Windows's Kerberos protocol helps ensure that client and server computers can validate one another's identities, making it nearly impossible for intruders to capture traffic (at least, between Windows 2000 and higher computers; older Windows versions don't use Kerberos and can be fooled into sending traffic to an unintended computer).

Intruders could still insert new records into DDNS, however, and potentially use those records in an attack against your network. In fact, when you create a new zone Windows Server 2003's DNS service warns you that allowing just any old dynamic updates is a significant security vulnerability, as shown in Figure 4.10. The DNS service does offer an option for secure updates that accepts updates only from computers that have successfully authenticated to the domain. However, the secure option is available only when the DNS service is running on an Active Directory domain controller, thereby providing DNS with access to authentication information. For that reason alone, we always recommend that your DNS servers also be Active Directory domain controllers and that you enable DNS to use secure DDNS updates.

When you install the DNS service on a Windows Server 2003 computer, a new DNS-specific event log is added, along with the built-in application, security, and system event logs. A regular part of your maintenance routine should be to analyze the DNS log for potential security problems such as a large number of unauthenticated update attempts, which can indicate a potential security attack.

Dynamic Host Configuration Protocol

Dynamic Host Configuration Protocol (DHCP) doesn't offer many security vulnerabilities because its only task is to hand out DHCP addresses. However, some especially secure organizations, including banks and government agencies, often take steps to deny DHCP services to network intruders. By preventing DHCP from providing an IP address to unknown computers, intruders have that much harder a time working on the network. Of course, an intruder can always make up an IP address; finding one that will work and that isn't already in use can take time, though, and might discourage some attackers.

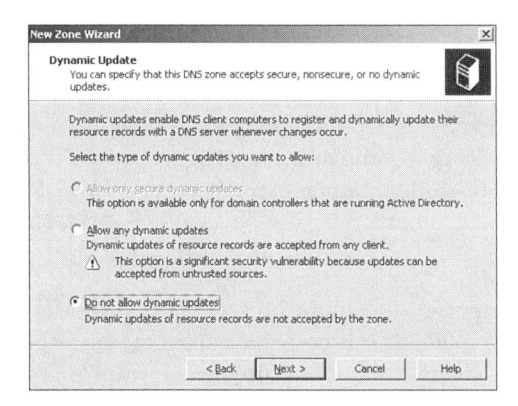

Figure 4.10 Secure updates are possible only on a domain controller.

Securing DHCP in this fashion requires that you configure your computers to use DHCP and then configure DHCP with a reservation for each computer. By ensuring that each DHCP scope contains just enough addresses to fulfill your reservations, you ensure that no extra computers will be capable of obtaining addresses. Of course, using reservations in this fashion largely defeats the "dynamic" part of DHCP; what you're really doing is reverting to static IP configurations that are centrally managed on the DHCP server. This isn't a step most organizations feel is necessary, but it's available as an option if your organization needs to use it.

Network Monitor

Network Monitor (NetMon) is a network packet-capture tool included with almost every version of Windows since Windows NT (it's not included with Windows 9x versions). We won't go into NetMon's operations in detail; the product has been around since early versions of Windows NT and is also included in Microsoft Systems Management Server. What you need to be aware of is how NetMon can be used to compromise network security.

NetMon captures and displays raw network data, meaning anyone with NetMon can analyze practically anything that crosses your network. The most obvious concern, then, is it giving attackers the ability to pick up passwords from your network. For domain authentication, that's not a worry because even older versions of Windows NT and Windows 9x use some pretty powerful encryption techniques. However, for any internal Web sites, FTP sites, or other services that might not use Windows-integrated authentication, password stealing is a very real problem. NetMon also makes pulling other confidential information across the network relatively easy. For example, if someone in your human resources department copies a salaries spreadsheet to a file server, an intruder could capture the traffic with NetMon and reassemble what should have been confidential information.

Microsoft helps prevent NetMon abuses in a couple of ways. First, the version included with Windows captures only traffic sent to or from the machine on which NetMon is running. That limits the user to capturing whatever is coming and going from his own computer, so he won't likely pick up anything he couldn't have accessed otherwise. However, the so-called "full" version of NetMon, included with Systems Management Server, can pick up anything that passes on the network segment, making it a much more dangerous tool. The full version isn't actually hard to come by apart from Systems Management Server; several Microsoft Official Curriculum courses in the past included it, and several less-than-legitimate Web sites make it available for download.

Fortunately, Microsoft anticipated that unauthorized use of NetMon might be a problem. Every running copy of NetMon sends out occasional packets in a special protocol called *bone*. The protocol name is actually something of an in joke: NetMon's product code-name is "Bloodhound," so naming its internal protocol "bone" is intended to be cutesy. The practical use of the bone protocol is that it enables you to see other copies of NetMon running on your network. You should regularly run the full version of NetMon (yes, you'll probably need to purchase Systems Management Server to get a legal copy) and check for bone broadcasts from other copies. To do so, follow these steps:

1. Perform a network capture with NetMon. Let it run for several minutes, at least.
2. View the completed capture and add a new filter by clicking the **Filter** icon in the toolbar.
3. Double-click the filter's **Protocol** line and disable all but the bone protocol, as shown in Figure 4.11.

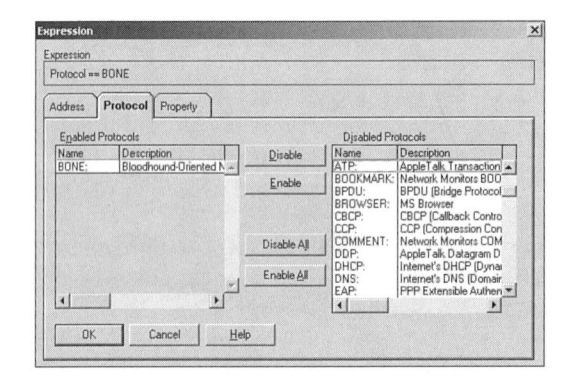

Figure 4.11 Disabling all but bone makes spotting bone packets in a large capture easier.

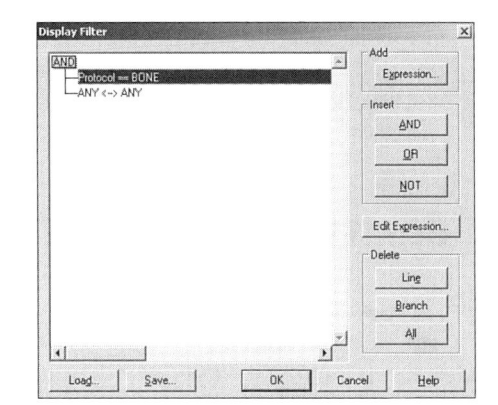

4. Close the dialog box, and ensure that your filter looks like the one in Figure 4.12.

Figure 4.12 A properly configured filter makes spotting bone broadcasts without missing any important data easier.

5. Review any packets shown in the capture. Bone packets include the IP address of the computer that sent it, helping you to track down the unauthorized user.

> **Caution** Don't see any bone frames in your capture? Don't relax. Even the full version of NetMon can capture only the traffic on your local network segment, so you'll need to perform a capture on each segment. In a switched environment, you can usually configure your switches to forward all traffic to one switch port, where you can plug in your NetMon computer to capture everything.

Finally, keep in mind that NetMon is not a unique product. Even though it's relatively easy to acquire, plenty of other commercial packet sniffers are available that an attacker can use to pull information from your network as it passes by on the wire. Not all these other products include something similar to the bone protocol, so you won't be able to detect their use. The best way to keep these packet capture tools under control is to firmly control what software your users can run on their computers and to guard all physical connections to your network that an intruder might use to gain access.

Internet Information System

IIS has come to be known as one of Microsoft's more serious security flaws, primarily because it's installed by default on so many operating systems. Several viruses, including the now-famous "Code Red" worm, attack IIS directly, set up shop on the attacked computer, continue to attack other computers from there, and eventually spread throughout the network.

Although IIS isn't installed by default on Windows Server 2003, it's still the default option on older versions of Windows. You can go a long way toward securing your environment by removing IIS from computers on which it isn't necessary and by applying the latest service packs and security updates to computers that must run IIS. A vigorous antivirus plan, including frequent updates to virus definitions, can help protect both servers and clients from viruses that attack IIS.

Developing a Security Strategy

As we've mentioned a couple of times already, security is not something you worry about once and never again. It's a constant process, and to make that process as efficient as possible, you need to have a battle plan. We find that the ongoing work of security falls more or less into two areas: auditing and maintenance. That's not to say no other security-related tasks exist; on the contrary, most of what we cover in this book is security configuration. But configuration is more of a one-time thing: You configure some security settings and you're done. Auditing and maintenance, however, are two security-related tasks that are never finished.

Auditing

Auditing is the process of reviewing something—in this case, security-related somethings—to ensure they comply with some standard. Windows Server 2003 provides several types of auditing:

- **You can configure auditing on file and folder access**—This enables you to review who is accessing files. This auditing takes place in the security event log, and you have to decide which files and folders to audit.
- **You can audit domain events such as user logons**—As with file access, you have to decide which events to audit, and the events themselves are listed in the security event log.
- **You can audit IIS log files to look for errors, potential security problems, and much more**—You have to configure IIS to create a log file, and you must manually review the log. It's just a text file (not a regular event log), although you can purchase third-party applications to help summarize log information and call your attention to possible problems.
- **You can audit the DNS log**—This is included in the Event Viewer snap-in. This log can alert you to potential security problems as well as operational errors.

Of course, there are many more. You should also make it a regular habit to audit things other than logs. For example, you might occasionally look at the membership of your company's Enterprise Admins, Domain Admins, and Schema Admins user groups. The members of these groups have powerful built-in permissions, and an occasional check to ensure the groups contain only authorized users is a good practice. Your organization might set up other sensitive groups, and you should check them on a periodic basis, too.

Auditing can be a daunting task, with so many things to look at. Consider creating a checklist that helps you remember which things to look at.

> **Tip** Remember, only you can prevent forest fires and only you can prevent security breaches. Microsoft has given Windows Server 2003 the capability to be as secure as you need it to be; it's your job to implement those capabilities and to ensure they continue to meet your organization's ongoing needs.

Security Maintenance

Unfortunately, securing your servers isn't a one-time task. Hackers are constantly finding new ways to compromise common security measures, and you'll always need to implement new measures to maintain your environment's security levels. Also, despite Microsoft's Trustworthy Computing initiative, rest assured that Windows Server 2003 does contain bugs, and some of those bugs will affect the product's security. As those bugs are discovered and squashed, you'll need to apply the appropriate fixes to your servers. Bear in mind that Microsoft offers a few types of fixes:

- **Service packs**—These roll up several months' worth of fixes, along with new features, into a single, cumulative package. Each service pack contains all prior fixes, so that installing service pack 2, for example, also installs the fixes contained in service pack 1. Service packs go through an extensive beta-test cycle and are fully regression-tested, so they shouldn't introduce new bugs. In practice, of course, Microsoft rarely releases a perfect service pack; we recommend waiting a few weeks after the release of a new service pack to ensure it's relatively well-behaved.

> **Note** One of the reasons service packs can be buggy is that Microsoft uses them to deploy new features. Every so often, Microsoft resolves to stop doing that and to include only bug fixes. To my knowledge, that has never actually happened and service packs continue to introduce new features and changes to existing features along with a host of bug fixes.

- **Hotfixes**—Also called *quick-fix engineering updates (QFEs)*. These generally correct very specific bugs in the operating system and don't receive the benefit of a full beta-test cycle. Microsoft recommends that you install a hotfix only when you're experiencing the specific problem the hotfix addresses. We concur with this recommendation; don't treat hotfixes as something you casually deploy because they can sometimes break things. If you're not experiencing the specific problem the hotfix solves, wait until the next service pack. Every service pack rolls up the preceding hotfixes and tests them in a full beta-test cycle.

- **Security updates**—These are basically hotfixes that address security issues. One supposes that Microsoft puts a bit more effort into testing these than a typical hotfix, but because security updates are nearly always released too quickly to fix a problem, don't assume a full beta-test cycle has been completed. Nonetheless, given that they fix security holes, you should regularly apply the latest security updates and just take the risk that they might break something, too. SUS can help automate security update deployment to Windows 2000, Windows XP, and Windows Server 2003 computers.

In short, your security maintenance plan must include constant vigilance, constant updates, and constant education about new threats. You can start by signing up for Microsoft's Security Bulletin, a free periodic email newsletter, at www.Microsoft.com/security.

➤ For more information on using Software Update Services, **see** Chapter 14, "Maintenance," **p. 231**.

➤ For an overview of the Framework, **see** Chapter 9, "Web Development," **p. 145**.

➤ For more information on software restrictions, **see** Chapter 13, "Management," **p. 215**.

➤ For details on how IIS has been made more secure, **see** Chapter 7, "Internet Information Services," **p. 101**.

➤ To learn about Active Directory changes, including Active Directory's role in security, **see** Chapter 5, "Active Directory," **p. 65**.

➤ To see what's new and changed in Group Policy, **see** Chapter 6, "Group Policy Changes," **p. 81**.

5

ACTIVE DIRECTORY

In This Chapter

- Understanding Active Directory functional levels, **page 66**.
- Using new tools and utilities, **page 68**.
- Administering Active Directory, **page 69**.
- Expanding your organization's security, **page 76**.

What's New

Windows Server 2003 brings a number of feature improvements and new capabilities to Active Directory. One of the biggest surprises of Windows 2000's lifecycle was the number of companies that adopted Windows 2000 but continued to run Windows NT-based domains, rather than moving to Active Directory. In Windows Server 2003, Microsoft has attempted to address some of the issues that discouraged companies from adopting Active Directory, while maintaining full backward-compatibility with Windows 2000 Active Directory as well as Windows NT-based domains.

Active Directory's new features fall into five basic categories: tools and utilities, administration, architecture, security, and operations. None of Active Directory's changes or new features are really earth-shattering; instead, they're the type of sensible, gradual improvements you'd expect in a version release of a product.

Note | You can migrate directly from Windows NT domains to Windows Server 2003 Active Directory or from Windows 2000 Active Directory. However, Windows Server 2003 doesn't make Active Directory planning any less important to a migration process. If anything, Active Directory's new features make planning even more important.

Active Directory Functional Levels

Windows 2000 Active Directory domains can run in one of two modes: mixed and native. Mixed mode provides support for Windows NT backup domain controllers (BDCs) while preventing the use of certain NT-incompatible Active Directory features, such as universal security groups. Windows Server 2003 takes the concept of modes a step further, and it renames them *functional levels*.

Similar to Windows 2000 Active Directory modes, functional levels enable Active Directory to remain compatible with older versions of Windows while preventing the use of certain features that would compromise backward-compatibility. Every Windows Server 2003 Active Directory domain starts in the Windows 2000 mixed functional level, which is identical in functionality to the Windows 2000 mixed mode. Domain functional levels include

- **Windows 2000 mixed**—In this mode, you can have Windows NT, Windows Server 2003, and Windows 2000 domain controllers.
- **Windows 2000 native**—In this mode, you can have only Windows 2000 and Windows Server 2003 domain controllers.
- **Windows Server 2003**—In this mode, you can have only Windows 2003 domain controllers.

Note | If you upgrade from a Windows 2000 domain that's in native mode, Windows Server 2003 Active Directory starts in the Windows 2000 native functional level.

Because Windows Server 2003 also introduces new forest-wide functionality to Active Directory, forests have their own functional levels, as follows:

- **Windows 2000**—This mode supports a forest containing Windows 2000 or Windows Server 2003 domains running at any domain functional level.
- **Windows Server 2003**—This mode supports only Windows Server 2003 domains running in the Windows Server 2003 domain functional level.

Various features and functionality are available only in the higher-end functional levels. All the features that are available only to Windows 2000 domains running in native mode are available only if a Windows Server 2003 domain is in the Windows 2000 native functional level or a higher functional level. Of the new Windows Server 2003 features discussed in this chapter, the following have functional level restrictions:

- Domain controller rename requires the Windows Server 2003 domain functional level.
- Domain rename and restructure requires the Windows Server 2003 forest functional level.
- Schema class and attribute deactivation requires the Windows Server 2003 forest functional level.
- The Update Logon Timestamp feature requires the Windows Server 2003 domain functional level.
- Cross-forest trusts and authentication require the Windows Server 2003 forest functional level.
- Global catalog (GC) replication improvements require the Windows Server 2003 forest functional level.

Assuming your domain meets the requirements for upgrading, you can raise its functional level. However, Windows Server 2003 doesn't allow you to raise the functional level of any domain that contains domain controllers that would be incompatible with the new level. To raise the domain functional level, open Active Directory Domains and Trusts. Then, right-click the domain and select **Raise Functional Level** from the pop-up menu. You'll see the dialog box shown in Figure 5.1, which enables you to select a new functional level.

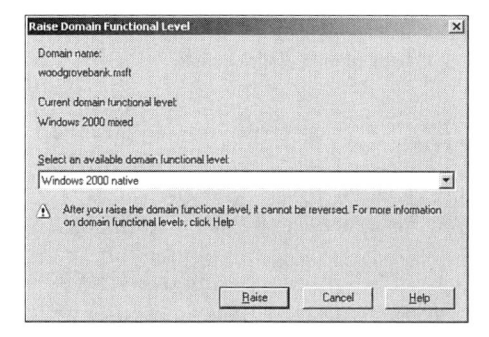

Figure 5.1 This dialog box shows the current functional level and allows you to select a new one.

Caution | Raising the domain functional level is a one-time operation that cannot be reversed. So, be sure you're serious about raising the level before you take this step.

You can also use Active Directory domains and trusts to raise the forest's functional level. Notice in Figure 5.2 that Windows Server 2003 won't allow you to raise the forest functional level if all the domains in the forest aren't at the proper functional levels themselves. This prevents you from raising the forest to a functional level that would be incompatible with one or more domains.

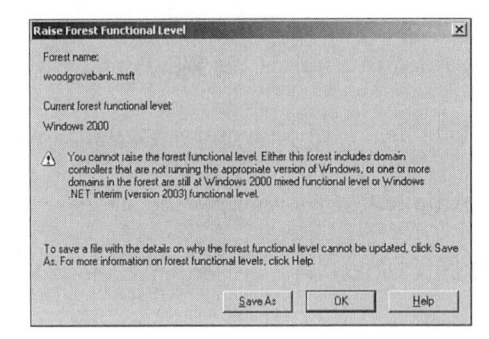

Figure 5.2 This dialog box displays a warning, rather than allowing you to raise the forest functional level.

Throughout the rest of this chapter, we'll call your attention to features that require a Windows Server 2003 domain or forest functional level.

> To see which domain features are limited by the Windows 2000 mixed and native functional levels, log on to www.samspublishing.com and enter this book's ISBN number (no hyphens or parenthesis) in the Search field; then click the book cover image to access the book details page. Click the Web Resources link in the More Information section and locate article ID# **A010501**.

Tools and Utilities

Active Directory includes two major new tools for Windows Server 2003: the Active Directory Migration Tool (ADMT) 2.0 and the new Group Policy Management Console (GPMC).

ADMT 2.0 is a beefed-up version of Microsoft's bundled Active Directory migration tool. New features include the capability to migrate user passwords along with their accounts and the capability to migrate users from Windows 2000 domains as well as from Windows NT domains. Interestingly, Microsoft left the password migration capability out of ADMT 1.0 because it said it wasn't possible. Shortly after Windows 2000 shipped, though, Aelita Software (www.aelita.com) shipped a third-party migration product that handles password migration. Realizing its error, Microsoft hurried to include the much-demanded feature in ADMT 2.0. Password migrating capabilities aside, ADMT 2.0 is still relatively limited in functionality. It's suitable primarily for smaller migrations involving only a few servers or client computers. For larger migrations, we strongly recommend a more powerful, third-party migration solution. Solutions are offered by Aelita, NetIQ (www.netiq.com), and others.

The new GPMC interface is integrated into the existing Active Directory administration tools: Active Directory Users and Computers and Active Directory Sites and Services. This and other Group Policy improvements are covered in Chapter 6, "Group Policy Changes."

Administration

Windows Server 2003 brings several much-needed administrative enhancements to Active Directory, including improvements to Active Directory's administrative tools and features that enable you to change what used to be one-time, irreversible domain design decisions.

Administrative Tool Enhancements

All the Active Directory administrative tools have been updated with new features. These features are most noticeable in Active Directory Users and Computers, which is where administrators typically spend most of their time. These features include

- **Drag and drop**—Finally, you can drag and drop items in Active Directory. For example, Figure 5.3 shows several users being dragged from one organizational unit (OU) to another. This change makes Active Directory administration much faster and more intuitive.

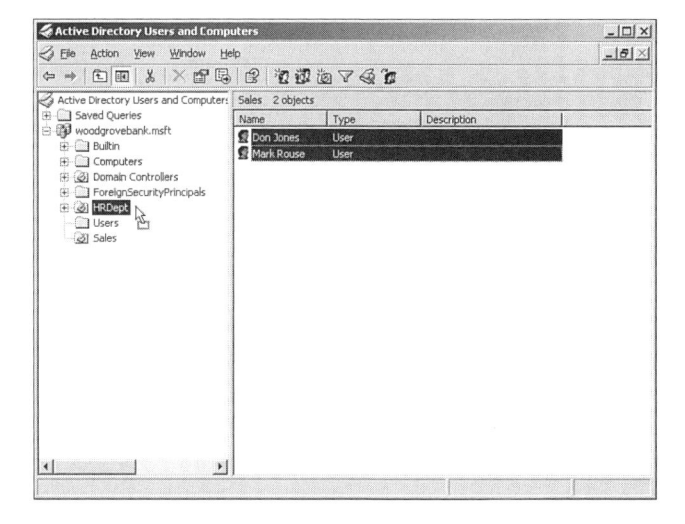

Figure 5.3 Drag and drop makes keeping your domain organized easier.

- **Show effective permissions**—This feature enables you to select an object and see the effective permissions a given security principal will have on that object. Extremely useful for security troubleshooting, show effective permissions is a fast way to sort through complex chains of permissions inheritance to see exactly which permissions a user or group has.
- **Show inheritance parent**—This feature shows the parent from which an object inherits its permissions. Previously, Active Directory simply showed you which permissions were inherited; it didn't show you from where the permissions came. This new feature makes locating the source of an undesired permission and correcting it easier.

- **Multiselect**—You can now select multiple objects in Active Directory and change specific attributes for all the objects at once. For example, Figure 5.4 shows several user objects selected and the resulting Properties dialog box. You can use check boxes to determine which attribute changes will be applied to all the selected users.

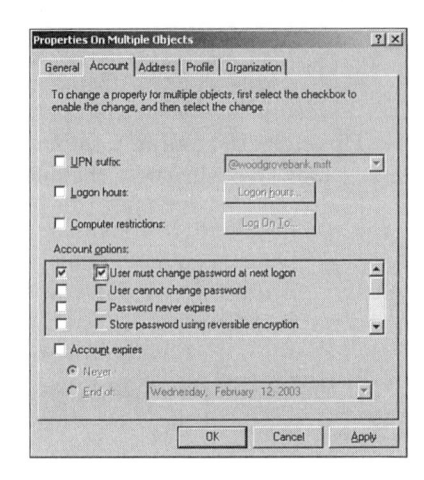

Figure 5.4 Multiselect lets you quickly change several objects' attributes to a consistent setting.

These new improvements seem relatively minor, but they will make a big difference in your day-to-day administrative tasks.

Saved Queries

Another valuable new feature in Active Directory Users and Computers is Saved Queries. This feature lets you create Active Directory queries, effectively filtering Active Directory for specific objects. You can then save the queries and execute them as often as necessary. Query results appear in the right pane of the console, where you can use multiselect to immediately alter the objects' attributes. For example, Figure 5.5 shows a saved query that selects all users who haven't logged on in the past 30 days. You could then multiselect those users and disable their accounts, expire their passwords, and so on.

Resultant Set of Policy

A new feature of Active Directory Users and Computers, Resultant Set of Policy (RSOP) lets you quickly analyze the policies that would apply to a specific security principal given their locations in a specific container in Active Directory. To start the tool, you can click any container or security principal and select **RSOP (Planning)** from the pop-up menu. You'll see a screen similar to the one in Figure 5.6, which enables you to select both a user and a computer account or a container in which you want to place a user or computer account.

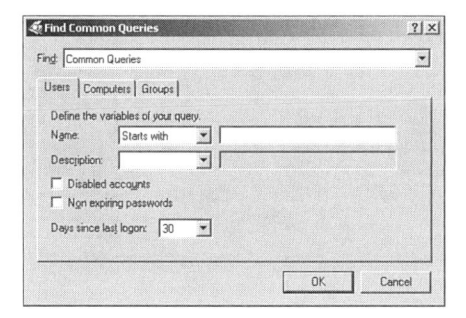

Figure 5.5 Saved queries are an efficient way to quickly locate and work with a subset of objects in Active Directory.

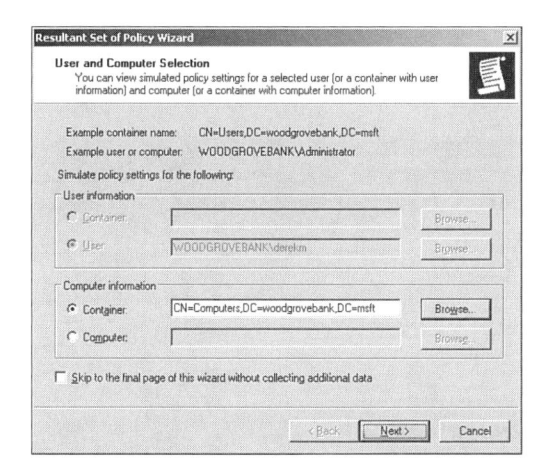

Figure 5.6 The new RSOP tool works with both user and computer accounts in Active Directory.

Next, you can set various options. For example, in Figure 5.7, you can decide whether to simulate the security principal being dialed in or over a slow network connection. Keep in mind that Active Directory now supports slow link detection and therefore doesn't send the same policies over a slow link that it would over a higher-speed link. The RSOP tool has about a half-dozen option screens. When you've selected all the options you want, check the **Skip to the Final Page** check box to accept the defaults on the remaining options.

Finally, you'll see a screen similar to the one in Figure 5.8. This is a standard security template editor console, where you can browse the policies that will apply to your security principal under the conditions you've specified. You'll be able to see the exact results of their locations in Active Directory, their logon conditions, and so forth—all without moving (or even having) an actual user or computer account.

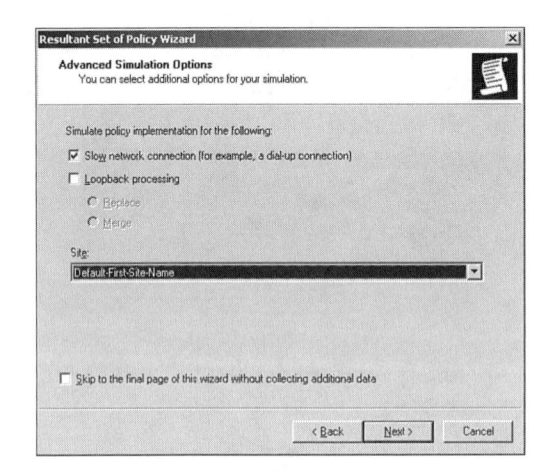

Figure 5.7 Simulating various logon conditions enables you to fine-tune your RSOP results.

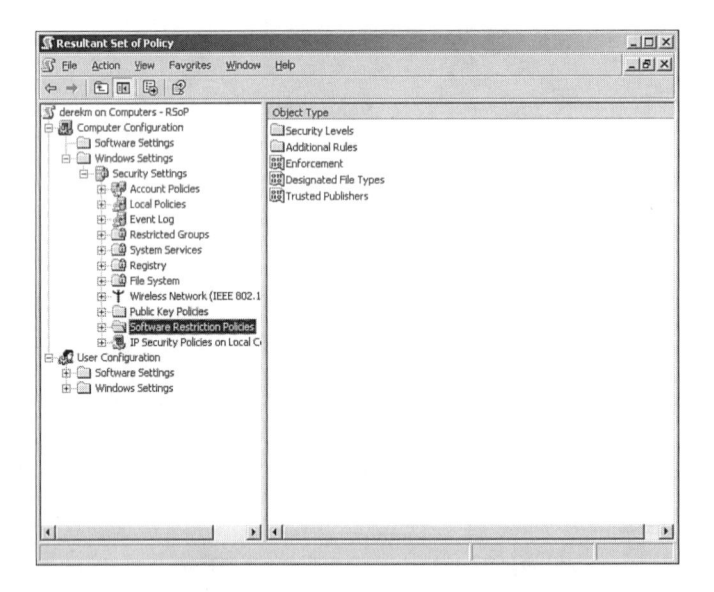

Figure 5.8 RSOP results are displayed in their own window.

The RSOP tool is a great time-saver and can help you avoid embarrassing mistakes that result from misapplied Group Policy.

Domain and Domain Controller Rename

For domains running in the Windows Server 2003 functional level, you can rename domain controllers. Previously, this was an impossible task: To rename a domain controller, you had to demote it, rename it, and then repromote it to domain controller status. Now, you can use a simple command-line utility to rename the domain controller. The process includes reregistering the domain controller with DNS and all other steps necessary to keep the domain controller functioning smoothly. For detailed steps on renaming a domain controller, consult Windows Server 2003's online Help and Support Center.

> **Caution** Don't try to rename a domain controller without carefully reading the instructions and precautions first. You need to be aware of several things about domain controller renames depending on your environment and operational needs.

You can also rename entire domains, provided your forest is in the Windows Server 2003 functional level. Renaming domains enables you to restructure domains in your forest. For example, you could rename `east.braincore.net` to `research.west.braincore.net`, perhaps responding to a change in your organization's political structure.

Renaming a domain, however, isn't something you do casually; it's a serious process with a number of different steps. You'll need two tools that are provided on the Windows Server 2003 CD but are not installed; they're located in the `\Valueadd\Msft\Mgmt\Domren` folder on the CD. You'll also need the step-by-step instructions provided by Microsoft. Those instructions are provided online; refer to the Readme document included with the domain rename tool on the CD-ROM for the current URL.

> **Tip** The Microsoft link also provides a download for the latest version of the domain rename tool. We strongly recommend using the version from the Web site rather than the one on the Windows CD because the one on the Web site contains all the latest bug fixes and improvements made by Microsoft.

One of our most frequently asked questions is, "Does domain rename work?" After all, it's a pretty novel concept in the world of Microsoft domains, and it seems like a serious operation. The answer is, "Yes, it does work." Of course, that's provided you carefully read the instructions and follow them to the letter. Because renaming a domain requires so much information in Active Directory and DNS to change, the process can be time-consuming, so you should allow the necessary time. You should also test the rename process by using an offline backup domain controller to ensure your domain doesn't contain any data that will cause the process to fail halfway through.

Architecture

Active Directory includes a number of architectural changes. Although most of these are invisible if you don't look for them, it's valuable to understand what they do and how they work so you can manage and plan your domains more effectively.

Partitioning

A new feature of Active Directory in Windows Server 2003 is the capability to support *application partitions*. These partitions are sections of Active Directory that don't have to be replicated to every domain controller in a domain.

For example, suppose you have a new line-of-business application that stores information in Active Directory. Only two of your branch offices use this application, and they each have their own domain controllers. You can instruct the application to store its information in a separate Active Directory partition and then configure that partition to replicate only to those two branch offices' domain controllers. You'll reduce replication traffic to other domain controllers, as well as saving hard drive space and memory on other domain controllers.

You create and manage partitions entirely from the command line using the Ntdsutil utility (hopefully, a future update to Windows will include a GUI for this functionality). The process isn't complicated, but you do have to be careful because Ntdsutil doesn't provide much in the way of error-checking or undo capabilities. For step-by-step instructions, consult Windows Server 2003's online Help and Support Center and search for "application partitions."

You'll also need to do some planning for your partitions because they get their own names. For example, in a domain named braincore.net, you might create an application partition named application.braincore.net. The fact that the partition looks like a child domain lets applications—even those that don't know about partitions—easily store information there, but you need to be careful not to conflict with your domain naming scheme. Again, planning details can be found in the Help and Support Center.

Schema Deactivation

In Windows 2000, you can extend the Active Directory schema to include custom classes and attributes. Many applications, including Microsoft Exchange 2000 Server, take advantage of this capability to store application data in Active Directory. The problem is that you can't subsequently delete the custom classes and attributes if you stop using the application.

Windows Server 2003 still doesn't allow you to delete classes and attributes, but it comes one step closer. As shown in Figure 5.9, you can use the Active Directory Schema console to make classes or attributes defunct. To do so, you modify the properties for the attribute or class and simply clear the Active check box. You'll receive a warning message and, if you click OK, the class or attribute will be made *defunct*, meaning it cannot be used to create any new objects.

Architecture 75

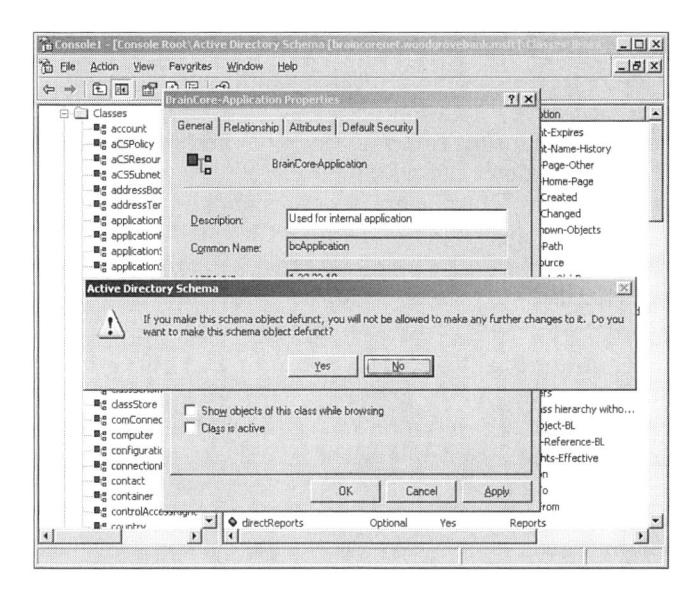

Figure 5.9 Use the Schema console to mark classes and attributes as defunct.

Note that no Schema console is configured by default. You must follow these steps to get to this new feature:

1. Open a command-line window and change it to the Windows\System32 folder.
2. Type `regsvr32 schmmgmt.dll` and press **Enter**.
3. Type `mmc` and press **Enter**.
4. From the File menu, select **Add/Remove Snap-Ins**.
5. Click **Add**.
6. Locate and double-click the **Schema** snap-in.
7. Close all dialog boxes, and you'll have a new Schema console ready for use. Be sure to save the console for future use by selecting **File**, **Save As**.

Even though you still can't delete schema classes and attributes, you can at least ensure that they won't be used in new object definitions. Perhaps a future version of Windows will allow you to remove defunct classes after a period of time.

Replication Improvements

Windows Server 2003 offers some major improvements to replication, providing better performance in Windows Server 2003 domains. The major improvements include the following:

- **Under Windows 2000, global catalog (GC) replication is very inefficient whenever changes occur to the Active Directory schema**—Any schema changes require every GC server in an entire forest to dump the GC completely and rebuild it from scratch, which is a significant operation in large forests. In Windows Server 2003, with forests running in the Windows Server 2003 functional level, GC servers are capable of replicating schema changes. That means schema changes are no longer the nightmare they once were, requiring special planning and all-night sessions waiting for replication and GC rebuilds to complete. Instead, schema changes can be replicated change-by-change to each GC in the forest, creating less replication traffic, user impact, and administrator stress.
- **In Windows 2000, changing the membership of a group requires domain controllers to rereplicate the entire group**—Therefore, adding a new user to a group with 5,000 members requires a lot more replication traffic than you might think. Windows Server 2003 domain controllers are capable of replicating the changes only to group members and adding a new user or removing a user one at a time, rather than rereplicating the entire group. This improved replication occurs only between Windows Server 2003 domain controllers; any Windows 2000 domain controllers in your domain will continue to replicate the entire group when changes to its membership occur.
- **Windows Server 2003 includes new replication algorithms that improve performance and help decrease latency between domain controllers**—It also includes a new Intra-Site Topology Generator (ITSG) that generates the replication topology between Active Directory sites. You must be running an all-2003 domain to take advantage of these improvements, however, because they're enabled only in domains running in the Windows Server 2003 functional level.

Security

Windows Server 2003 introduces *cross-forest trusts*, the capability of one Active Directory forest to trust another and for users to access resources in a trusting forest. You create and manage these trusts using Active Directory Domains and Trusts. After a trust is established, you can include user and group accounts from a foreign, trusted forest in the access control lists (ACLs) of Active Directory and NTFS permissions.

> **Note** Internet Authentication Service (IAS), Windows Server 2003's bundled RADIUS-compatible server, is now compatible with cross-forest authentication. An IAS server running in one forest can authenticate dial-in users who have accounts in another, trusted forest.

Cross-forest trusts enable organizations to more easily use forests, rather than domains, as their basic units of security when designing their Active Directory deployments. In the past, Microsoft suggested that domains would be the basic security boundary between parts of an organization with different security requirements. However, the presence of the all-powerful, forest-wide Enterprise Admins groups made many organizations uncomfortable; they felt they needed a way to completely separate the security used by different parts of their organizations. With cross-forest trusts, you can now deploy many more forests within a single organization and use trusts to provide resource access between forests as necessary.

One disadvantage of cross-forest trusts is that they have the potential to create the large, complex webs of trust relationships that made NT domains difficult to manage. If organizations begin to use large numbers of forests, administrators will have to manage the large number of subsequent intraforest trusts.

Note | Keep in mind that cross-forest trusts are available only when the forests involved in the trust are running Windows Server 2003 and are in the Windows Server 2003 forest functional level.

Operations

Finally, this section covers the Active Directory changes and improvements that affect day-to-day operations. Fortunately, most of these features enable themselves automatically when your domain or forest is in the correct functional level. Even though you don't need to enable these features, it's good to know about them so that you can take advantage of them.

Active Directory Application Mode

Microsoft has been disappointed with the rate at which companies have adopted Active Directory. Actually, the problem has been the rate at which companies *aren't* adopting Active Directory and are instead remaining on Windows NT-based domains. This hesitation on the part of Microsoft users is understandable: Active Directory represent a massive change in the way domains are planned, implemented, and managed, and not every company is convinced of the value Active Directory offers.

Aside from sad faces at Microsoft stockholder meetings, Active Directory's slow adoption has had a major impact on Microsoft's other product divisions. Exchange 2000 Server, for example, has had the slowest and lowest adoption rate of any version of Exchange, due primarily, we suspect, to its reliance on Active Directory. Other Microsoft products, such as Internet Security and Acceleration Server, require Active Directory for advanced functionality and can operate only in a limited fashion without it. This growing reliance on Active Directory, coupled with Active Directory's slow acceptance, has created a general slowdown in product adoption throughout Microsoft.

Microsoft's answer is Active Directory Application Mode (AD/AM). Essentially, AD/AM is a nondomain version of Active Directory designed to support applications that require Active Directory. You can implement AD/AM on regular servers and use it within an NT-based domain or without a domain at all.

AD/AM is considered part of the Windows Server 2003 product, but it isn't delivered on the product CD. It's a separate piece of Windows you can obtain directly from Microsoft or one of its certified partners.

Updating Logon Times

A helpful new feature of Windows Server 2003 domains running in the Windows Server 2003 functional level is the last logon timestamp attribute. This attribute is present for all security principals in a domain and is replicated to all domain controllers in the domain. It is updated each time the security principal logs on and can be useful in conducting security audits for unused or rarely used user and computer accounts. You can query this attribute in Active Directory Users and Computers, as described earlier in this chapter, in the section "Saved Queries."

Remote Office Logons

Windows 2000 domains have a significant weakness with respect to branch offices. Many organizations have deployed domain controllers to branch offices on the assumption that users would be able to log on to the local domain controller if the network connection between the branch office and the main office was unavailable. Unfortunately, these organizations didn't realize that Windows clients require a GC server to even find a domain controller. Without a GC at each branch office, the local domain controller can't be used for logging on when the network connection to the main office is unavailable.

An easy solution is to simply add a GC to each branch office. After all, any domain controller can be a GC. However, adding a GC simply to ensure logon capabilities is overkill, resulting in additional over-the-WAN network traffic.

Windows Server 2003 provides a better solution by supporting the capability of branch office clients to log on to a local domain controller even if a GC server isn't present. Organizations can now decommission GC servers located in remote offices, assured that their domain controllers will be capable of handling local logon traffic even if the WAN connection to the main office is unavailable.

Replication from Media

Whenever you build a new domain controller in a remote office, waiting for it to perform its first replication of Active Directory can be scary and time-consuming. WAN links don't offer the best bandwidth for whole-directory replication, but that's what a new domain controller requires.

Windows Server 2003 supports a new feature called replication from media. Essentially, you back up the domain database to a CD, tape drive, or some other removable media. You can then physically carry the media to the new remote domain controller running Windows Server 2003 and allow it to perform its first replication from that media. Subsequent replications include only changes and therefore are much smaller.

➤ For more information on Windows Server 2003's new security features, **see** "What's New," **p. 45**.

➤ For details on the new Group Policy user interface, **see** "Group Policy Management User Interface," **p. 86**.

➤ For information on what's new and changed in Active Directory Group Policy, **see** "What's New," **p. 81**.

➤ For a list of new Active Directory command-line utilities, **see** "New Command-Line Tools," **p. 225**.

➤ For differences between 32-bit and 64-bit editions of Windows, **see** "Significant Differences," **p. 259**.

6

GROUP POLICY CHANGES

In This Chapter

- Application Deployment Editor, **page 84**.
- Group Policy Management Console, **page 86**.
- Resultant Set of Policy, **page 87**.
- Software Restriction Policies, **page 93**.

What's New

Microsoft introduced Group Policy in Windows 2000. Group Policy is a mechanism for administration of computers in Active Directory domains. Group policies allow administrators to specify settings for everything from user environment configuration to software distribution to password policies. The basics of Group Policy have not changed with Windows Server 2003. However, several enhancements make the management and implementation of group policies easier. The existing Group Policy MMC snap-in has been redesigned and two new management consoles have been introduced (Resultant Set of Policy and Group Policy Management Console) to make Group Policy administration much more robust. In addition, general changes such as WMI filtering, cross-forest support, and tweaks to software distribution further improve the flexibility of Group Policy, making it more feasible to deploy. The Group Policy settings themselves have been extended and reorganized—there are more than 150 new or revised Group Policy settings, including whole new categories of policies such as Terminal Services,

Software Restriction Policies, and so forth. All in all, these changes are designed to make Group Policy in Windows Server 2003 more useful and manageable.

> For a brief technical overview of Group Policy, visit www.samspublishing.com and enter this book's ISBN number (no hyphens or parenthesis) in the Search field; then click the book cover image to access the book details page. Click the Web Resources link in the More Information section, and locate article ID# **A010601**.

General Group Policy Changes

Even though Group Policy fundamentals are untouched in Windows Server 2003, a few general Group Policy tweaks can have huge consequences for the implementation of group policies.

WMI Filtering

A new feature for controlling the scope of group policies is the ability to filter the Group Policy based on WMI settings. As shown in Figure 6.1, a new WMI Filter tab is available on the Group Policy Object (GPO) for specifying *WMI filters*. Windows Management Instrumentation (WMI) is Microsoft's implementation of the Web-Based Enterprise Management (WBEM) initiative, which is intended to define standards for gathering and sharing enterprise management information. Both Windows 2000 and, to a greater degree, Windows Server 2003 contain several built-in WMI providers for gathering information about the system. WMI filters enable you to gather environment-specific information such as hardware, software, and configuration settings about machines or users. By using WMI filters, you can more finely control the scope of your group policies.

For example, a patch needs to be applied to a particular software application, but there are different patches for different operating systems: one for Windows 95, one for Windows 2000, yet another patch for Windows XP, and so on. Previously, if you wanted to do this with Group Policy, you had to come up with some way of determining the affected systems, and then add the computers to an organizational unit (OU) or group, and either apply the GPO to the OU or filter it based on the group. With WMI filters, you can simply create one Group Policy for each patch and filter each Group Policy to apply to the appropriate operating system. How's that for ease of administration?

> Note: The trick with WMI filtering is writing the WMI script on which the filter is based. Figure 6.2 shows a sample WMI filter that detects whether Windows 2000 is installed.

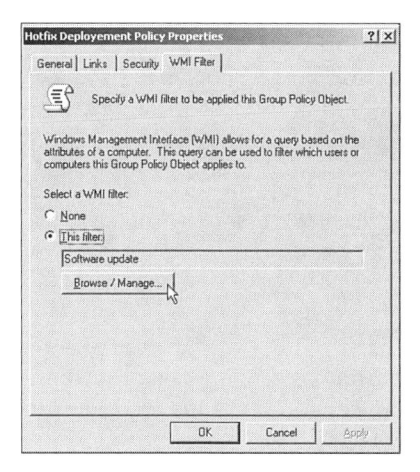

Figure 6.1 Controlling the scope of Group Policy with WMI filtering.

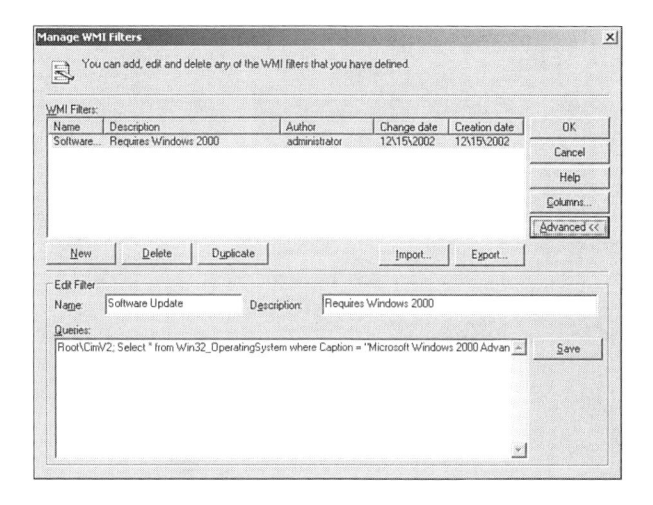

Figure 6.2 Configuring a WMI filter to detect whether Windows 2000 is installed.

Cross-Forest Support

Group policies in Windows Server 2003 now have cross-forest support. Before you get too excited, this does not mean that you can link GPOs created in a domain in one forest to objects (sites, domains, or OUs) in another. What it does mean, however, is that after root trusts are established, GPOs from trusted forests can be detected and processed. For example, when a user (Mary) from one forest (Forest1) logs on to a machine (ComputerA) that is a member of another forest (Forest2), the resulting group policies are those applied to ComputerA in Forest2 and those applied to Mary in Forest1. Additionally, you can allow cross-forest profiles so the user in the previous example would get his roaming profile as well.

> For more information on the new cross-forest root trusts and how they are used, **see** Chapter 5, "Active Directory," **p. 65**.

Software Deployment

On the surface, the Software Installation section looks the same as Windows 2000. However, a few subtle alterations exist in the software package creation process that can dramatically affect software deployments.

The first is merely a cosmetic change. When creating packages in the Software Installation section of Group Policy, you can now modify the Support Information URL. As shown in Figure 6.3, the support information URL is displayed when you click the support information link for an application in Add or Remove Programs.

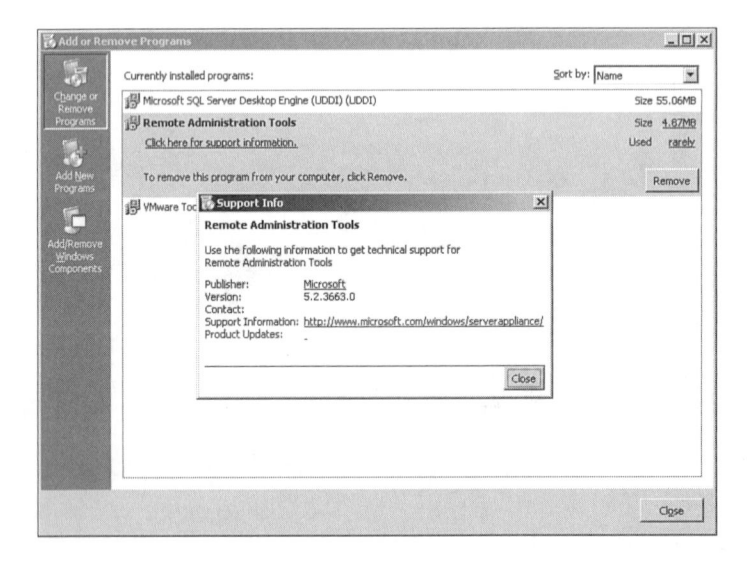

Figure 6.3 The support information URL link for the Remote Administration Application in Add or Remove Programs.

Previously, the support URL information was specified in the software distribution package file being loaded. Therefore, to specify a different URL, you had to create a different package. The ability to customize the URL when creating the software distribution in Group Policy enables administrators to provide users with support information regardless of the package. For example, the same software package can be used and the users directed to different support centers simply by specifying different support URLs when creating the package in the GPO.

A new choice for assigning applications to users is the option called Install This Application At Logon. This option fully installs the assigned application when the user logs on instead of on first use. This is particularly useful for users who are not always connected to the network. They can connect once and have the software installed immediately. Previously, applications assigned to users were installed on first use or from Add/Remove Programs. In the case of mobile users, they might not actually use it for the first time until much later, after they have disconnected from the network. In that case, the software would attempt to install but would be unable to do so because the network would no longer be available. This new option prevents this scenario because the software is installed when the policy applies and the user is still connected to the network.

> Caution | Be careful when implementing this policy: You might not want your users to get the application over dial-up. Imagine installing a 500MB application over 56K lines. It'll be done sometime next week. You can use other Group Policy settings to mitigate this by detecting slow WAN links and preventing the installation of software.

The Software Installation section of Group Policy has added support for 64-bit operating systems because a 64-bit version of Windows is available now. Specifically, the following options are available:

- You can make 32-bit x86 Windows Installer applications available to Win64 machines.
- You can make 32-bit x86 down-level (ZAP) applications available to Win64 machines.

These options enable the installation of regular 32-bit applications on their 64-bit cousins.

> Caution | Use these options only if you have already tested the 32-bit application and know it works on your 64-bit systems. Poorly performing 32-bit applications can severely impact the performance of your 64-bit systems.

➤ For more information on 64-bit operating systems, **see** Chapter 15, "64-bit Windows," **p. 253**.

Another new option when loading packages to be deployed with Group Policy is Include OLE Class and Product Information. This option specifies whether to deploy information about the Component Object Model (COM) components the application might need. By specifying this option, the application can dynamically install any of the required COM components if necessary by simply querying Active Directory.

Note Although it is still in the documentation of Windows Server 2003 RC1, the option Remove Previous Installs of This Product from Computers (or for Users), If the Product Was Not Installed by Group Policy-Based Software Installation is no longer available. This feature was always iffy at best. Sometimes it worked; sometimes it didn't depending on the application and how it was originally installed. As of this writing, it looks as if Microsoft will not include this option, although it could change its mind and leave it in.

Group Policy Management User Interface

In Windows 2000 only one utility is available for managing Group Policy—the Group Policy MMC snap-in. Windows Server 2003 not only expands on this utility, but also introduces some additional utilities for Group Policy management.

Group Policy Object Editor

The old Group Policy snap-in has been renamed Group Policy Object Editor. The MMC interface has been improved to use a Web style interface. Two choices of view exist for the right policy list pane: Standard, which is the old Windows 2000 style, and Extended, which is the new style. When using the Extended style, an explanation of what the policy does is displayed when a policy listed in the right pane is clicked. This helps you more easily determine what each of the policies does. As shown in Figure 6.4, in addition to a description of the policy, a Requirements section lists the systems that support the policy (Windows 2000, XP, 2003, and so on). This enables you to easily tell which policies apply to particular systems.

Note The new Extended tab is not available for the Security Options section, and no Description or Requirements headings exist. The policies in this section are viewed the same as in Windows 2000.

Because Group Policy is now supported by multiple operating systems (Windows 2000, Windows XP, and Windows Server 2003) and some policies are applicable only for some of these operating systems, a new Filtering option is available on the View menu for Administrative Templates. This option enables you to limit the policies that are displayed in the Group Policy Editor MMC. They can be filtered to do the following:

- **Filter by Requirements Information**—Shows only those policies supported by a particular operating system or specific applications. For example, by clicking the check boxes for At Least Windows 2000 Service Pack 1 and At Least Internet Explorer 6 Service Pack 1, you display only those policies that can be used on systems with Windows 2000 SP1 and IE6.
- **Only Show Configured Policy Settings**—Displays only policies that are currently configured in the particular GPO.

- **Only Show Policy Settings that Can Be Fully Managed**—Hides Windows NT 4.0 system polices that might have been loaded as administrative templates.

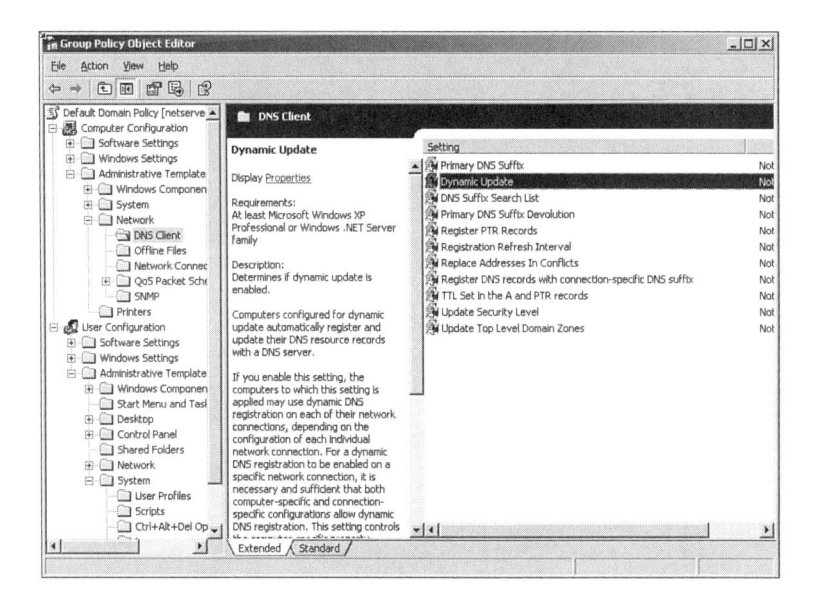

Figure 6.4 The Group Policy Object Editor (Formerly the Group Policy snap-in) displaying the OS requirements and descriptive information for the DNS dynamic update policy.

Resultant Set of Policy

By now, you can probably get a sense for the bewildering array of Group Policy settings. Because of all the Group Policy application rules—inheritance, block inheritance, no override, filtering (by group or WMI filter), and so on—troubleshooting Group Policy applications can be a nightmare. A new utility can help: the Resultant Set of Policy (RSoP) MMC snap-in. RSoP enables you to see the effects of group policies. As shown in Figure 6.5, the RSoP console displays each Group Policy setting that applies as well as the source GPO from which the policy was obtained.

Note | No Resultant Set of Policy console is available on the default Administrative Tools menu. You must therefore create your own RSoP MMC console. Additionally, the first time the snap-in is used, no data is displayed because no queries have been run yet. You have to launch the Resultant Set of Policy Wizard by right-clicking **Resultant Set of Policy** and selecting **Generate RSoP Data**. This launches the wizard, which walks you through the prompts for generating the scenario for which you want to examine Group Policy data.

88 Chapter 6 Group Policy Changes

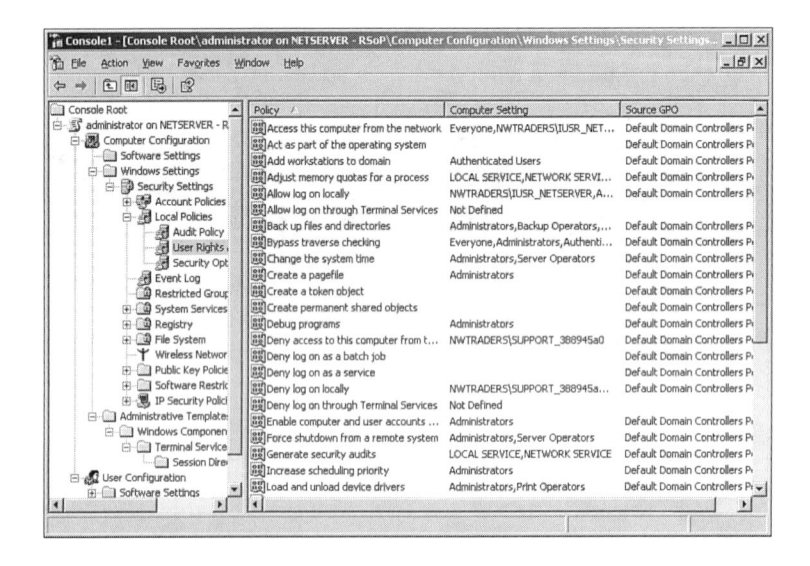

Figure 6.5 The Resultant Set of Policy console displays effective user rights policy settings and the GPOs from which they were applied.

> For a tutorial on how to create Microsoft Management Consoles (MMC), visit www.samspublishing.com and enter this book's ISBN number (no hyphens or parenthesis) in the Search field; then click the book cover image to access the book details page. Click the Web Resources link in the More Information section, and locate article ID# **A011301**.

Additionally, youcan right-click any of these settings and select **Properties**. This brings up the configurable options for the policy setting, just like in Group Policy Editor. However, a Precedence tab is also available, as shown in Figure 6.6. This tab shows all the GPOs that apply that setting. This helps determine whether any kind of GPO conflict exists and whether policies are being applied as expected. In this case, two policies (Default Domain Controller Policy and Security Settings) configure the Allow Log on Locally setting. From Figure 6.6 you can see that the Default Domain Controller Policy wins the conflict.

The RSoP console has two modes for displaying policy data, Logging and Planning. Logging mode enables you to see the current policies applied to a particular user and machine. Planning mode, on the other hand, enables you to run what-if scenarios to see the effective policies. The variables that you can manipulate in the what-if scenarios are as follows:

- User configuration policy settings for a particular user or container
- Computer configuration policy settings for a particular computer or container
- Group Policy environment settings—slow WAN link, loopback processing, Active Directory site

- Group membership
- WMI filters

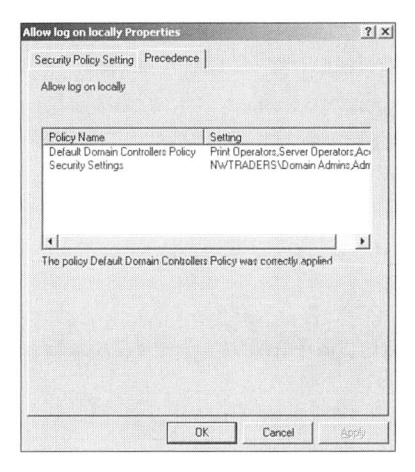

Figure 6.6 The Precedence tab for policy settings allows you to determine at a glance whether a policy conflict exists.

By manipulating these variables, administrators can determine the effects of Group Policy changes without actually performing them. For example, how are policies affected if a user is moved from one OU to another? What if she accesses the network from a different site? What if you add her to a particular group or apply a WMI filter? And so on.

Planning mode needs to query Active Directory to determine the policies applied in these various circumstances. Consequently, Planning mode is available only if the machine running the RSoP console is a member of an Active Directory domain.

In the following example, you will use RSoP to examine the user configuration policy applied to a particular user. Then you will run RSoP again to see what would happen if you moved the user to a different OU.

Note: For this scenario, I have created a user called Mary in the Users container. Mary is only a member of the default Domain Users group, and the only policies are the default policies (Default Domain Policy applied at the domain level and Default Domain Controllers Policy applied at the Domain Controllers OU) with the default settings. I have also created an OU called Employees that has a Group Policy (Disable Instant Messenger) that is configured with a User Configuration Administrative Template setting to not allow Windows Messenger to be run. To get the same results when following along with this example, you should also create these objects (in a test environment, of course).

First, let's see what settings are currently being applied to Mary. Do the following:

1. Create an MMC console with the Resultant Set of Policy snap-in.
2. Right-click **Resultant Set of Policy** and select **Generate RSoP Data**.
3. On the Welcome to the Resultant Set of Policy Wizard screen, click **Next**.
4. On the Mode Selection screen, make sure **Planning Mode** is selected and click **Next**.
5. Select **User** and then click **Browse**.
6. Make sure **Current User** is selected and click **Next**.
7. On the Select User screen, type in `Mary` in the **Enter the Object Name to Select(Examples):** field and click **Check Names**. The name should resolve to something like `Mary(mary@nwtraders.msft)`. Click **OK**.
8. Because you are not interested in changing anything and just want to see the user's current settings, select **Skip to the Final Page of This Wizard Without Collecting Additional Data** and click **Next**.
9. Click **Next** on the Summary of Selections screen.
10. Click **Finish**.

As shown in Figure 6.7, the RSoP console displays all the User Configuration policy settings that are being applied to Mary. There are no Administrative Template settings at all, so the user currently has no policy restricting Windows Messenger.

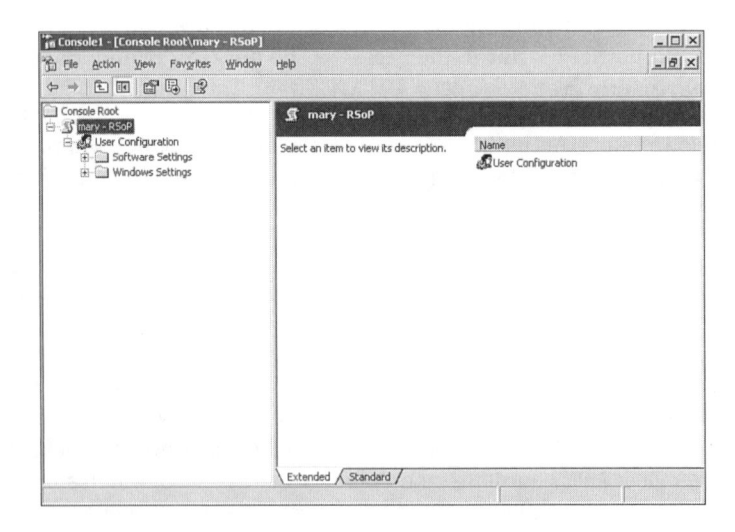

Figure 6.7 The Resultant Set of Policy in logging mode displaying all the policies applying to the user.

Next, let's look at what happens to the policy settings if you move Mary to the Employees OU. Follow these steps:

1. Because you have already run a query once in the RSoP console, right-click the username (mary-RSoP) and select **Change Query**.
2. On the Resultant Set of Policy Wizard screen, click **Next**.
3. Because you're not doing anything with her site or WAN links, on the Advanced Simulation Options screen, click **Next**.
4. On the Alternate Active Directory Paths screen, select **Browse**. This is where you get to move Mary to a new OU.
5. On the Choose User Container screen, find and select the **Employees** OU; then click **OK**. On the Alternate Active Directory Paths screen, the distinguished name of the Employees OU should now be listed under User location. Click **Next**.
6. Because you're only moving Mary to a new OU and not making any other changes, click **Next** on the User Security Groups screen.
7. Click **Next** on the WMI Filters for Users screen.
8. Click **Next** on the Summary of Selections screen.
9. Click **Finish**.

Now, as shown in Figure 6.8, RSoP displays the effective Group Policy settings when the user is moved to the OU. Note that there is now an Administrative Templates section. In addition, the Do Not Allow Windows Messenger to Run policy is enabled, and it was obtained from the Disable Instant Messenger GPO. Also, remember that you did not actually move Mary's account—this just lets you see what would happen if you did.

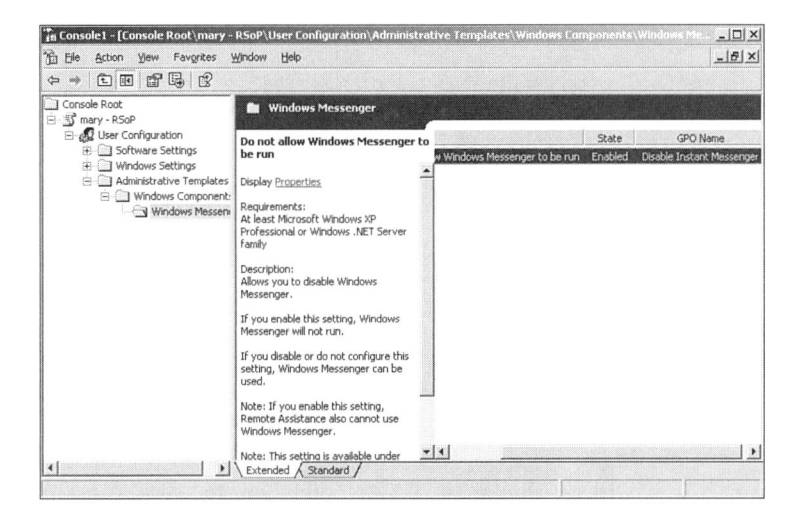

Figure 6.8 The Resultant Set of Policy in Planning mode displaying the policies that would be applied to Mary if you moved her account.

Group Policy Management Console

Yet another new utility is available for Group Policy management—the *Group Policy Management Console (GPMC)*. Unfortunately, it is not included with Windows Server 2003. However, it is supposed to be available as a free download when Windows Server 2003 is released. Once installed, GPMC replaces the existing Group Policy Object Editor on the Group Policy tab objects (sites, domains and OUs) in Active Directory Users and Computer.

GPMC provides a single console for managing GPOs across multiple forests. As shown in Figure 6.9, the tree pane view shows all the Group Policy objects throughout the entire forest. For each forest, there is a display of the domain, OU, and site hierarchies, which allow you to see all the GPOs linked at each level. Additionally for each domain, a Group Policy Objects and WMI Filters section shows all existing GPOs and WMI filters, respectively, whether they are linked or not.

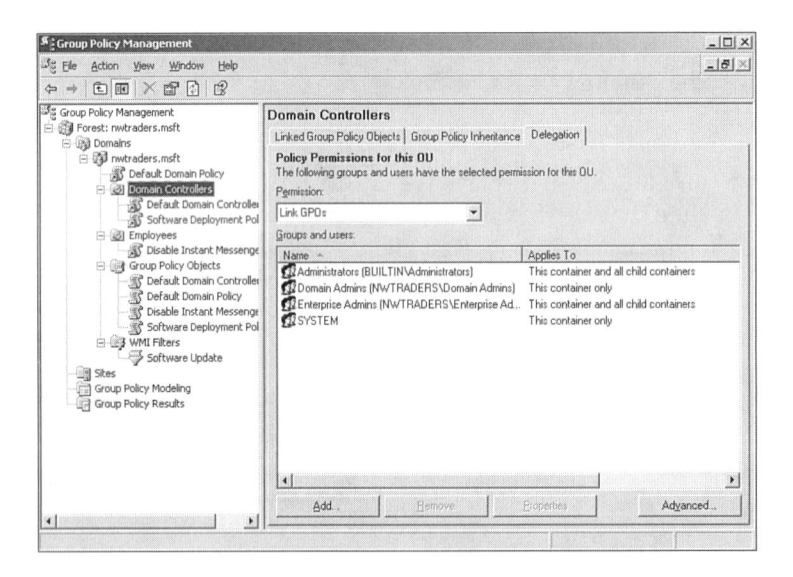

Figure 6.9 The Group Policy Management Console displaying GPOs for a single domain forest.

In the tree-pane view of the hierarchy, you can see which policies are linked to each location simply by clicking the location, such as the Domain Controllers OU, and viewing the Linked Group Policy Objects tab. The Group Policy Precedence tab displays all the group policies that will be processed at the particular location, including those inherited from parent containers, and the order in which they will be processed. This enables you to see at a glance whether any conflicts might arise. The Delegation tab displays who has permissions (Link GPOs, Perform Group Policy Modeling Analysis, and Remotely Access Group Policy Results Data) to manage the GPOs at that particular level (site, domain, or OU).

By selecting a GPO, you can see where it is linked, whether it is enabled at the linked location, any filters that might be applied (by group or WMI filter), as well as any other permissions for the GPO. You can also right-click the policy and edit it, just like in Group Policy Object Editor. However, be careful because editing a GPO affects all locations where the policy is applied, just like when you edit with Group Policy Editor (it actually launches the Group Policy Object Editor to perform the edits).

Clicking a GPO in the Group Policy Objects container displays the same information as mentioned previously, but this section enables you to back up and restore your GPOs as well as import settings from previous backups into existing GPOs. Similarly, the WMI Filters container lists all the WMI filters configured—whether linked or not—and allows you to import and export them.

GPMC also integrates with RSoP via the Group Policy Modeling and Group Policy Results sections to provide reporting of RSoP data and GPO settings. The Group Policy Modeling and Group Policy Results sections correspond to RSoP Planning and Logging modes, respectively (they actually launch the RSoP wizards).

To top it all off, the GPMC is fully scriptable, so anything you can do in GPMC you can automate with a script. It also includes several sample scripts (`C:\Program Files\GPMC\Scripts`) for automating common GPO administrative tasks, such as creating and deleting GPOs.

The Group Policy Management Console is a complete rework of the Group Policy user interface and extremely simplifies Group Policy management. I strongly recommend every Group Policy administrator download and install the GPMC when it is available. If nothing else, it provides a unified view and centralized console for running all your Group Policy management utilities.

New Group Policies

Windows Server 2003 introduces more than 160 new group policies. Because there are so many new ones, we will assume familiarity with existing policies and just concentrate on the new ones, particularly the new categories of policies. Some of the new policies are more appropriately covered in other chapters and are referenced there. In typical Microsoft fashion, not only are there a ton of new policies, but a lot of existing policies have been renamed, moved to other sections, or otherwise reorganized.

For example, the Computer `Configuration\Windows Settings\Security Settings\Local Policies\Security Options` section has been completely rearranged and all the policies have been renamed. Each policy name now starts with a general category description, such as

Accounts or Network Access. Similarly, the Shut Down the Computer when the Security Audit Log Is Full policy has been moved from the Computer Configuration\Windows Settings\Security Settings\Event Log\Settings for Event Logs section to the Security Options section mentioned previously and is now called Audit: Shut Down System Immediately if Unable to Log Security Audits.

> **Tip** Group Policy is no longer refreshed using secedit /refreshpolicy. This function is now performed by the new command-line utility gpupdate.

This reorganization, although initially confusing, is helpful going forward in that it lets you more easily determine the scope of the policy setting. However, it is confusing coming from Windows 2000 because it makes finding the policies with which you might already be familiar more difficult.

New Computer Configuration Policy Sections

The following are whole new sections in the computer configuration section of group policies.

Windows Settings\Security Settings

This broad category is for configuring general Windows security settings. The new security related categories are

- **Wireless Network (IEEE 802.11) Policies**—This new section is used to configure a wireless policy for your network. You can configure such things as the type of network devices to access (access point preferred, ad hoc, or infrastructure). Additional settings are for configuring the network name (SSID), Wireless Encryption Protocol (WEP) encryption, as well as the 802.11x configuration specifications (transmit parameters, authentication, and so on).
- **Software Restriction Policies**—This is a new section for controlling which applications are allowed to run on the machines in the scope of the Group Policy. This provides essentially the same functionality as the previous Windows 2000 user configuration policy settings Run Only Allowed Windows Applications and Don't Run Specified Windows Applications, but it is more flexible and can be applied as a computer configuration policy.

  Software Restriction Policies are implemented by first specifying a default security level, such as unrestricted (where anything is allowed to run) which is the default or disallowed (where nothing can run), and then creating Additional Rules that provide exceptions to the default security level to either allow or deny (depending on the default) specific programs from running.

Administrative Templates\Windows Components

Administrative templates are just that: templates for configuring H-Key Local Machine (HKLM) and H-Key Current User (HKCU) Registry key settings. Because this is the Computer Configuration section, these settings manipulate HKLM Registry keys. The Windows Components section is used for configuring settings for built-in Windows applications:

- **Application Compatibility**—This section is for configuring the new Application Compatibility features of Windows XP and Windows Server 2003. Application Compatibility enables you to configure an operating environment to allow applications that wouldn't ordinarily run on XP or 2003 to run. It is essentially lying to the application so it thinks it is running under Windows 95, 98, NT 4, and so on. This section enables you to turn on or off application compatibility globally. You can also specify whether to allow 16-bit applications to run.
- **Terminal Services**—Terminal Services enables you to remotely connect to Windows Server 2003 via a graphical console as if you were physically at the box.

   ➤ For more information on Terminal Services Policies, **see** "New Administration," **p. 186**.

- **Windows Messenger**—Windows Messenger is Microsoft's Instant Messaging client. These Group Policy settings can be use to determine whether to allow Windows Messenger to run and whether it should be launched at startup.
- **Windows Update**—Windows Update allows you to configure the Automatic Updates feature. If enabled, you can specify the amount of user interaction you want with the download and installation process: whether to notify before downloading updates and then again before updating, to notify after downloading but before installing, or to download and install on a particular schedule without notifying. Additionally, you can also specify whether to redirect the Windows Update to a URL of your choice. This affects all occurrences of Windows Update: in Internet Explorer, off the Start menu, in updating printer drivers, and so on. Redirecting the URL enables you to use your own Windows Catalog for dispensing updates, presumably after you've tested them, rather than directly downloading from Microsoft. This gives you, the administrator, more control of what gets updated.

Administrative Templates\System

The following new categories contain settings for defining the behavior of various Windows system components:

- **User Profiles**—This section contains a number of settings concerning profiles: from whether to detect slow WAN links, to what to do with roaming profiles if a slow WAN link is detected. Other settings include whether to allow changes to be saved back to the server (thus making them mandatory read-only profiles), to cache roaming profiles locally, to only using local profiles, and so on.
- **Scripts**—These are settings for configuring the behavior of some scripts, such as whether logon scripts should run synchronously (one after the other) and whether startup scripts should run asynchronously (all run at the same time). If logon scripts run synchronously (the default), they all must complete before the desktop is available. If, on the other hand, startup scripts run asynchronously (the default), they all run at the same time before the logon screen is displayed. Other options are how long to wait for startup, logon, logoff, and shutdown scripts to process before killing them and whether to show startup and shutdown scripts.
- **Net Logon**—This section determines various settings for domain logon, such as dynamic registration of DNS SRV records for domain controllers, which records how frequently they should be refreshed. It also includes compatibility of the SYSVOL and NETLOGON shares, meaning whether to allow exclusive locks. Other settings are used to configure discovery options, such as how frequently computers attempt to discover domain controllers, and other maintenance tasks. One particularly beneficial setting is the designation of site name. By specifying the site name, the computer will not attempt to determine it from Active Directory. Thus, you can use Group Policy to specify in which site a computer thinks it is regardless of its actual IP address. In addition, a subcategory of this section, DC Locator DNS Records, enables configuration of the behavior of DNS service records for Active Directory. Among the settings you can configure are whether to dynamically register the records and whether records should be automatically created to cover all sites.
- **Remote Assistance**—Allows the configuration of the new Remote Assistance feature in Windows XP. The two settings are Solicited Remote Assistance and Offer Remote Assistance. Solicited Remote Assistance allows users to open a Remote Assistance session and send a request to support personnel (called *helpers*). These helpers can then remote control (using the RDP protocol like Remote Desktop) into the Remote Assistance session and help the user. The Group Policy settings can be configured to enable Solicited Remote Assistance, and if enabled, they specify which helpers are allowed to connect to the machine. You can also control whether they can only view the desktop or interact with it. The other setting is for configuring Offer Remote Assistance, which is essentially the same, but if it's configured, it allows helpers to initiate Remote Assistance sessions. Remote Assistance is a potentially powerful new feature, particularly for remote help desk support. It is similar to Remote Desktop (Terminal Services), but the user can see what the support person is doing and disconnect at any time.
- **System Restore**—System Restore is a new feature in Windows XP that performs automatic backups of critical system files under certain conditions, such as right before installing an application. The Group Policy settings in this section allow administrators to enable or disable the System Restore feature. They also can be used to determine whether users are allowed to configure the System Restore settings.

- **Error Reporting**—A new feature of Windows XP and Windows Server 2003 is Error Reporting. If this setting is enabled (which it is by default), whenever an application crashes, it prompts to send information to Microsoft. This policy can be configured to turn this off altogether or only for certain programs. This section also has a subcategory called Advanced Error Reporting. The settings in the Advanced Error Reporting subfolder enable configuration of error reporting for specific applications. Additionally, you can use them to specify whether to report operating system errors and whether to report unplanned shutdown events.

- **Remote Procedure Call**—Includes various configuration settings for troubleshooting RPC connections, such as maintain state information, generate extended error information, and whether to ignore delegation failure. Another setting specifies the timeout values for RPC over HTTP.

- **Windows Time Service**—Used to configure a Network Time Protocol (NTP) time service (client and server) to control automatic time synchronization across your network. This section contains a subcategory called Time Providers, which enables configuration of the NTP service. This allows you to configure whether time is synchronized via the domain hierarchy (the default) or via other NTP servers you specify.

Administrative Templates\Network

These new sections contain settings for configuring various network-level properties:

- **DNS Client**—This category was formerly under the Net Logon section and was only a setting for Primary DNS Suffix. Now several settings exist for configuring the DNS client. These settings allow configuration of the DNS client properties over and above what can be set using DHCP—for example, DNS suffix search order, whether to dynamically register DNS records, what to do if a conflict occurs when registering DNS records, whether to register PTR (reverse lookup) records, how long the records should be registered (Time To Live [TTL]), and the like.

- **Network Connections**—This section was formerly called Network and Dial-up Connections and now contains additional settings for controlling network connections over and above the previous setting of whether to allow Internet Connection Sharing (ICS). You can specify whether to allow Internet Connection Firewall (ICF) and network bridging, which are new features in Windows XP. ICF enables clients to block ports on their machines. Because most corporate networks have their own firewalls, ICF on individual machines is usually redundant and serves only to cause support headaches. So, having a global way to shut it off can be an advantage.

- **QoS Packet Scheduler**—Just as its name implies, this section is used for configuring the Quality of Service features of Windows XP and Windows Server 2003. Included are settings for specifying limits to the amount of bandwidth to reserve for QoS as well as settings for manipulating layer 2 and layer 3 priority values.

- **SNMP**—This section enables administrators to easily configure SNMP community strings and trap servers, which is beneficial for network management applications. A lot of management infrastructures use SNMP for gathering information. Previously these settings had to be manually configured in the SNMP service properties of each machine, which meant changing them was difficult. Now they can be done once and applied globally.

New User Configuration Policies Sections

The following are new sections in the computer configuration section of group policies.

Administrative Templates\Windows Components

The user configuration Administrative Templates section configures H-Key Current User (HKCU) Registry settings. Like its counterpart in the Computer Configuration section, the Windows Components section is used to configure built-in Windows applications. The following are the new categories in this section:

- **Application Compatibility**—The only setting in this category is to prevent access to 16-bit applications, which disables the MS-DOS subsystem (ntvdm.exe). It is used more for disabling unnecessary application compatibility features than for making applications compatible. If all your applications are 32-bit, there is no need for the MS-DOS subsystem and disabling it with this setting frees up system resources.
- **Help and Support Center**—The only setting in this section is Do Not Allow "Did you know" Content to Appear. The new Help and Support Center in Windows XP and Windows Server 2003 replaces Windows Help. The "Did you know" section on the Help and Support Center home screen is dynamically updated from the Internet for providing tips and hints. Currently, it displays as "Top Issues," not "Do you know" and is in the bottom-right portion of the screen.
- **Terminal Services, Windows Messenger**—These new User Configuration Policies sections contain similar configuration settings as previously discussed in the "New Computer Configuration Policy Sections" section. The settings are used for the same functions, but they apply based on the user accounts instead of the computer accounts. Additionally, because they are user configuration settings, they are usually applied after any computer configuration settings.
- **Windows Update**—The setting in this category is Remove Access to Use All Windows Update Features, which effectively disables the entire Windows Update Service. It is no longer on the Start menu, in Internet Explorer, or in updating printer drivers.
- **Windows Media Player**—These settings are for configuring Windows Media Player. They include such options as proxy settings (HTTP or MMS), protocols to use for streaming media (multicast, UDP including which ports, TCP, or HTTP), and whether to prevent users from changing these settings by hiding the network tab. You can even configure the look and feel of Media Player by specifying skins.

Administrative Templates\Shared Folders

This section determines whether to allow shared folders and DFS roots to be published in Active Directory.

> For more information on shared folders and DFS, **see** Chapter 8, "Network Services," **p. 125**.

Administrative Templates\System

Similar to its counterpart in the Computer Configuration section, the System section is used to configure the behavior of Windows system components. The following are the new categories in this section:

- **User Profiles**—These user profile configuration settings differ from those in the computer configuration section. These settings are user specific and allow specification of the home directory as the root path for folder redirection. This helps ease the transition from environments currently using home folders because you can transition to using Group Policy to do the same thing as the Home Folder user property setting. Other settings enable administrators to place restrictions on the user's profile by specifying a maximum profile size and which directories to include in roaming profiles to improve performance.
- **Scripts**—Similar to the computer configuration section on scripts, the user configuration section enables configuration of script behavior. The settings configured here are whether to display legacy logon scripts (the scripts configured in the user's properties page, not Group Policy) and whether they should run synchronously. Additional settings are for whether to display logon and logoff scripts.
- **Ctrl+Alt+Del**—This section can be used to configure which options appear when Ctrl+Alt+Del is pressed (Task Manager, Lock Computer, Change Password, Logoff).

Note | Disabling the Shutdown button from the Ctrl+Alt+Del security screen is still configured via a Start menu and Taskbar setting, only now it is called Remove and Prevent Access to the Shut Down Command.

- **Power Management**—The setting in this section is Prompt for Password When Resume from Hibernate/Suspend. This essentially locks the computer when it goes into a low power state, requiring the user (or an administrator) to reenter his password when coming out of sleep or hibernation. Presumably, because this is a section unto itself, additional policies will eventually be added for managing power settings.

Windows Server 2003 extends the Group Policy infrastructure introduced in Windows 2000 and includes several changes to make Group Policy administration and troubleshooting easier. All these improvements enhance the usefulness of Group Policy as a management tool. They also give administrators more control over their networks, yet at the same time provide additional flexibility to customize to end user needs. Can it be that Windows desktop management has finally come of age?

7

INTERNET INFORMATION SERVICES

In This Chapter

- Understanding IIS's new architecture, **page 104**.
- Administering IIS 6, **page 108**.
- Migrating from IIS 5 to IIS 6, **page 118**.
- Configuring the SMTP and POP3 services, **page 120**.

What's New

A quick glance at the IIS console reveals the tip of the huge iceberg of changes contained within IIS 6. As Figure 7.1 shows, the console sports a slightly different graphical look, using the more photorealistic icons first introduced in Windows XP. The changes are more than skin deep, though, as indicated by the console's Application Pools and Web Service Extensions folders.

Of all of Windows Server 2003's major features, IIS 6.0 is perhaps the biggest set of changes over Windows 2000. IIS has been completely revamped to be a more powerful, reliable, and secure Web server platform.

102   Chapter 7   Internet Information Services

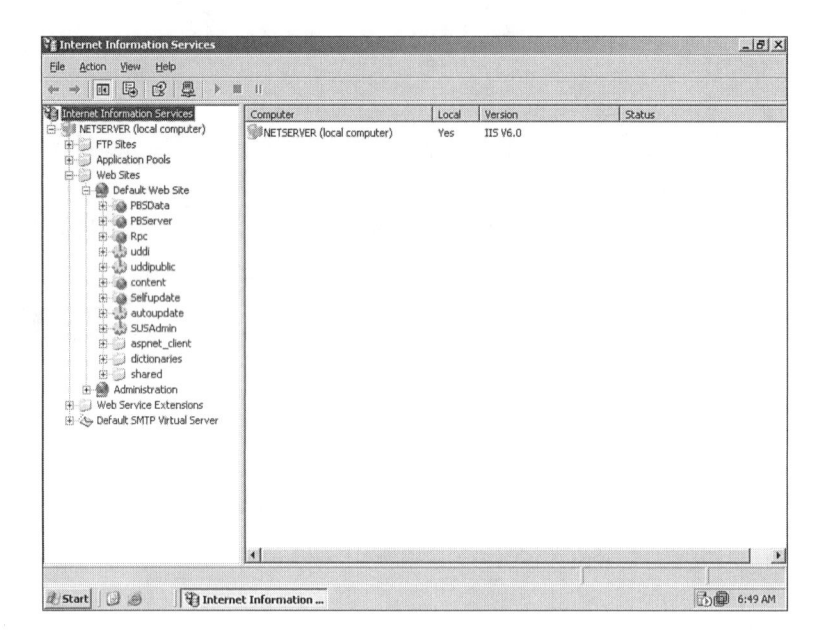

Figure 7.1 The new IIS snap-in sports a revised look and entirely new areas of functionality.

Note | As we've mentioned elsewhere in this book, Windows Server 2003 is the server equivalent to Windows XP. However, Windows XP Professional contains IIS 5.1, which is a relatively minor revision over the IIS 5.0 contained in Windows 2000.

Briefly, IIS 6.0's major improvements include

- Built-in application health monitoring, enabling Web server administrators to more effectively monitor the status of their Web applications.
- Changes to the way IIS processes incoming HTTP requests make the product more secure and less vulnerable to the many request-based attacks used against earlier versions of IIS.
- IIS is completely locked down by default, requiring manual steps to enable advanced technologies that might create security vulnerabilities.
- IIS's *metabase*, the database that contains IIS's configuration settings, is now fully XML based and includes new management tools that make it easier for administrators to directly manipulate the metabase.
- Microsoft's .NET Framework is included with Windows Server 2003, making it an out-of-the-box solution for .NET-based Web services applications built on IIS 6.

These changes are all designed to address fairly major functional deficiencies found in earlier versions of IIS. One of the most important alterations is the complete change in Microsoft's philosophy regarding IIS because IIS is not a default installation option in Windows Server 2003. Instead, administrators must specifically decide to install IIS. And, after installed, IIS is by default configured in a fully locked-down model, requiring administrators to take additional steps to enable more advanced features.

> **What's an Application Server These Days?**
>
> You'll see documentation from Microsoft referring to *application servers*. In the past, administrators used this term to refer to any server running an application, such as Microsoft SQL Server or Microsoft Exchange Server. In Microsoft's new terminology, *application server* refers to a server that provides a platform for applications, namely IIS, ASP.NET, COM, the Microsoft Data Engine (MSDE), and so forth. This new application server role replaces the role of Web server in Microsoft's universe.

To learn more about prior versions of IIS, and for a brief overview of IIS, visit www.samspublishing.com and enter this book's ISBN number (no hyphens or parentheses) in the Search field; then click the book's cover image to access the book details page. Click the Web Resources link in the More Information section, and locate article ID# **A010701**. You can also check out http://support.microsoft.com/default.aspx?scid=KB;EN-US;q224609&, which includes an IIS version comparison chart.

IIS: Not Installed by Default

This new installation behavior deserves some explanation. In all previous versions of Windows, Microsoft's goal was to make the product as easily managed as possible. In general, that meant installing all common network services—including IIS—by default, so that those services would be instantly available if needed. Those services were also configured to be fully operational by default, so that practically no administrative action was necessary to take full advantage of the product. IIS wasn't the only network service installed in this fashion, but it was the most talked about because IIS was plagued by security vulnerabilities. Most of these vulnerabilities stemmed from the product's advanced features, such as Active Server Pages (ASPs). Because IIS was installed in earlier versions of Windows by default, all Windows servers became victims of IIS security holes, even servers that weren't being used as Web servers. Further, even though Microsoft always responded to security vulnerabilities by quickly providing patches, many administrators patched only their Web servers, forgetting that every Windows server running IIS carried the vulnerabilities. As a result, many Windows servers continued to be vulnerable to IIS security flaws, even though fixes were readily available.

By not installing IIS by default, Microsoft allows administrators to avoid being blindsided by any future vulnerabilities. And, by configuring IIS to use a default locked-down configuration, Microsoft enables inexperienced administrators to install IIS while still avoiding the complex security issues associated with the product's more advanced features. Still, Microsoft's new security philosophy is no guarantee of a totally secure IIS. As an administrator, you must still keep up with Microsoft security bulletins and security updates to Windows Server 2003. Because IIS is most often used as an Internet Web server, it's placed in a position where it is more open to attacks than many other Windows network services, and Internet-based hackers are sure to discover any vulnerabilities that do exist. Visit Microsoft's Security Web site at www.Microsoft.com/security for more information on recent security updates and to subscribe to Microsoft's free security update email bulletins.

Architecture and Memory Management

IIS's architecture has always had a lot of challenges. Think about it: IIS is designed to execute applications written by other software developers with varying levels of experience. The learning curve for Web development isn't that steep, so relatively inexperienced developers are often in the position of creating corporate Web applications. As a result, those applications often contain the types of errors normally associated with inexperienced developers, including memory leaks, imperfect code access violations, and so forth. As the host process, IIS has to be reliable and scalable even when running these imperfect applications. Prior versions of IIS had certain design limitations, such as their use of memory and their interaction with the Windows operating system; IIS 6 revises much of IIS's underlying architecture to provide a more reliable, scalable application hosting environment.

IIS 5 uses a single process, Inetinfo.exe. This process can accept incoming HTTP requests and farm them out to one or more other processes by using dllhost.exe. This architecture limits the amount of exception handling that IIS can perform and also limits its overall capability to deal with poorly written Web applications. IIS 6, on the other hand, uses a new architecture built around a kernel-mode driver, http.sys. This driver listens for incoming HTTP requests and handles them. By running in kernel mode, rather than user mode, http.sys can interact with Windows at a much lower level, providing better performance. Essentially, http.sys provides the core functionality for a generic Web server; application handling is done by completely separate pieces of code, ensuring that Web applications have no effect on the core Web server code.

Two other new concepts are worker processes and application pools. IIS 6 contains a new Web service DLL, which is loaded into memory by one or more *worker processes*, which are separate processes from the core Web server process running http.sys. These processes can load Internet Services Application Programming Interface (ISAPI) filters and extensions, such as the ISAPI extensions used to implement ASP and ASP.NET. By keeping these filters and extensions in the separate worker processes, the core Web server process remains protected against poorly written applications. *Application pools* accept incoming HTTP requests from http.sys and deliver those requests to one or more Web applications based on the applications' URLs. A single application pool can feed multiple worker processes and provide a means for administrators to manage the separation between multiple Web applications running on a single server.

Putting It All Together

So, here's how it all works: The http.sys driver listens for incoming requests and queues them up. The driver maintains one request queue for each configured application pool, so that each pool's requests can be delivered independently. For example, suppose you're running Application A and Application B on the same server. Users access Application A by using the URL http://servera, and they access Application B by using http://serverb, although both URLs point to the same physical Windows Server 2003 server. The http.sys driver separates incoming requests by their destination URLs, lining up the requests in the application pool for each application (assuming each application is configured to use a separate application pool). Any poorly written code in Application A will not affect http.sys because it runs in kernel mode and contains 100% Microsoft code. Even if Application A completely crashes, http.sys will continue to queue up incoming requests for Application B. This process is illustrated in Figure 7.2, which shows two application pools configured to handle three applications.

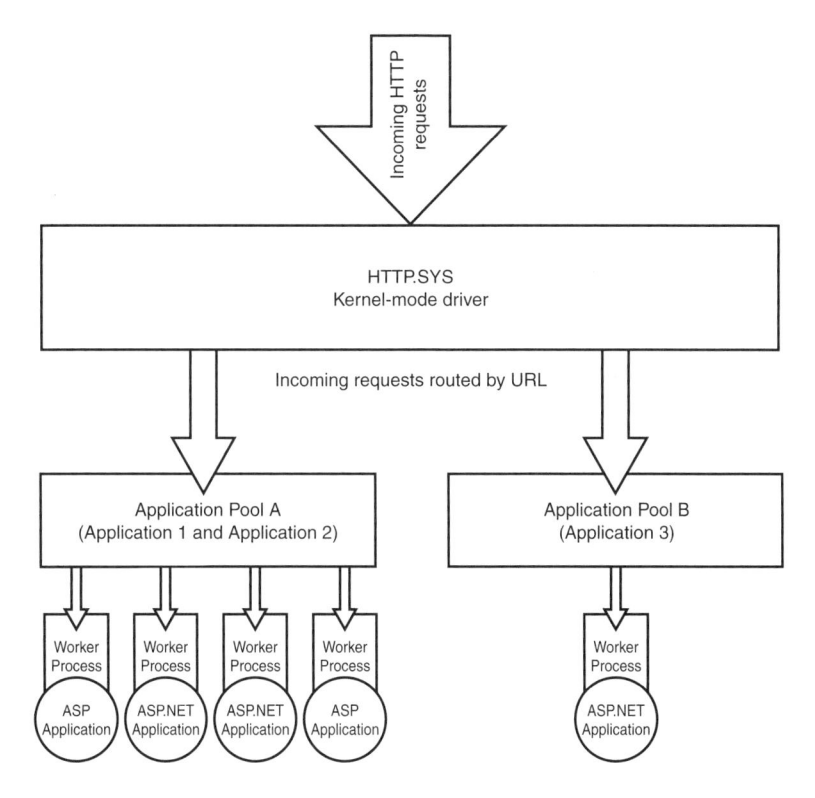

Figure 7.2 Applications within a pool can be completely different, such as the first pool shown, which runs an ASP application and an ASP.NET application.

Each application pool can be serviced by multiple worker processes, which actually execute the Web application's code, such as an ASP or ASP.NET application. If one of the applications does crash, the WWW service will eventually notice that the worker process is no longer servicing requests from its application pool. In response, the WWW service creates a new, identical worker process to service any outstanding requests. The failed process will eventually be terminated after a set amount of time (which we'll discuss later).

Another key architectural component is the new WWW Service Administrator and Monitoring component. Like http.sys, this component contains 100% Microsoft code and never loads third-party code, helping to ensure its reliability. This component is primarily responsible for configuring IIS and managing IIS's processes. The component reads IIS configuration information from the IIS metabase and initializes the http.sys driver's namespace with one entry for each configured application. This initialization informs http.sys that there is an application pool that responds to each namespace entry, so that http.sys can start new worker processes for the application pool. Note that http.sys requests worker processes only when there is a demand for them; if you have configured eight applications on your Web server, worker processes will exist only for applications that are actually receiving HTTP requests. This behavior conserves server resources for applications that are actually being used.

Worker Process Isolation

IIS 6's new worker process isolation mode enables IIS to run application code in an isolated section of memory, without the negative performance hit experienced in previous versions of IIS.

Note   IIS 6 also supports a backward-compatible process isolation mode, called *IIS 5 isolation*, which I'll discuss later.

The http.sys driver routes requests to the appropriate application pool queue, and worker processes running in user mode pull those requests directly from http.sys. This behavior eliminates unnecessary communication between the separate processes; normally, such cross-process communication is a major contributing factor to slow application performance. In fact, previous versions of IIS handled cross-process communication so poorly that many application developers created in-process applications to avoid the performance problems. *In-process* applications ran in IIS's main memory space, and if the application crashed, so did IIS. IIS 6 doesn't offer this as an option, ensuring the integrity of the core http.sys driver. Because all application code executes in isolated worker processes, applications can crash (or be deliberately unloaded) all they want, without affecting the core Web server code.

Isolating these worker processes has side benefits, as well, such as the ability to throttle the CPU utilization that a particular process can consume. This capability enables you to limit (to a degree) the server resources consumed by a particular Web application, without crippling the core Web server code in http.sys.

Keep in mind that multiple applications can be assigned to a single application pool. For example, Web hosting companies might create a unique application pool for each customer, assigning all of that customer's applications to one pool. Any failed application might take down the entire pool, but only that one customer would be affected.

> **Tip** As we'll describe later in this chapter, applications can be assigned or reassigned to an application pool on-the-fly, without restarting the application or the Web server.

IIS 6's complete isolation of applications suggests interesting new load-balancing capabilities in the future. For example, suppose you administer a Web farm that runs two different Web applications and contains three Web servers. If Application A on Server 1 crashes, IIS could communicate that to load-balancing software, which could direct all incoming Application A requests to Servers 2 and 3. Incoming requests for Application B could still be load-balanced across all three servers, providing maximum load-balancing efficiency.

> **Tip** You can configure a new IIS 6 features known as *rapid fail protection* to completely disable processes that fail frequently. For example, if a particular worker process fails and is subsequently restarted 10 times in a short period of time, the application is obviously misbehaving. IIS can disable the application pool, returning a `503: Service Unavailable` error to users and preventing the application from consuming any additional server resources. You can also manually place applications in this out-of-service mode for maintenance or to stop runaway applications.

Bear in mind, too, that a single application pool can be serviced by multiple independent worker processes. Microsoft refers to this as a *Web garden* because it's a bit like a Web farm where multiple servers handle a single Web site. In this case, the so-called garden exists entirely on a single server, with multiple isolated processes responding identically to incoming requests for the application's services. IIS automatically handles the distribution of requests between worker processes.

Backward Compatibility

IIS 6 also supports an IIS 5.0 Isolation Mode, a backward-compatible architecture that retains the `http.sys` kernel-mode driver but runs all user-mode processes within a single process hosted by `Inetinfo.exe`. This mode is designed to support multiple-instance applications, applications that rely on session state being persisted in-process, and so forth. Essentially, `http.sys` delivers all incoming requests to `Inetinfo.exe`, which operates similarly to the architecture in IIS 5.0. Your Web developers should be able to tell you whether their applications require this backward-compatible architecture. Be advised, however, that IIS 5.0 Isolation Mode does not include the additional reliability of IIS 6's native architecture, and you can't use both isolation modes at the same time on a single computer.

Administrative Changes

Most IIS administration is accomplished through the IIS console, a Microsoft Management Console (MMC) snap-in. There are a number of other administration interfaces, though, such as Windows Management Instrumentation, scripts, command-line tools, and so forth. All these interfaces, however, interact with IIS's Administration Base Objects (ABOs), a set of COM components that modify the IIS metabase. The metabase contains all IIS's configuration settings, making them universally available. Figure 7.3 shows the relationship between the administrative interfaces, ABO, and the metabase.

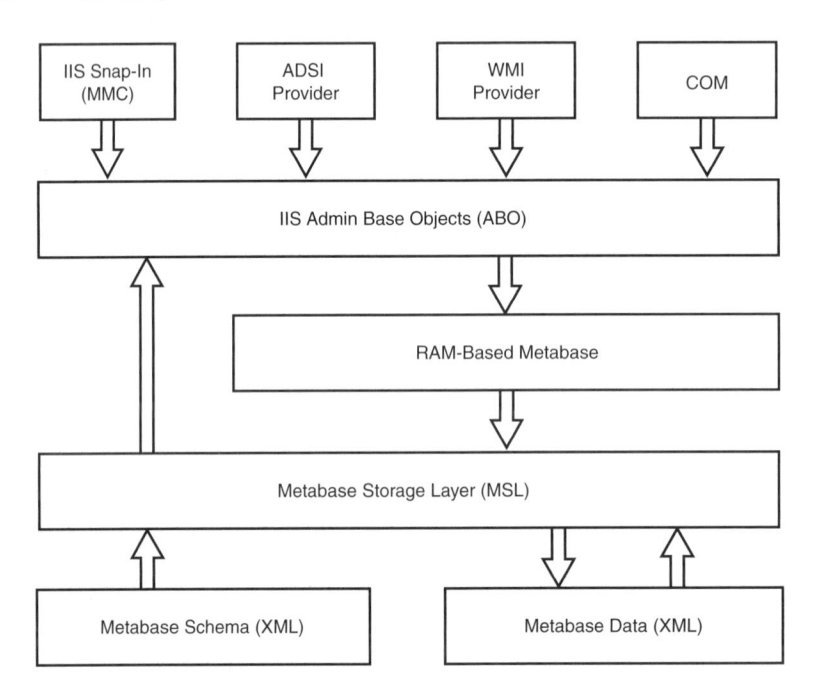

Figure 7.3 The metabase is XML based and contains all of IIS's configuration settings.

Administering IIS 6 is similar to administering earlier versions of IIS; the next few sections cover the major changes, especially those that relate to IIS 6's new architecture and security enhancements.

Configuring Server and Web Site Options

One major change to IIS Web sites is the capability to support Microsoft .NET Passport authentication, in addition to the familiar Integrated Windows authentication, Basic authentication, and Digest authentication. Passport authentication can be enabled in the properties of a Web site, as shown in Figure 7.4. Keep in mind that Passport authentication requires a .NET Passport infrastructure, which you have to set up with Microsoft for additional fees. Visit `www.Microsoft.com/passport` for more details.

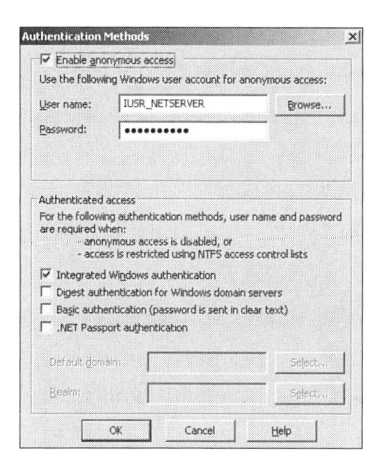

Figure 7.4 Passport authentication makes creating Internet Web sites that use Microsoft's popular authentication mechanism easier.

You'll find that most other Web site and server administrative options are unchanged from Windows 2000: Logging, directory security, digital certificates, document paths, and other settings work the same as in IIS 5.0. Note that the Default Web Site enables additional document types for the default document, as shown in Figure 7.5. Now, `Default.aspx` joins `Default.asp`, `Index.htm`, and `Default.htm` as default pages that IIS looks for. `Default.aspx` is an ASP.NET file type.

Another important change is to a Web site's general properties: The ability to specify the application pool with which the site is associated. IIS is configured with a couple of default application pools to which you can assign your applications, but you'll more than likely want to create your own pools for full control over IIS's behavior and performance.

Configuring Application Pools

To configure a new application pool, simply right-click **Application Pools** and select **New Application Pool** from the pop-up menu. Each application pool's properties dialog box includes four tabs: Health, Recycling, Performance, and Identity.

Figure 7.5 Default.aspx is last on the list, meaning any other default page is loaded instead, if one is present.

The Recycling tab, shown in Figure 7.6, is where you tell IIS how to treat worker processes. You can tell IIS to automatically recycle worker processes after a specified number of minutes, after they handle a certain number of requests, or a combination of the two. You can also specify that processes be recycled at specific times, such as idle times for your application. Finally, you can tell IIS to recycle worker processes after they've consumed a specific amount of memory, forcing IIS to clean up and terminate any processes that are no longer being used.

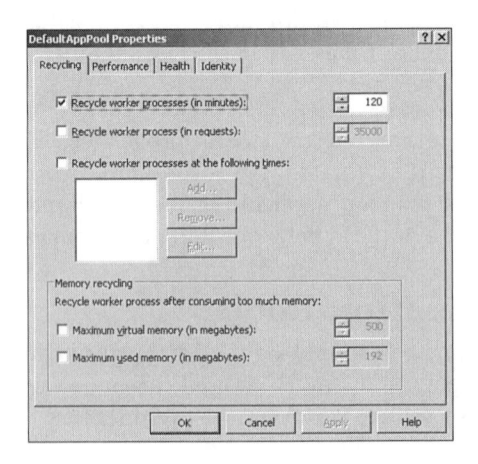

Figure 7.6 IIS defaults to recycling worker processes every two hours, which is sufficient for most applications.

Figure 7.7 shows the Health tab, which is where you tell IIS how to determine whether a worker process within the application pool is healthy. By default, IIS pings each process every 30 seconds to see whether it responds; processes that don't respond are considered unhealthy and are normally terminated. This dialog box also enables you to configure IIS's rapid-fail protection feature by specifying a maximum number of failures within a specified period of time. Application pools that exceed these thresholds are permanently disabled. Finally, you can specify the maximum amount of time, in seconds, that a worker process should take to start or stop. You'll need to take into account the initialization time for any ISAPI filters or extensions the processes must load. Any process exceeding these time limits is assumed to be unhealthy and is terminated.

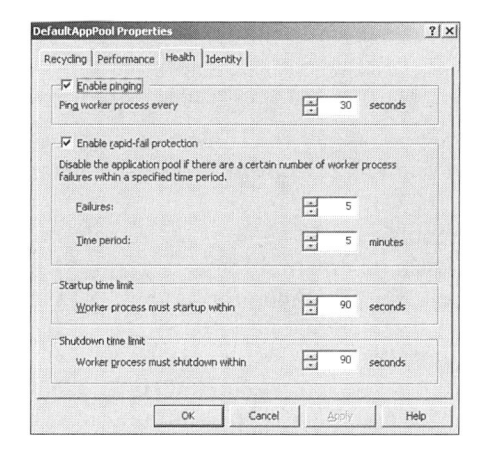

Figure 7.7 The default health settings are sufficient for most Web applications.

Figure 7.8 shows the Performance tab, which enables you to configure the performance for an application pool. You can specify that IIS automatically terminate worker processes that have been idle for a specific amount of time (the default is 20 minutes). This dialog box is also where you specify the maximum number of worker processes for the application pool's Web garden. The default is 1, which means the pool will be served by a single worker process.

The Performance tab also enables you to configure the application pool's request queue length, and the default is 1,000 requests. As worker processes pull requests from the queue, it empties. New requests are placed onto the queue by http.sys. When the queue fills, http.sys automatically responds to new requests with an error message until the queue empties out. You can use the queue limit setting to restrict the number of requests that can stack up for a slow-running Web application; in many cases users might prefer to receive an "unavailable" error message rather than wait for your application to catch up and service their request. Also, forcing the server to queue more requests for a slow application requires http.sys to maintain a larger number of open HTTP connections, which consume server resources.

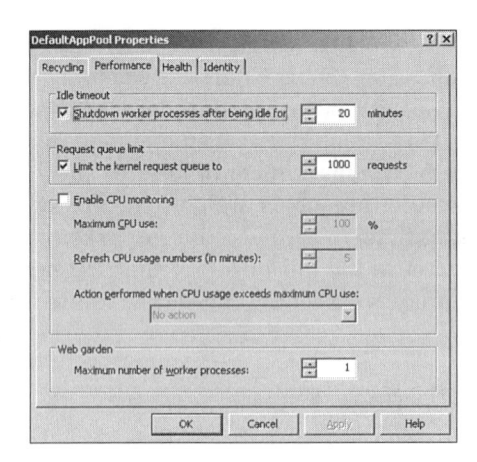

Figure 7.8 A single worker process is not the same as a single thread; one process can still be multithreaded to support multiple simultaneous users.

Finally, the Performance tab enables you to monitor the amount of CPU that the application pool uses. Simply enable a CPU threshold, and then specify an action to be taken if that threshold is exceeded. By default, the CPU monitoring feature is disabled.

Finally, Figure 7.9 shows the Identity tab, which is where you can configure the security context of the application pool. You can use a predefined identity, such as the default `Network Service` or configure a custom user account the application pool will use.

> **Caution** Be very careful when configuring application pool identity. If the pool runs under a high-privilege user account, or even an ordinary domain user, hackers might be able to exploit IIS security flaws and perform unauthorized actions on your servers.

Configuring Web Services Extensions

Web Services extensions enable you to more easily configure extensions such as ASP and ASP.NET. Figure 7.10 shows the Web Service Extensions container in the IIS console, listing all the extensions configured in IIS by default. Notice that many extensions are configured but set to be Prohibited (the figure does not reflect the default prohibited/allowed status for each extension). The Prohibited setting allows Microsoft to ship IIS with a number of useful extensions but to ensure that those extensions are disabled until an administrator specifically enables them.

Administrative Changes **113**

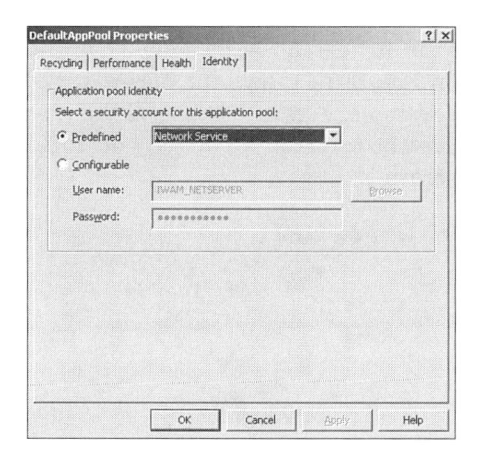

Figure 7.9 By default, all application pools run under a low-privileged, anonymous user account.

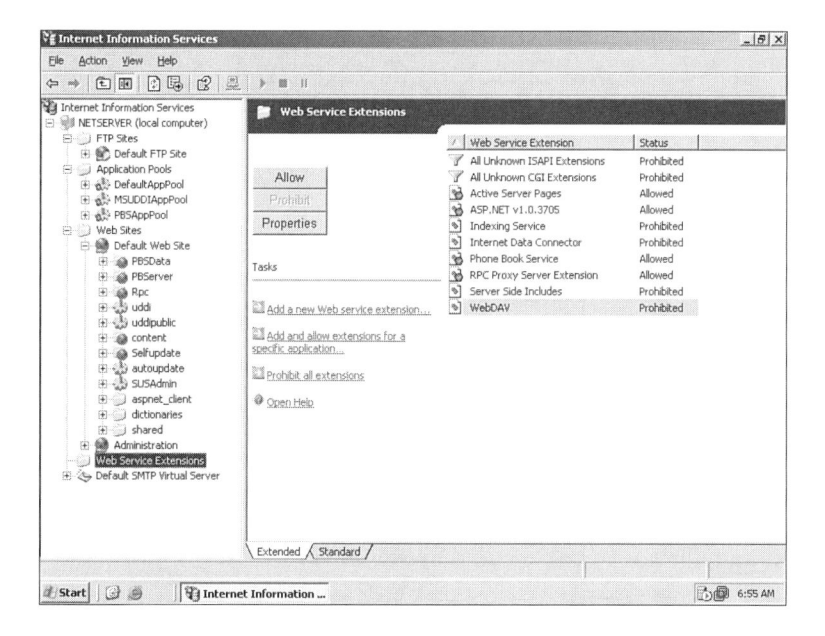

Figure 7.10 Notice the filter extensions for unknown ISAPI extensions and CGI extensions, which are prohibited by default.

You can modify the properties for any extension by double-clicking it. The extensions' Properties dialog box, shown in Figure 7.11, lists the files required for the extension to operate and the status of the file. For example, Figure 7.11 shows the properties for the Internet Data Connector extension, which uses the `httpodbc.dll` file. By default, this file is prohibited, preventing the extension from operating.

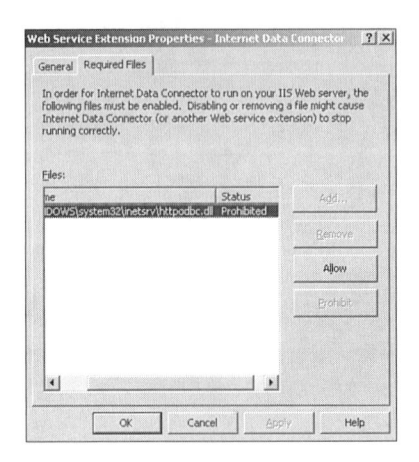

Figure 7.11 A single extension can have any number of associated files; the Internet Data Connector extension shown here has only one associated file.

You can also create your own extensions. For example, one popular alternative to ASP is PHP (www.php.net), an Open Source scripting language designed specifically for creating dynamic Web pages. Most PHP pages use PHP as their filename extension and are processed by a special ISAPI DLL. IIS 6 makes configuring PHP as a Web Service extension easy, enabling your Web server to host PHP pages.

To create a new Web Service extension, right-click the **Web Service Extensions** container in the IIS console and select **New Web Service Extension** from the pop-up menu. As shown in Figure 7.12, provide the extension's name and required files and select the check box that sets the extension's status to Allowed. Click **OK**, and IIS will immediately recognize the new Web Service extension and allow it to be executed by worker processes.

Web-Based Administration

IIS 6 also supports full Web-based administration as part of Windows Server 2003's Web-based administration console. The Web-based console is accessible only to administrators and uses a built-in digital encryption certificate to provide secure HTTPS connections. To access a server's administrative Web page, simply type the server's name, followed by **:8099**, in your Web browser. For example, type **http://ServerA:8099**.

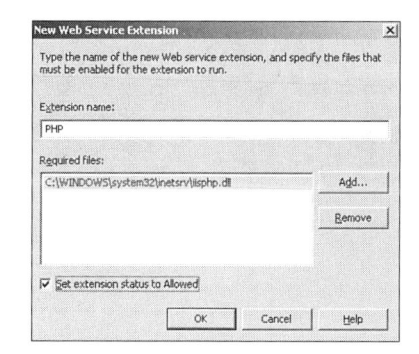

Figure 7.12 Remember that any extensions not specifically defined as Allowed are automatically prohibited and not allowed to execute.

Tip | Don't try to access the administration site by using the URL http://localhost. The site requires encryption and can enable encryption only when you use the server's actual name.

Figure 7.13 shows the Web-based console, opened to the Web Server administration screen. Notice that the server is displaying a status of Warning in the upper bar, just below the server name. This warning is present on all new Windows Server 2003 computers and is a reminder to you to replace the server's preconfigured encryption certificate with a valid certificate of your own.

Only members of the server's local Administrators group can access this Web site by default. In a domain, the local Administrators group includes the domain's Domain Admins group, allowing any domain administrator to access the Web site.

If, for any reason, the Web site is not capable of using a secure HTTPS connection, you'll see the error screen shown in Figure 7.14. You should never try to bypass this security check; the administrative Web site contains a great deal of confidential information, and if you use it to reset user passwords or deal with other sensitive data, the HTTPS encryption will protect that data as it travels across your network. Without the HTTPS encryption, your sensitive data can be easily compromised.

As an additional security precaution, you might want to reconfigure the Administration Web Site to use a different port number. Doing so will help deter attackers who might try to access the site on its default port number. Additionally, if you don't plan to use the Administration Web Site, use the IIS console to stop it completely, preventing an attacker from accessing it at all.

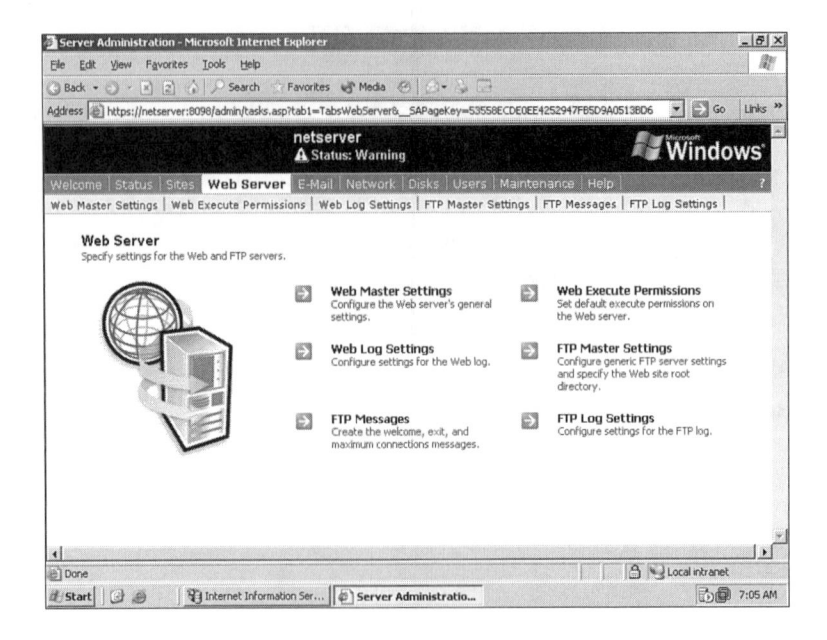

Figure 7.13 The Web-based administration console provides access to several administrative functions.

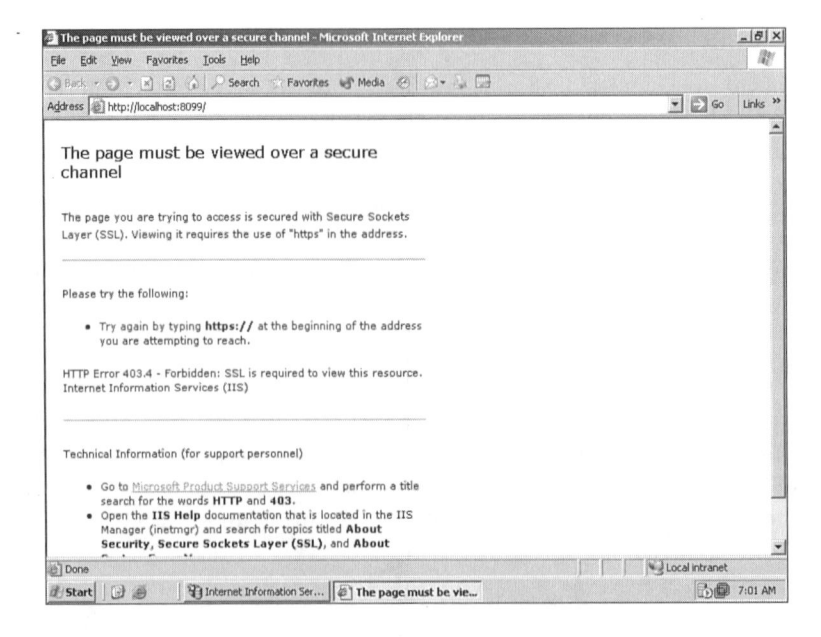

Figure 7.14 Notice that encryption could not be enforced here because the `localhost` URL was used rather than the server's actual name.

Security Enhancements

Microsoft has introduced several changes to IIS 6 to enhance security, including

- As we've already discussed, Windows Server 2003 doesn't include IIS by default. By eliminating IIS as a default installation option, Windows Server 2003 lets you more easily keep track of your Web servers for security and update purposes.
- By default, IIS serves only static Web page types. All dynamic Web page types (ASP, ASPX, and so forth) are disabled by default. Many security vulnerabilities are associated with the incorrect use of dynamic Web pages, so administrators must take specific actions to make them accessible.
- When upgrading to Windows Server 2003, the Setup process actually disables any IIS 5.0 installation that is configured only with the default settings. This feature turns off IIS on any servers where it doesn't appear to be used, removing a potential security vulnerability.

Note | Be sure to carefully review every Windows 2000 server you upgrade to Windows Server 2003. The feature that disables IIS is a new philosophical direction for Microsoft, and you should follow up on its caution with a thorough review of the upgrade to ensure that your server is configured to meet your needs and to provide maximum security for your environment.

- A new group policy in Windows Server 2003 enables domain administrators to prevent users from installing any version of IIS on their computers. You might apply this to your client computers to prevent users from installing IIS locally and opening a potential security hole in your network.
- By default, IIS is configured to run worker processes in the security context of a low-privilege user account. This feature helps prevent worker processes from performing dangerous actions in the event that a hacker manages to place unauthorized code on the server.
- All requests for unrecognized file extensions are rejected. In the past, IIS would attempt to process unknown file extensions as text or HTML pages; IIS 6.0 responds with an error message. This behavior helps prevent hackers from uploading and executing malicious code.
- The Web server process cannot execute any IIS 6 command-line tools. Having the Web server execute command-line tools was an often-used security vulnerability in prior versions of IIS, allowing hackers to reconfigure IIS remotely.
- Previous versions of IIS used timeouts that were pretty generous, opening the server to a broader range of attacks. IIS 6 defaults to fairly aggressive timeouts, preventing long-running scripts and other security vulnerabilities.
- IIS 6 worker processes can detect and terminate applications that generate a buffer overflow. Buffer overflows are a frequently used security attack because they can cause poorly written applications to overwrite unintended areas of memory.

- The `http.sys` kernel-mode driver verifies that the content requested in an HTTP request actually exists before handing the request off to a worker process. This behavior helps protect poorly written applications that don't gracefully handle unexpected conditions, such as missing content.

> For a brief history of IIS's security problems and solutions, visit `www.samspublishing.com` and enter this book's ISBN number (no hyphens or parentheses) in the Search field; then click the book's cover image to access the book details page. Click the Web Resources link in the More Information section, and locate article ID# **A010702**.

Migrating from IIS 5 to 6

After upgrading a Windows 2000 Server computer to Windows Server 2003, most Web applications will run normally. Although IIS 6 includes ASP.NET, it also includes the so-called Classic ASP, which is included with IIS 5. Both ASP.NET and Classic ASP can run side by side with no problems because they differentiate between each other by using different filename extensions: ASP for Classic ASP and ASPX for ASP.NET.

One of the biggest problems in moving from IIS 5 to IIS 6 is that IIS 5 enables session state by default and IIS 6 does not. On a server upgrade, IIS 6 should retain the equivalent IIS 5 settings. However, if you're moving your Web site from an IIS 5 server to a new IIS 6 server, you might need to enable session state maintenance in the IIS 6 server properties, as shown in Figure 7.15.

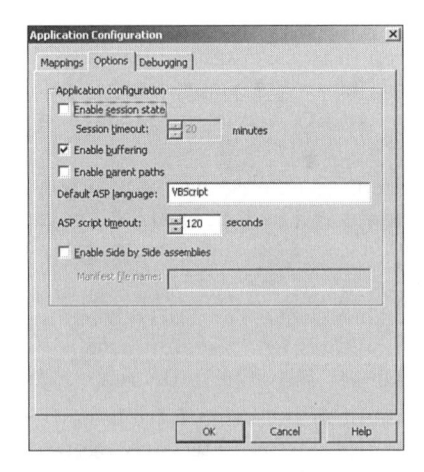

Figure 7.15 Session state is disabled by default on IIS 6. Also, buffering is enabled, which is also the default on IIS 5, but not on IIS 4.

Other than session state issues, most ASP and ASP.NET Web applications will migrate with no modification. Certain types of applications, as we've already discussed, can require IIS 5.0 Isolation Mode to be enabled in the server's properties. Your Web developers should be able to advise you if this will be necessary in your environment.

Metabase and Management Enhancements

IIS's metabase contains all of IIS's configuration settings. As was described earlier (and shown in Figure 7.3), the metabase can be accessed through a variety of administrative interfaces, including the familiar MMC snap-in, Microsoft Active Directory Services Interface (ADSI), Windows Management Instrumentation (WMI), and much more. By default, administrators cannot modify the metabase while IIS is running. Instead, changes to the metabase must come through a registered administrative interface such as the IIS console. However, as shown in Figure 7.16, you can modify IIS's properties to allow direct editing of the metabase XML file while IIS is running.

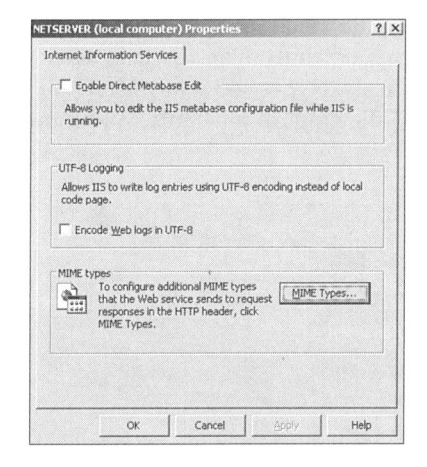

Figure 7.16 Direct metabase editing is off by default.

The ability to directly manipulate the XML metabase file can be useful for troubleshooting because the file enables you to see exactly which IIS settings are configured and how they are configured. The fact that the metabase is XML based enables Microsoft and third-party vendors to more easily extend the metabase to meet future application needs. Note that IIS 4 and 5 binary metabase files will upgrade to the new XML file with no problems when you install Windows Server 2003.

The metabase automatically keeps a history of changes, making it easy to track configuration changes made to IIS and to more easily roll back to a prior version of the metabase. By default, IIS stores the current metabase in a file named Metabase.xml, along with a version number. A copy is saved in a History folder each time the metabase is changed, and each copy is given a unique version number. You can directly view or edit any of these files in a simple text editor, such as Windows Notepad.

The POP3 and SMTP Services

IIS 6 includes an optional SMTP service, and Windows Server 2003 includes a related POP3 service. The SMTP service enables IIS to send email by using the Simple Mail Transport Protocol (SMTP). The POP3 service enables you to create mailboxes that can receive and store incoming email. Users can then log on to their mailboxes to retrieve their mail, much as they would for a regular Internet service provider (ISP).

IIS 6's SMTP service is very similar to the SMTP service provided in IIS 5. Of particular importance, however, is the Relay Restrictions, shown in Figure 7.17. This dialog box can be accessed by right-clicking the SMTP virtual server, selecting Properties from the pop-up menu, and then clicking the Relay Restrictions button on the Access tab. By default, IIS is configured to relay email only from computers on the list, which, as shown, is empty by default—preventing relaying entirely. Notice, however, that the check box at the bottom of the dialog box is selected by default, allowing all authenticated computers and users to relay email.

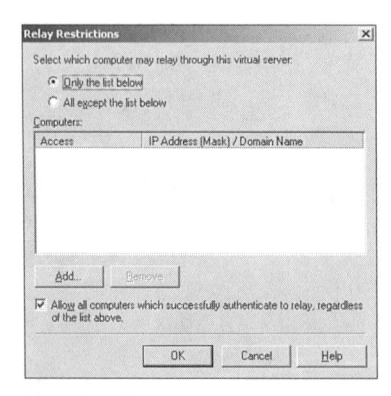

Figure 7.17 SMTP relaying is a major cause of network saturation, server overutilization, and security issues.

Why is relaying bad? SMTP relaying enables a user to connect to an SMTP server, compose an email destined for a recipient who doesn't have a mailbox on that server, and then disconnect. The server automatically relays the message, making it seem as if the message came from within your organization. In effect, relaying enables an SMTP server to be "hijacked," and it enables the hijacker to send free email that's practically untraceable. Much of the Internet's unsolicited email is sent through SMTP relaying. SMTP relaying increases network traffic, increases your servers' resource utilization, and decreases the availability of your server for your own users. Relaying can also land you in legal trouble because many ISPs take legal action for unsolicited email against the owners of the SMTP server from which the mail originated.

SMTP has one legitimate use: Users with POP3 email clients, such as Outlook Express, need an SMTP server to send outgoing email. Therefore, IIS defaults to allow authenticated computers to relay because it allows IIS to accept outgoing email from legitimate users and deliver that email to its final destination (or to another SMTP server that will handle the final delivery).

Windows Server 2003 also includes a POP3 service, which you administer through its own MMC snap-in. Figure 7.18 shows the basic properties for the POP3 service, which include the server's authentication method, server port, and logging level. The standard POP3 port of 110 shouldn't usually be modified because most users' POP3 client software looks for the server on port 110. You do need to select an appropriate authentication mode, so the POP3 service can provide users with access to their mailboxes. In a domain, the default Active Directory Integrated authentication method is best because it allows users to access their mailboxes by using their domain user accounts.

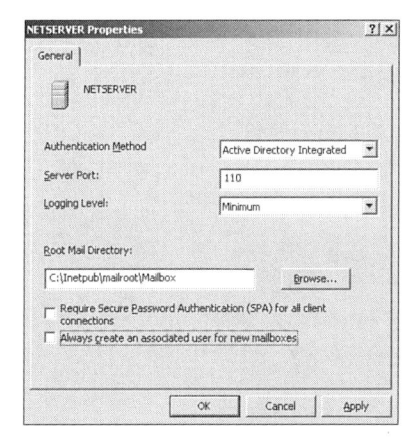

Figure 7.18 Note the option to require Secure Password Authentication (SPA), which is supported only by Microsoft Outlook and Outlook Express.

POP3 is designed to associate a single mailbox with a user. As shown in Figure 7.19, you can create mailboxes for as many users as desired and monitor their mailbox usage. Because POP3 mailboxes store messages as text files on disk (rather than in a database such as Exchange Server), you can use the built-in disk quotas feature of Windows to limit the size of a user's mailbox. See the POP3 service's online help file for more information on this technique.

122 Chapter 7 Internet Information Services

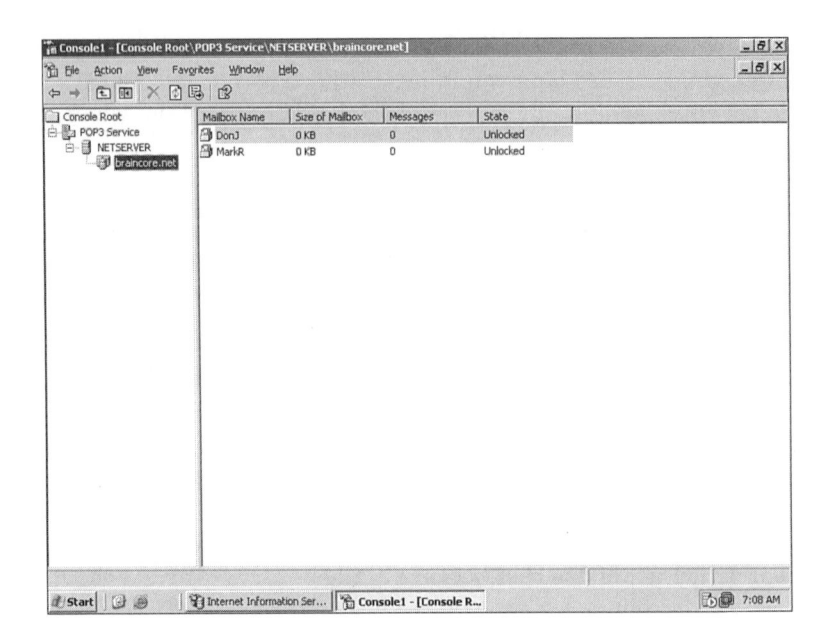

Figure 7.19 After a mailbox is created, the server accepts incoming email for that user and stores the email in the mailbox.

The relationship between the POP3 and SMTP services is illustrated in Figure 7.20. Users use the POP3 service to retrieve email that the server received on their behalf, and they use the SMTP service to send outgoing email. Each service provides half of the total email equation.

With its SMTP and POP3 service, can Windows Server 2003 completely replace mail servers like Microsoft Exchange? Hardly. The SMTP and POP3 services provide the minimum functionality necessary for a working email system and don't provide anywhere near the level of features offered by full messaging systems such as Exchange, Lotus Notes, and other products.

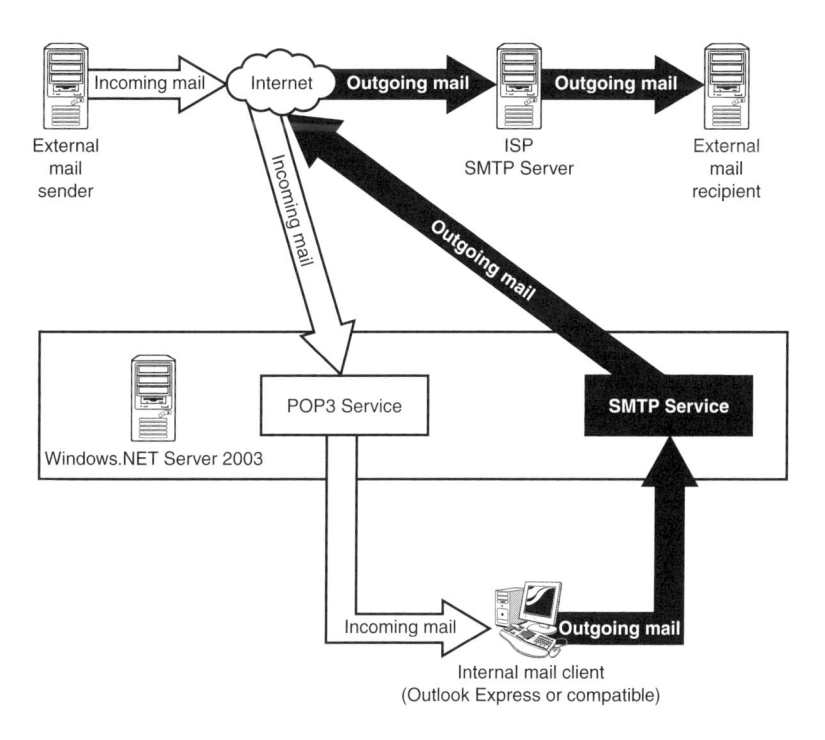

Figure 7.20 POP3 and SMTP work together to provide a complete, very basic email system for very small organizations.

8

NETWORK SERVICES

In This Chapter

- Basic Network Services, **page 126**.
- Using Windows Server 2003 as a fax server, **page 132**.
- Working with Shadow Copies, **page 135**.
- Sharing secured files, **page 141**.

What's New

One of the basic functions of any network operating system is to provide network services. In a TCP/IP-based network, the most basic of these services range from the core services such as DHCP, WINS, and DNS (which provide connectivity and the capability to locate resources) to accessing those resources via methods such as file sharing.

Windows Server 2003 introduces a number of enhancements to these network services. The majority of these enhancements are changes to the various core network service consoles (DHCP, WINS), whereas others add increased functionality (application partitions in AD-integrated DNS). Additional improvements with other network-accessible services have been made primarily to make those services more accessible (fax sharing, shadow copies, EFS file sharing, and sharing of files across the Web). This chapter looks at the improvements to each of these services.

WINS, DHCP, and DNS

Windows Internet Naming Service (WINS) in Windows Server 2003 is largely unchanged from Windows 2000. There are some minor display improvements primarily for performance, but the service itself functions the same. Dynamic Host Configuration Protocol (DHCP) introduces a few new management features, but it too is largely unchanged. Domain Naming Service (DNS), on the other hand, has some significant improvements.

WINS

WINS is the service used for locating network basic input output system (NetBIOS) resources. It provides a dynamic database for maintaining associations between NetBIOS names and Internet Protocol (IP) addresses. The changes to the WINS service in Windows Server 2003 are primarily enhancement to the Microsoft Management Console (MMC) snap-in for administering WINS. The first notable improvement is in the way WINS records are displayed. In Windows 2000 you had to choose which records to display in the console. You could select to find records by name, owner (the WINS server on which the record was created), or type (which was a sub-choice of finding by owner). It is pretty much the same in Windows Server 2003, but now you simply select **Display Records** and enter the criteria for the records to display: **by Record Owner**; **by Record Type**; or **by Record Mapping**. Filtering by record mapping includes filtering by name, by IP address, or both. The real improvement is in what the console does when you choose to display the records.

When choosing to display records, you have an option labeled Enable Result Caching, as shown in Figure 8.1. If you don't select this check box, the query is run against the WINS server (or servers if multiple owners are queried) and the results are displayed. Subsequent queries are also run against the WINS servers(s). Depending on the size of the WINS database and the network connectivity between the servers, a significant delay could occur before displaying the results of each and every query as the query traverses the network. By selecting this check box, the WINS records are downloaded to the local machine and cached in memory. Subsequent queries can then find those records in memory without having to query the WINS server across the network again. Thus, with the results cached, subsequent queries to the same data are faster. The caveat is that if the WINS database is particularly large, the amount of memory consumed for caching can actually degrade performance. What actually gets cached depends on the query: If you query WINS records by owner, all the records from that owner are downloaded to the local machine and cached. Any subsequent queries for records from that owner are returned from the cache without querying the WINS server again—the queries are faster but potentially outdated if anything has changed on the WINS server queried. If the WINS records are queried through a filter (by name, IP address, or type), only those records in the query result set are cached. Subsequent queries for the same result set (or subset) are cached, but queries for other records have to again access the WINS server (across the network).

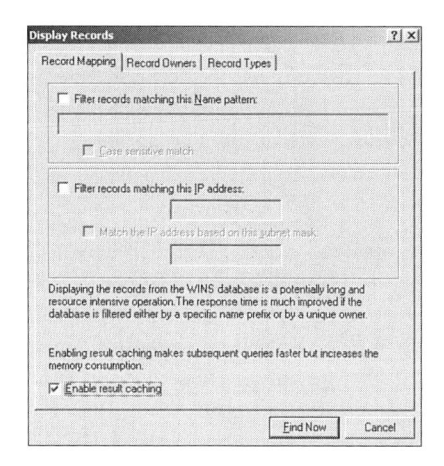

Figure 8.1 Caching WINS results improves the performance of queries.

Another change in the WINS server is in the designation of valid replication partners. In previous versions of WINS, administrators had to manually configure push/pull partners to enable replication between two WINS servers. To ease this administrative burden, Windows 2000 introduced a new feature called Automatic Partner Configuration, which allows WINS servers to detect other WINS servers on the network and automatically configure push/pull relationships. If a lot of WINS servers are on the network, this autodiscovery and autoconfiguration could potentially lead to WINS replication chaos because any WINS server could replicate with any other WINS server. Administrators can gain some control over this by specifying a list of WINS servers from which a given WINS server would block replication of records. Windows Server 2003 improves on controlling Automatic Partner Configuration by enabling administrators to designate acceptance of records from particular owners. This is basically the same thing, but instead of having to specify all the servers with which you don't want to replicate, you can simply specify the few servers you do.

Note | The capability to block replication from particular WINS servers is not exclusive to Automatic Partner Configuration. You can block WINS servers even if you don't use Automatic Partner Configuration; however, there is really no reason to do so because you would be manually configuring the replication partnerships anyway. The new ability to specify servers from which to accept replication can also be used to improve the security of your WINS infrastructure. This could prevent someone from putting up a rogue WINS server and replicating with your WINS servers. Previously, the only way to do this was to find out the name or IP address of the rogue server and explicitly block it. However, by the time you have that kind of information, the damage has already been done.

For an introduction to WINS, visit www.samspublishing.com and enter this book's ISBN number (no hyphens or parenthesis) in the Search field; then click the book cover image to access the book details page. Click the Web Resources link in the More Information section, and locate article ID# **A010801**.

DHCP

DHCP is the service used to automatically issue IP addresses and configuration information. Like WINS, DHCP is largely unchanged in Windows Server 2003. Most of the improvements are with the DHCP service snap-in. One of the nicest enhancements is the capability to back up and restore the DHCP database right from the console. In previous editions, DHCP could be configured to back up its database; however, these configurations were performed either by modifying the Registry or with the netsh command. The netsh command still exists and is still used to configure an automated backup interval, but the DHCP snap-in now has the capability for performing a manual backup. More importantly, it provides an easy way to restore a corrupted DHCP database. Simply right-click the DHCP server, select **Restore** from the pop-up menu, and select the location from which to restore. It even prompts you to automatically restart the DHCP service to make the "new" database available.

Some additional niceties in the console are new descriptions on the Dynamic DNS tab, clarifying what each option does. Additionally, it provides the capability to specify the credentials used to authenticate to the DNS server for DNS dynamic updates. There is also a new predefined option (249 - classless static routes) that enables definition of static routes for configuring alternative routing paths over and above the default gateway.

There is a significant change in the Windows XP and Windows Server 2003 DHCP client. The Internet Protocol (TCP/IP) properties for the network adapter have a new Alternate Configuration tab that allows finer control over the Automatic Private IP Addressing feature. The Windows 2000 DHCP client introduced a new feature called *Automatic Private IP Addressing (APIPA)*. APIPA is the capability of the DHCP client to assign itself an IP address. Basically, if a Windows 2000 client configured for DHCP does not receive a response when it attempts to obtain a lease from a DHCP server, the client automatically assigns itself an IP address in the 169.254.x.x class B address range.

Note | If two clients assign themselves the same IP address, an IP address conflict occurs and one of the clients is incapable of communicating. To prevent this, the APIPA-configured DHCP client broadcasts the IP address it randomly picked. If it doesn't receive a response that anyone is using it, it assigns itself the IP address.

This is great for small businesses and SOHOs on a single network segment. Their clients can make up IP addresses and communicate without needing a DHCP server. In that environment, with everyone on the same subnet, all machines would use the 169.254.x.x address space and could communicate with each other.

> **Note**   Clients using APIPA on the same subnet would not be able to communicate with anything off their local subnet, such as the Internet. They would have to use some type of proxy server of network address translation for that.

Although APIPA works well for small networks, it is not a very good option for large organizations that already have a DHCP infrastructure and multiple IP subnets. In such an environment, if a particular client comes up with a 169.254.x.x address, it might be able to communicate with other similar clients on its local subnet but not anything anywhere else, such as the servers, Internet, and so on.

By default, the APIPA configuration is enabled in Windows 2000 but can be turned off via a Registry key. It's just one more potential headache for administrators. With Windows XP and Windows Server 2003 the DHCP client still defaults to using APIPA, but now you can configure an alternative IP address to use instead of the randomly determined 169.254.x.x address. Basically, it's like being able to configure a static IP to use in the event the client cannot obtain a DHCP address. You can think of it as a static backup address for when DHCP is unavailable. One common application for the new Alternate Configuration feature is for laptop users. Their computers can be set to use DHCP when they're in the office and be programmed with a static address for use at the user's home or other location.

Some administrators like to configure servers to use DHCP, too. They create a reservation in DHCP, so that the servers always get the same IP addresses, and rely on DHCP to change other IP configuration settings such as DNS servers, WINS servers, and so forth. However, if the DHCP server fails, servers might not obtain an IP address at all, which would interrupt network operations. By using the Alternate Configuration, you can take advantage of DHCP while still ensuring that servers will have an accurate IP address if the DHCP server isn't available.

For more information on the DHCP service, visit www.samspublishing.com and enter this book's ISBN number (no hyphens or parenthesis) in the Search field; then click the book cover image to access the book details page. Click the Web Resources link in the More Information section, and locate article ID# **A010802**.

DNS

DNS has received a minor makeover for Windows Server 2003, including how Windows Server 2003 handles Active Directory-integrated DNS zones and improvements to the DNS management console.

Active Directory-Integrated Zones

Probably the single greatest enhancement to the DNS service is a new feature of Active Directory (AD) integrated zones. Windows 2000 introduced Active Directory integrated zones, which store DNS records in the Active Directory database instead of in flat .dns files on the

DNS server (like primary and secondary zones). The major benefit of an Active Directory-integrated zone is that your DNS records are replicated to all domain controllers, so in the event of a DNS server failure, you simply install DNS on a domain controller and the zone appears, as if by magic. In effect, any domain controller has the capability to become a DNS server, and your zone records are protected by Active Directory's replication.

> **Note** The usual implementation of Active Directory-integrated zones is with multiple domain controllers as DNS servers in a primary/secondary hierarchy. That way, if the primary DNS server goes offline or is too busy, the secondary can immediately take up the slack.)

The big drawback to the way Windows 2000 implements Active Directory-integrated zones is that all DNS records in the zone are replicated to every domain controller throughout your domain. This can potentially generate a lot of unnecessary network traffic because not every domain controller is a DNS server and therefore doesn't need the DNS zone replicated. With the new Active Directory Application Partitions in Windows Server 2003, the replication of the DNS information can be more finely controlled.

▶ For more information on the Active Directory Application Partitions, **see** "Replication Improvements," **p. 75**.

When you use Active Directory Integrated zones on a Windows Server 2003 DNS server, Windows creates two application partitions—one called DomainDNSZones and one called ForestDNSZones—and used to replicate DNS information throughout the domain or forest. As shown in Figure 8.2, a given zone can be replicated as follows:

- To all DNS servers in the Active Directory forest.
- To all DNS servers in the Active Directory domain.
- To all domain controllers in the Active Directory domain. This is the only option compatible with replication to Windows 2000 domain controllers. Windows 2000 domain controllers know nothing about application partitions.
- To all domain controllers specified in the scope of the following application directory partition. This option enables you to load DNS into your own application partition (provided you have created one) for even tighter control of replication.

Enhancements for DNS Hierarchy

Several enhancement to DNS provide additional flexibility for designing a DNS infrastructure. One such enhancement is a new zone type: stub zone. A *stub zone* is simply a copy of a DNS zone, like a secondary zone. The difference between a stub zone and a secondary zone is that a stub zone can contain *glue records* for delegated subdomains.

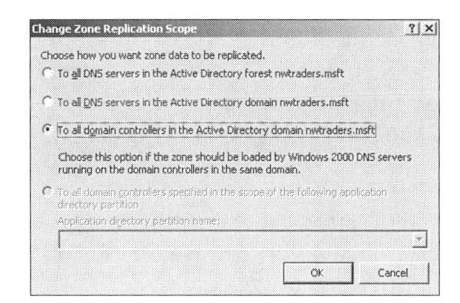

Figure 8.2 Windows Server 2003 enables you to control the scope of replication of Active Directory integrated zones.

> Tip A stub zone, similar to a secondary zone, can be a standard zone or an Active Directory-integrated zone.

Glue records are references to servers that are authoritative for the subdomain. These records enable the DNS server to send a referral directly to the DNS server authoritative for the child domain without having to forward the request up the DNS hierarchy, only to have it come back down again.

Another new infrastructure design feature is the capability to designate forwarders on a per-domain basis. A *forwarder* is a pointer to a particular DNS server for sending unresolved queries. Ordinarily, if a DNS server is not authoritative for the zone referenced in a DNS query, it contacts or forwards the query to a root ('.') server, which then sends the query to successive child domains down the tree until it gets to the authoritative zone. Forwarders enable you to pass the request to other DNS servers which might potentially have or know about the zone without having to start at the root servers. This gives administrators some control over how queries will be resolved, allowing them to design DNS hierarchies to more efficiently respond to queries. A potential problem is that you might want queries for some domains to start at the root but want other domains to send the queries to your internal DNS servers. With Windows Server 2003, you can do both. You can specify individual domains (or all domains) to forward and specify to which servers they get forwarded. You can also specify whether to use recursion for queries to those domains.

> Note *Recursion* occurs when the DNS server contacts the subsequent DNS servers and returns the response to the client. With no recursion, the DNS server simply tells the client which DNS server to query and the client queries the new server itself.

DNS Console Improvements

Similar to the other core networking services, the DNS console in Windows Server 2003 sports some improvements. One nicety is that the built-in DNS console provided includes the event viewer snap-in with the DNS event log for monitoring DNS service messages. Additionally, a new option on the server pop-up menu—Launch Nslookup—launches the `nslookup` command-line utility for testing DNS query resolution. The Debug Logging tab has also been redesigned with more detailed configuration information. Also, a new tab is available for specifying the types of events to be written to the event log (previously only available through editing the Registry).

An additional security improvement is the capability to manage DNS server permissions at the server level. This enables you to delegate server-wide control of your DNS servers instead of just at the zone level, such as in Windows 2000.

> For more information on DNS and how it works, visit www.samspublishing.com and enter this book's ISBN number (no hyphens or parenthesis) in the Search field; then click the book cover image to access the book details page. Click the Web Resources link in the More Information section, and locate article ID# **A010803**.

Fax Sharing

To understand the improvements in the fax service for Windows Server 2003, you need to understand how faxing works in Windows 2000. Because faxing in Windows 2000 is extremely limited, it might be unfamiliar to some administrators, so we'll go over the basics here.

Faxing the Windows 2000 Way

Windows 2000 doesn't make faxing very easy. Basically, you first have to install a fax printer, configure the device, and learn to live with the operating system's limited faxing capabilities.

Installing Fax Printers

In Windows 2000, the fax service is installed by default. To enable faxing, you simply install a modem. After a modem is installed, a printer called Fax magically appears in the Printers control panel. You can install additional modems, but they do not show up as additional fax printers in the Printers control panel. Instead, they appear in the Fax Administration console as additional fax devices.

Fax Device Configuration and Routing Options

Each device in the Fax Administration console can be configured to receive incoming faxes, send outgoing faxes, or both. Devices configured as outgoing simply send the fax via the fax device; devices configured to receive incoming faxes require further configuration to designate what to do with the incoming faxes. The Received Faxes configuration options are as follows:

- **Print On**—The fax gets printed to a local printer.
- **Save in Folder**—The fax is stored locally in a specified directory on the server.

- **Send to Local Email Inbox Profile Name**—The fax is sent to the inbox of a mail profile on the server.

> Note To be able to send to a local email inbox, the fax service needs to be configured to log on as a user with administrative privileges. Additionally, a mail client must be installed and a MAPI profile must be configured for the user profile used by the fax service account.

You might have noticed in this description that everything is local: Incoming options are the local printer, local file, or local profile.

Limitations

The biggest limitation of the Windows 2000 fax service is that it cannot be shared. This means that all outgoing faxes need to be sent from the server and all incoming faxes are stored locally on the server in some form. This is all well and good for a client machine, but generally you don't want to have to log on locally to your servers.

Faxing the Windows Server 2003 Way

Windows Server 2003 improves Windows' built-in faxing capabilities. It improves installation and offers the capability to share fax printers with network users, giving you an effective entry-level network fax solution.

Installing the Fax Service

The first clue that faxing in Windows Server 2003 is different from Windows 2000 is in the fax service itself. It is not installed by default. Installing a fax modem does not magically generate a fax printer in the Printers, now called Printers and Faxes, control panel applet. To enable faxing in Windows Server 2003, you need to install the fax service using Add/Remove Programs—Add/Remove Windows Components, just like any other service. After it's installed, a whole host of new features are available.

First, when a modem is installed, the fax printer appears in Printers and Faxes. Unlike Windows 2000, this fax printer queue *can* be shared out just like any other print share, enabling remote users to be able to print to it and thereby send outgoing faxes via the fax server.

Fax Device Configuration and Routing Options

The Fax Administration console, now called the Fax Service Management console, has been greatly improved. In addition to showing all the fax devices, it has several new configuration properties for controlling the behavior of faxes. For example, you can set different archival settings to maintain copies of sent or received faxes. You can also record incoming and outgoing events, as well as Activity Logging and Event Reporting. Activity Logging enables you to write incoming and outgoing activities to a special log, whereas Event Reporting controls the level of information written to the Windows Application Event Log.

> **Tip** The Fax Service Management console displays all fax devices installed on the server. However, if a new modem is installed, it does not show up as a device in the Fax Service Management console until the Fax Service is restarted.

The routing options for incoming faxes have also been extended. As shown in Figure 8.3, you can still print directly to a local printer or save to a local folder as before; however, the incoming email routing option enables routing to any email address via an SMTP server that you configure in the fax properties. You can also arrange multiple devices into *device groups*. Devices groups are just that—collections of devices that enable you to treat multiple devices as a single unit. Another new feature is the ability to designate rules; you can create rules to designate faxes destined for a certain region/country and area code to use specific fax devices (or groups of devices).

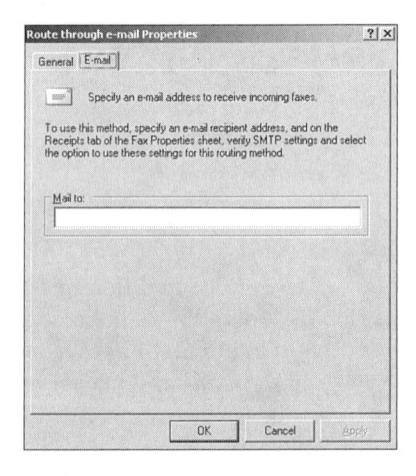

Figure 8.3 Routing incoming faxes via email.

The fax client, previously the fax queue application, has been replaced with the Fax Console. With the Fax Console, you can send and receive faxes, create cover letters, and so on. Another new console, the Fax Monitor, enables you to monitor the status of current faxes, and it can be configured to automatically pop up whenever a fax is sent or received.

> **Tip** Pre-Windows XP clients can also use the enhanced administration and faxing features of the Windows Server 2003 fax service by installing the fax client from *servername*\faxclient, which is physically located in \\%systemroot%\\SYSTEM32\clients\faxclient.

File Sharing

Probably the most significant new feature for file share management is the capability to create shadow copies. *Shadow copies* enable you to save point-in-time copies of files. These captures are performed at the file system level, so they even capture open files.

> **Caution** Even though shadow copies can capture open files, you should still be careful using shadow copies with databases. Check with the database manufacturer first to make sure it is safe.

The intended implementation for shadow copies is as a safety net to easily recover deleted or modified files without resorting to backups, not as the sole method for disaster recovery. Even better, a shadow copy enables the user to restore files, freeing the administrator from the headache of sifting through backup tapes to find a particular version of a file.

Shadow copies are enabled at the volume level (Volume Shadow Copies or VSS). To enable shadow copies for a particular volume, simply right-click the volume, click **Properties**, and then select the **Shadow Copies** tab. From this tab, you can create shadow copies for any given volume. When creating a shadow copy, you must choose where to store it. The default is to store shadow copies on the same volume as the original file, but you can configure (on a per-volume basis) the location of shadow copies. It is recommended that you save your shadow copies to a different volume so as not to consume more space on the original volume. Additionally, if the volume fails, you won't lose the files and the copies. You also can specify how much disk space to allow the shadow copies for a particular volume to consume (minimum 100MB). After they use up this space, previous shadow copies are overwritten and lost, so choose the amount of disk space carefully based on how much data is in your file shares.

> **Tip** Shadow copies can also be managed from the `vssadmin` command-line utility.

After shadow copies are enabled, the contents of all file shares (including the administrative shares, C$, IPC$, and so on) are saved as shadow copies. The Shadow Copies tab lists the existing volumes, when the next shadow copy is scheduled to run (if enabled), the number of shares (not including administrative shares) on each volume, and the amount of disk space used by shadow copies. For each volume you can enable or disable shadow copies of all shares on that volume.

> **Caution** Shadow copies can be enabled only for entire volumes. They cannot be enabled per share—it's either all or nothing).

You can also schedule when to perform shadow copies (the default is twice per day—weekdays at 7 a.m. and 12 p.m.) or perform one manually.

After shadow copies are enabled, clients can view them. This essentially provides a type of versioning capability, where a user can compare changes between an existing file and a shadow copy of the same file.

136 Chapter 8 Network Services

Note Clients prior to Windows Server 2003 can also view shadow copies, but they will need to install the shadow copies client, which is in the \\%systemroot%\system32\clients\twclient directory.

It can also be used for a type of disaster recovery. Consider the following scenario:

Mary creates a file in a shared folder that has been enabled for shadow copies. The file is there long enough to be captured by a scheduled shadow copy. Another user, Jim, overwrites the original file. Mary accesses the file and realizes her changes are gone. She can simply click the file and then select **View Previous Versions** under File and Folder Tasks in Windows Explorer. This opens a dialog box that displays a list of the shadow copies where she can choose to view, copy, or restore her original file. Alternatively, she could select the folder (not the file), select **View Previous Versions**, and she would once again be given the option to view, copy, or restore (see Figure 8.4). In this case, clicking View opens a new window and displays the contents of the entire folder from the selected shadow copy. This method is particularly useful for recovering multiple files or deleted files.

Tip To see the option to View Previous Versions, the user must connect to the folder via a file share. (\\servername\sharename). The file share has to be enabled for shadow copies, of course. One more requirement is that the user's Windows Explorer must be configured to Show Common Tasks in Folders, not Use Windows Classic Folders.

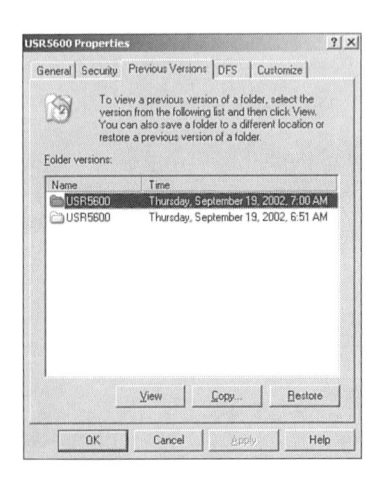

Figure 8.4 Recover accidentally deleted files with shadow copies.

Windows Server 2003 provides some enhancements to the Computer Management console for file share administration. One such enhancement is the new Publish tab on the shared folder properties. This enables resource administrators to publish and maintain information about their file shares in Active Directory, without giving them the Active Directory Users and Computers snap-in. The new File Share wizard has also been improved: The folder path and selection options are clearer, as are the folder caching (now simply called Offline Settings) options.

> **Caution** One thing that could potentially cause confusion is that the default permission for file shares is all users (Everyone) read-only—not full control as in Windows 2000.

Distributed File System

Distributed file system (DFS) is a technology that provides easier access and availability for file shares. The two types of DFS are server-based and domain-based. *Server-based* DFS resides on a single server. Administrators designate a DFS root, which is just a pointer to a file share, and underneath the DFS root administrators can create DFS links that point to other file shares. These file shares can be on the same or different servers. This enables administrators to provide a logical shared folder hierarchy regardless of the actual underlying folder structure.

Domain-based DFS has the same structure of DFS roots and links, but you can create multiple roots. Domain-based DFS also gives you the ability to provide redundant shares called *replicas*.

Replicas are copies of the DFS root and link on another server. By having replicas on multiple servers, clients can always access the DFS shares. For example, consider a domain called `braincore.net` with a DFS root (`Software`) that points to a file share on a server (`Netserver`). An additional replica is created on the server `Netserver2`, which provides fault tolerance for the `Software` share. Clients access the share via `\\braincore.net\Software`. The DFS client queries Active Directory and determines the replica server closest to the client. If one of the servers is down, the client is still capable of accessing the other server. The multiple DFS replicas not only provide fault tolerance for the `Software` share, but also potentially bring the share closer to the user. Site-aware DFS clients (Windows 2000 or better) are directed to the DFS link in their own sites.

> **Using DFS for Software Deployment**
>
> DFS is particularly useful for software deployment shares. We once had to deploy Internet Explorer (IE) to an entire organization. There was no infrastructure for software deployment, so the only choice was to automate through logon scripts. To ensure local installation and minimize traffic across WAN links, we created the software distribution share for IE on servers in every location. We then had to create special scripting to detect where the client was located and direct it to the appropriate server for downloading IE. Pretty complex! DFS handles all this automatically. With DFS, we could simply create a DFS root called `Software` and then create DFS links for the software application share. We could create replicas of the root and links on multiple servers across the organization. The File Replication Service (FRS) would automatically replicate the content of the application share to all the replicas, providing a consistent copy

(Continued)

of the share across all the participating servers. The software installations could be performed by simply connecting to *domain**software**application*. DFS would direct the client to a participating server in the client's own site, so the installation would be performed without crossing WAN links and without complex scripting to detect the client's location.

New DFS Features

At first glance, DFS in Windows Server 2003 appears to be the same as in previous versions. However, some subtle enhancements dramatically increase its functionality. First, you can now create multiple DFS roots on a single server. Previously, although you could create multiple DFS roots in domain-based DFS, each server could host only one root. This meant that to have multiple DFS roots in a domain, you had to use different servers for each of the roots, thus increasing the number of servers required for DFS. Additionally, DFS roots can now be published in Active Directory, to make them easier for users to find. DFS links can also be made available for offline access by Windows XP clients.

You can now designate the DFS replication topology in domain-based DFS (full ring or hub and spoke). In Windows 2000, DFS replication is either automatic or manual. Manual is just that—the administrator must manually keep the replicas in sync (such as by using robocopy or xcopy). With automatic replication, one server (by default the first one) is designated as the master and all other replicas synchronize with the master. With Windows Server 2003, the administrator can designate the DFS replication topology. Four choices are available:

- **Ring**—One replica replicates with another and so on in a chain until the last one replicates back with the first.
- **Hub and Spoke**—Similar to Windows 2000 in that there is a central server with which everyone replicates.
- **Full Mesh**—Everyone replicates with everyone else.
- **Custom**—The administrator can choose who replicates with whom. This provides much more flexibility in the traffic between replicas.

For additional flexibility, you can designate a replication schedule and designate certain files that should not be replicated (called a *replication exclusion list*).

When multiple replicas exist for a DFS root or link, a client has to choose one of the replicas with which to connect. The way it determines which replica to use is by looking up site information in Active Directory. In Windows 2000, if no DFS replica exists in the same site as the client, the client could choose to connect to a replica in any site. Therefore, a client could potentially attempt to connect to a replica on the other side of the world when there might be a closer replica. Windows Server 2003 includes the capability to specify costs for DFS links. This provides an alternative mechanism for determining which link to use.

Network Attached Storage and Storage Area Network Management

Further file system improvements in Windows Server 2003 include enhancements for Network Attached Storage (NAS) and Storage Area Networks (SANs). Discussions about NAS and SANs can sometimes be confusing because they are two similar acronyms for similar technologies.

Too Many Acronyms

You'd think with all the letters in the alphabet that the information technology industry could come up with unique acronyms. However, to add to the confusion, both NAS and SAN are acronyms for two unrelated technologies—Network Access Server (NAS) and System Area Network (SAN). This section discusses the differences between these four technologies and then looks at the enhancements in Windows Server 2003 for Network Attached Storage and Storage Area Networks in Windows.

NAS: Network Attached Storage Versus Network Access Server

Network Attached Storage is a storage device that provides file share access across the network. It is essentially a file server in a box. There is even a class of NAS devices called *filers*, which are file server appliances. You simply plug them into the network and access the storage device via network shares as if it was a file server. Clients and servers can directly access the data stored on a NAS device across the same network. NAS devices can be used to expand storage capacity of existing file servers. The file servers map file shares to the NAS storage device. The clients connect to a share on the file server, which redirects to the NAS storage device.

Network Access Server is a method of providing authentication for access to remote networks. Generally, NAS servers are used by ISPs to provide authentication for Internet access. Network Access Servers have nothing to do with Network Attached Storage other than sharing an acronym.

SAN: Storage Area Network Versus System Area Network

Storage Area Network is a technology for connecting multiple servers and storage devices (hard drives) over a network. Generally, it consists of one or more hard drive enclosures accessed via fibre channel or Small Computer System Interface (SCSI) with partitions carved out for one or more servers, with no sharing of data between servers. To the server operating system it appears as a hard drive. Storage Area Networks are an extension of traditional high-speed direct attached storage devices, but it allows more flexibility in that it can be expanded more easily or repartitioned to more efficiently use the available storage.

A *System Area Network*, on the other hand, is a special technology for providing high-speed *network* connectivity between systems. In Windows 2000 and Windows Server 2003, Datacenter Edition, System Area Networks can be used to connect data center servers to each other using special System Area Network adapters and reliable high-speed Gigabit fibre channel connections. Additionally, System Area Networks use Winsock Direct, which provides Winsock applications direct access to the System Area Network devices without having to go through the TCP/IP protocol layer. This reduces network overhead and provides high-speed connections between servers.

Windows Server 2003 Improvements for NAS and SAN

Windows Server 2003 provides improvements to all these technologies. In this section we will touch on the improvements for Storage Area Networks and Network Attached Storage.

Storage Area Network Improvements

Windows Server 2003 supports "multipath failover" when connected to a SAN, which enables redundant paths from the host server." What does this mean? It means you can have multiple physical connections between the server and the storage array. If a given path (connection) fails, it dynamically uses the remaining path(s), thus providing fault tolerance for the connection between the server and SAN devices.

Windows Server 2003 also provides built-in APIs, called *Virtual Disk Services (VDS)*, for managing SAN devices. Previously, SAN vendors had their own set of APIs for manipulating their SAN devices. So, to add more storage devices or to repartition the SAN, you had to use special applications provided by the SAN vendor. With Windows Server 2003, each vendor provides a VDS provider that translates the Windows 2003 APIs to the vendor-specific APIs. VDS is an abstraction layer, which makes developing storage management applications for SANs easier because you no longer have to worry about the vendor-specific details. Therefore, SANs can be managed through the Disk Management console or command-line utilities, such as `diskpart`, just like any other disk.

For example, you can connect your SAN storage arrays as if they were regular disks. You can create volumes or partitions and assign them drive letters, or not—just like local disks.

Network Attached Storage Improvements

Windows Server 2003 natively supports connecting to NAS devices. This support isn't immediately obvious because connecting to a NAS is implemented by simply mapping a file share, just like Windows 2000. With the native support—unlike Windows 2000—you don't necessarily need any vendor-specific applications to connect to the NAS device. The Configure Your Server Wizard can be used to install a Web-based console for configuring NAS devices. Additionally,

Microsoft uses the Windows Server 2003 server operating system as the foundation for its Windows-powered NAS devices, which will be available from a number of vendors.

Encrypting File System

Encrypting File System (EFS), a feature of the NTFS file system first introduced in Windows 2000, enables increased security of files by encrypting them so only those with the correct encryption key are able to view them. *Encryption* is the process of scrambling something (in this case a file) in a particular way such that you are the only one who can unscramble it. The two types of encryption are *symmetric key*, in which the same key is used to encrypt and decrypt, and *asymmetric key*, in which one key (a *public* key) is used to encrypt and a different key (the *private* key) is used to decrypt.

EFS Implementation

EFS uses a combination of both types of encryption. Each file has its own unique encryption key that is used for encrypting and decrypting the file (symmetric). Additionally, each user has her own public/private key pair that is used to encrypt/decrypt the file encryption key. The following is what happens when a user encrypts a file:

- The operating system encrypts the file using the file's unique encryption key.
- The file's encryption key is then itself encrypted using the user's public key and is stored in the data definition field (DDF) of the file.
- The file encryption key is also encrypted with the public key of a recovery agent (by default the administrator) and stored in the data recovery field (DRF) of the file. This provides the ability to decrypt the file in case the user loses her private key.

This process ensures that the data is secure because only the private key of the user (or the recovery agent) can decrypt the key used to encrypt the file. The problem with this implementation is that it prevents the sharing of encrypted files—even to trusted personnel. In Windows Server 2003 (and Windows XP), the encryption model used by EFS has been expanded to allow the user to designate one or more authorized users. The user can add additional users' public keys to encrypt the file encryption key, thus enabling multiple users to be able to decrypt the file.

Storing Encrypted Files Remotely

Going along with the concept of making encrypted files more available, Windows Server 2003 supports storage of encrypted files on remote servers without having the user's digital certificate installed on the server. Several requirements exist for this to work. First, only Windows XP and Windows Server 2003 support this feature. Additionally, both the client and the server must be in the same Windows 2003 forest. After the domain is in Windows 2003 native mode (meaning there are no more Windows 2000 or Windows NT 4 domain controllers), a new delegation tab is available for computer accounts in Active Directory Users and Computers. Selecting Trust This Computer for Delegation to Any Service (Kerberos Only) allows the computer to support encrypted files remotely. This option enables the computer to impersonate the user. Therefore, the computer account then has access to the user's private key and is capable of encrypting and decrypting the user's files.

> **Encrypted Files on Remote Servers**
>
> There are a couple of things to be aware of if you're using encrypted files on remote servers. First, improper use of the Trusted for Delegation option could pose a security risk. Secondly, the file is not encrypted across the network; it is decrypted on the server and then transmitted across the network just like any other file. One thing you can do to mitigate this is to use some type of network encryption, such as IPSec, to encrypt the network traffic. You also can connect to the remote share via Web Distributed Authoring and Versioning (WebDAV), which can have its own encryption. Connecting via a WebDAV share has the additional benefit that you don't have to designate the computer as being trusted for delegation.

Additional improvements to EFS include the ability to use stronger encryption algorithms (DESX in Windows 2000 versus DESX or 3DES in Windows Server 2003) and the capability to encrypt offline files.

WebDAV and Remote Sharing

Another benefit for file sharing in Windows Server 2003 is an extension to WebDAV. The new WebDAV redirector allows file sharing using normal HTTP, which in turn enables access to network shares across the Internet through firewalls and proxy servers. This new feature is implemented as the Web Sharing tab on the properties of the folder to be shared. Simply select the Web site and click **Share This Folder**, as shown in Figure 8.5. (IIS has to be installed first.)

> ➤ For more information on IIS 6, **see** Chapter 7, "Internet Information Services," **p. 101**.

Next, give the Web share a name—the Alias—and designate the permissions (read, write, script source access, directory browsing, scripts, and scripts and executables). Doing so creates a new application (a virtual directory enabled as an application) in the specified Web site. Windows XP clients can then map a drive to this WebDAV-enabled virtual directory, which makes the file share available to any application without requiring anything special.

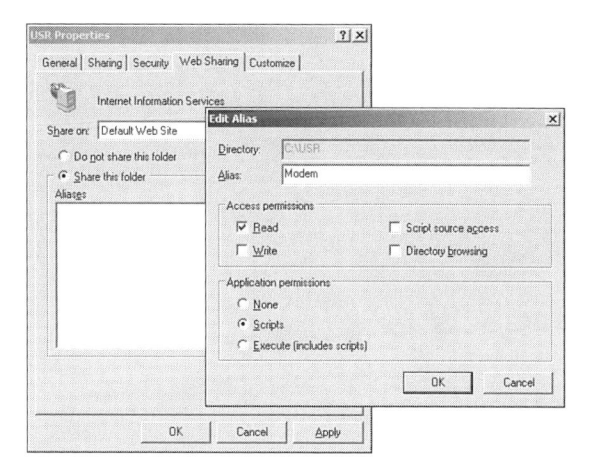

Figure 8.5 Enabling remote file sharing by creating a virtual directory that is accessible via WebDAV.

9

WEB DEVELOPMENT

In This Chapter

- Configuring .NET Framework applications and security, **page 146**.
- Implementing UDDI and other Web Services support, **page 154**.
- Understanding why developers are so excited about Windows Server 2003, **page 156**.

What's New

Windows Server 2003 comes out of the box with Microsoft's latest software development technologies. If you're reading this book, however, you probably consider yourself more of an administrator than a developer, so do you even need to worry about these technologies? The answer is an emphatic "Yes!" because Windows Server 2003, more than any previous version of Windows, is designed to host powerful, enterprise-class applications. You need to be familiar with these development technologies so that you can understand their impact on your servers, and so that you can install servers that provide the best possible support for your organization.

Windows Server 2003's most visible new development feature is the .NET Framework, which is an entirely new set of software development technologies. Software developers will use tools like Visual Basic .NET, C# (pronounced "C Sharp"), and Visual C++ .NET to create applications that use the .NET Framework.

One of the reasons software developers are so excited about the .NET Framework is that it makes creating *Web services applications* easier. Web services applications are designed to work in conjunction with Internet technologies, providing services over HTTP and other common Internet protocols. For example, a home insurance firm might offer a Web service that accepts home values, locations, and other information and provides insurance quotes. Real estate agents could incorporate this Web service into their own applications or Web sites, taking advantage of the capabilities offered by the Web service without having to write the complicated code themselves.

Of course, after companies start providing these Web services, they need a way to organize those services so that others—whether inside or outside the company—can locate and use the services. Windows Server 2003 provides a means for that organization of services in its included Universal Description, Discover, and Integration (UDDI) services. Other development enhancements that should catch your attention include Enterprise Services (the name for the latest version of Microsoft's venerable COM+ technology), Web farm technologies, and much more. We'll cover all these items in this chapter, focusing on them from a server administration point of view so you can better implement and use these new capabilities in your environment.

The .NET Framework

The .NET Framework represents an entirely new way of thinking about software development. You're probably familiar—even if you don't realize it—with the "old way" of creating software applications, which is illustrated in Figure 9.1. Developers would use a tool such as Visual Basic 6.0 to create software applications. When they were finished, the tool compiled their program code into *native code*, a form of program code that can execute directly on the operating system. Physically, Visual Basic code exists in simple text files, which the operating system can't execute. Compiled programs, however, exist in familiar EXE files, which can execute directly on the operating system. This software development technique has been around in one form or another since the beginning of computer programming and is capable of producing applications with very good performance.

There are a number of problems with this traditional programming model:

- **Executables produced in this fashion only run on a specific operating system and hardware platform**—As enterprises continue to implement a wider variety of hardware and operating systems—including portable devices like Pocket PCs—developers have to work harder to make their programs run throughout the enterprise. Each new operating system/hardware combination requires specialized development tools and often requires developers to start programming from scratch for each platform.
- **Very few popular programming tools take full advantage of the object-oriented nature of Windows**—Object-oriented programming saves time and money by allowing developers to create small sections of code to perform specific tasks and then easily

reuse that code in several different projects. A powerful object-oriented language also allows developers to reuse functionality inherent to the operating system, such as drawing windows and buttons, accessing files and networks, and so forth.
- **Different programming languages have different strengths and weaknesses, and developers have to choose one and pretty much stick with it**—Each language typically operates in a completely different fashion, making it very difficult for developers to switch back and forth between languages when working on different projects. As a result, developers tend to pick one language and stick with it, even if it isn't ideal for the task at hand.

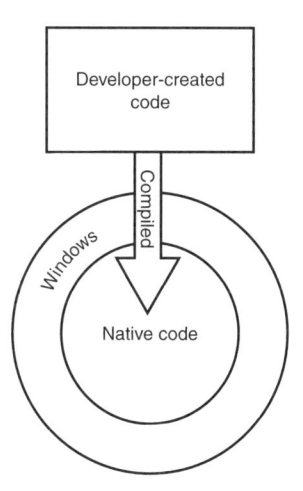

Figure 9.1 Traditional software development produces executables for a specific operating system and hardware platform.

The purpose of the .NET Framework is to address all these issues. For starters, Microsoft has provided new, .NET-compatible versions of its popular Visual Basic and C++ programming languages and introduced a new language named C#, which is similar in many respects to the popular Java programming language from Sun Microsystems. Although each of these languages has a different syntax, or *grammar*, they all offer the same basic capabilities. For example, developers who wanted to interface closely with the operating system used to choose Visual C++ as their language, often because languages such as Visual Basic didn't provide close operating system integration. Under .NET, that's no longer true: Each of the .NET languages provides the same capabilities, allowing developers to work in whatever language they're most comfortable with. Even better, all the languages can be used from within the same development tools (such as Visual Studio .NET), so that developers can switch languages without having to learn an entirely new set of tools.

148   Chapter 9   Web Development

The .NET Framework's changes go beyond developer convenience, though. When compiling a Visual Basic 6 application, developers produce an executable file. In Visual Basic .NET (or any other .NET language), however, compiling is simply an automated process in which the .NET Framework translates the developer's program code into a universal programming language called the Microsoft Intermediate Language (MSIL, or just IL). What's more, IL doesn't even execute directly on the operating system. Instead, IL is executed inside a virtual machine called the *common language runtime (CLR)*. The CLR actually reads the IL and compiles it into a form of native code. This final compilation occurs when the program is executed and is referred to as *just in time (JIT) compilation*. The CLR improves performance by saving the compiled program and reusing it until the original code is changed and recompiled into IL by the developer; at that time, the CLR recompiles the new IL and executes it. Figure 9.2 illustrates the new development environment the .NET Framework uses.

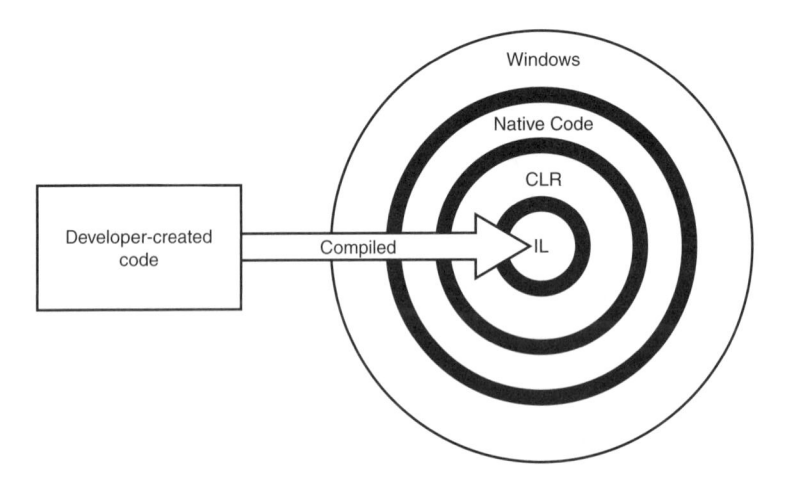

Figure 9.2   .NET applications have a number of extra steps involved in their execution.

So, what's the purpose of this extra complexity? Developers no longer write code for a specific operating system. Instead, they write for the CLR itself, which allows their code to execute more or less unchanged on any platform for which a CLR is available. Microsoft already provides a CLR for Windows and a Compact CLR for Pocket PCs and other Windows CE devices. The future might bring Linux- or Unix-compatible CLRs, allowing .NET applications to run (hopefully) unchanged on a completely different operating system. This capability solves another traditional development problem by allowing developers to write one program that runs on all of an enterprise's various computing devices.

This business with the CLR and cross-platform compatibility should sound familiar because it's what Java advocates have been preaching since their product was introduced. Java uses a similar development model in which developers write Java-specific code, which is executed by a Java Virtual Machine (JVM). So long as a JVM is available for a specific platform, that platform can run virtually all Java applications. If you've used Java applications, however, you might have noticed that they don't perform quite as quickly as native-code applications written in Visual Basic 6.0, Visual C++ 6.0, or other traditional programming languages. That performance decrease is inherent in any virtual machine technology: Rather than executing an application directly on the operating system, both Java and .NET execute the application within a virtual machine (the CLR in the case of .NET), and the virtual machine itself is executed by the operating system. In other words, the virtual machine represents an extra layer of code that has to be executed, which reduces performance.

Although .NET applications tend to perform pretty well, they can't compete with native-code applications, especially those written in Visual C++ (the language Windows itself is written in). For that reason, you won't see Microsoft using the .NET Framework to develop the next versions of its .NET Enterprise Servers, such as Exchange Server and SQL Server. Those will continue to be written in native code for a specific platform. Perhaps some future version of the CLR, combined with the ever more powerful hardware being created, will enable powerful server applications to be written in .NET, but that day is probably a long way off.

So, what does an administrator need to know about the .NET Framework? Prior to Windows Server 2003, the .NET Framework itself had to be installed before .NET applications could be installed and executed; Windows Server 2003, however, comes with the .NET Framework built right in, so your developers can immediately start installing and executing .NET applications on your servers. So, although deployment is a piece of cake, an additional administrative effort is involved because the .NET Framework adds whole new levels of security and management to your servers. In fact, Windows Server supports an entirely new console called the .NET Framework Configuration Console, shown in Figure 9.3.

This new console allows you to manage five aspects of the .NET Framework:

- **Assembly Cache**—*Assemblies* are basically modules of code that are shared by several applications. For example, a developer might create a logon routine and use it in all his corporation's custom applications. The Assembly Cache acts as a storage area for these assemblies, making them available to the applications running on the server.
- **Configured Assemblies**—Assemblies from the assembly cache can be organized into sets and associated with different rules. These rules determine which version of assemblies are loaded and which location is used to load the assemblies.
- **Code Access Security Policy**—The .NET CLR includes a complete set of code access security policies that control applications' access to protected resources. This extra layer of security ensures that only authorized applications can get to sensitive server and network resources and prevents unauthorized applications from wreaking havoc on your network.
- **Remoting Services**—These services enable applications to communicate with applications on other computers, and the console allows you to adjust the communications properties.

- **Individual Applications**—You can configure each .NET application with its own set of configured assemblies and remoting services, customizing the behavior of each application to meet your precise needs.

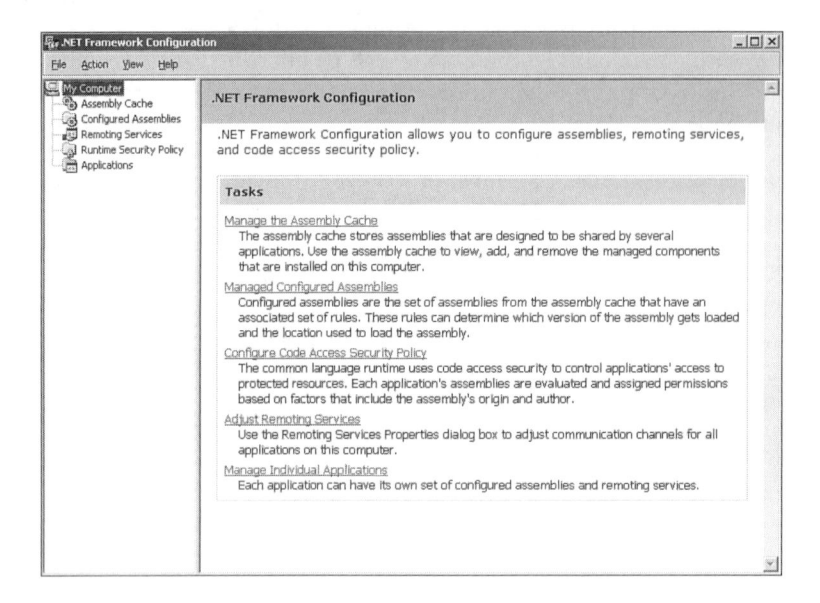

Figure 9.3 The .NET Framework Configuration console enables you to modify the behavior and other properties of the .NET Framework.

You might find yourself wondering whether many of these tasks are more properly suited to a developer rather than an administrator. Only time will tell if that's the case, but we firmly believe that administrators are responsible for the overall operation, efficiency, and security of the enterprise network, and that places these five configuration tasks firmly in the administrator's realm. Developers often become too focused on a particular task and don't take the health and well-being of the entire network into consideration, leaving it to the administrator to make sure everything is configured safely and efficiently. With that in mind, we'll spend the next five sections briefly covering each of the major .NET Framework configuration tasks.

Managing the Assembly Cache

Adding an assembly is pretty easy—just right-click Assembly Cache and select Add from the pop-up menu. As shown in Figure 9.4, the console displays a complete list of available assemblies. You'll need to rely on your developers to tell you which assemblies are required by their applications and to provide those assemblies for installation on your server.

The .NET Framework **151**

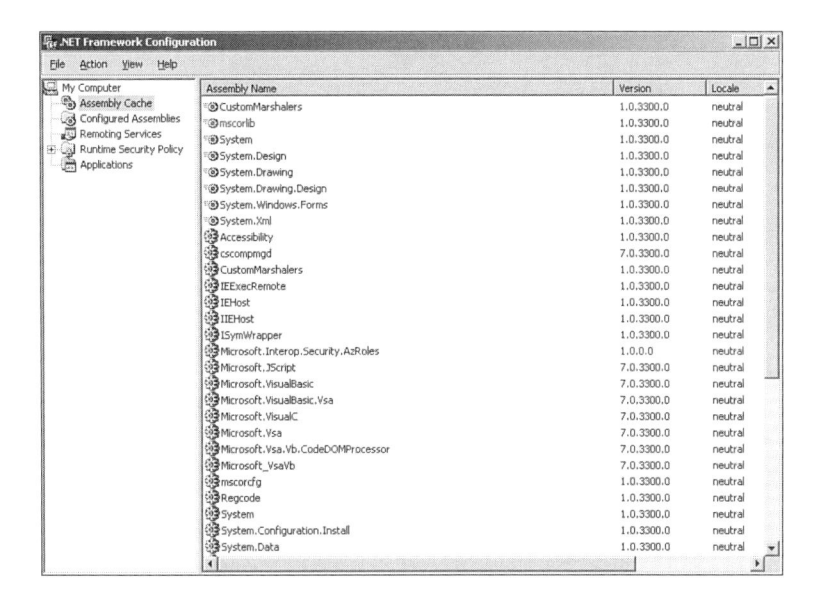

Figure 9.4 Windows Server comes with a long list of preinstalled assemblies.

Caution | Windows Server doesn't attempt to validate or verify the assemblies you add. Before adding an assembly, make sure it has been thoroughly tested and that it functions correctly, unless of course you're adding it to a test server for testing purposes.

One great feature about the assemblies list is the inclusion of each assembly's version number. This feature enables you to quickly determine which version of an assembly is running, thereby ensuring that the correct assemblies required by .NET applications are available on the server.

Tip | Ask your developers to maintain written documentation about with which assemblies and versions their applications have been tested. Such documentation can help narrow down application problems very quickly.

Managing Configured Assemblies

Adding a configured assembly is also pretty straightforward. Right-click **Configured Assemblies** in the console and select **Add** from the pop-up menu. Select an assembly from the assembly cache, and then specify the assembly's configuration properties, as shown in Figure 9.5.

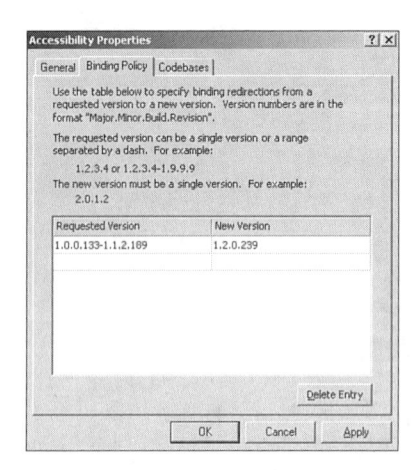

Figure 9.5 Assembly properties include a binding policy and codebase information.

A *binding policy* tells the server how to handle requests for different versions of the assembly. Multiple versions of an assembly can reside in the assembly cache at the same time; which version an application gets when it requests the assembly depends on the binding policy you set. The example in Figure 9.5 is for an assembly named Accessibility. Any application requesting version 1.0.0.133–1.1.2.189 of the assembly is given version 1.2.0.239, which must reside in the assembly cache. Binding policy enables you to actively manage backward compatibility because you can specify which version of the assembly will be used with a given request for a particular version.

> **Tip** Have your developers document the assembly versions their applications will request and provide you with a list of compatible assembly versions. This documentation will enable you to configure the proper binding policy for the .NET applications running on your servers.

Codebases are network-accessible versions of assemblies, which enable applications to load assemblies that aren't available in the server's assembly cache. You must specify the version of the assembly that an application might request and then provide a URL—either an http:// URL or a file:// URL—where a compatible assembly is located.

Managing the Runtime Security Policy

Windows Server groups security policies into three levels: per-enterprise, per-machine, and per-user. You can establish different security policies at each level. The security policy is basically a combination of code groups and permission sets. A *code group* simply organizes code into manageable groups. *Permission sets* define sets of permissions for code, such as the capability to access the file system, network, and other resources. It's important to understand that the effective permissions on any particular assembly are the combination of the enterprise, machine, and user policy levels. Each assembly might belong to different code groups at each level and will receive the most restrictive combination of permissions from all three levels. You can think of this behavior as similar to user groups and file permissions: Users can belong to multiple groups and receive the combination of permissions available to each group to which they belong.

Windows Server includes a default All_Code code group at each policy level. As shown in Figure 9.6, the membership condition of this group is simply All Code. You can define other code groups with different membership conditions, such as "all code in a certain folder" or "all code from a particular publisher." You then assign a permission set (Windows Server includes several predefined sets) to determine what the code within the group is allowed to do. There's even a default Nothing permission set, which prevents code from executing at all. This can be useful for preventing the execution of code that is known to be harmful.

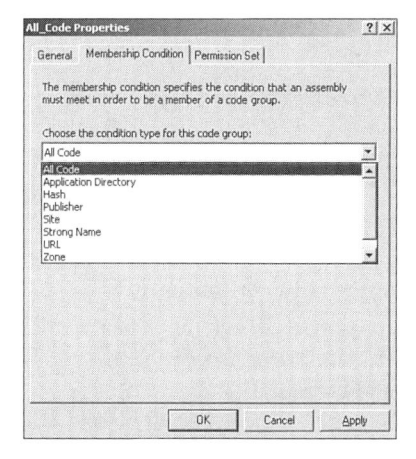

Figure 9.6 Code groups and permission sets enable you to define precisely what different applications can do on your servers.

> For more information on the .NET Framework security permissions, **see** Chapter 4, "Security," **p. 45**.

You can think of code groups as similar to domain user groups. Rather than explicitly placing applications within a code group, as you do with users, you specify rules. It's as if you could specify a rule that places all users whose names begin with *D* in a particular user group. And you can think of permission sets as preconfigured sets of file permissions. By assigning a permission set to a code group, you grant specific privileges to the code contained within the group.

Managing Remoting Services

Remoting Services allows applications to communicate with applications located on other computers. These communications take place via *communications channels*. By default, Windows Server provides two channels: TCP and HTTP. Neither of these channels provides any significant properties that you need to configure. Other communications channels can be installed on a server to allow communication over different networks or with different levels of security; these channels might provide properties that you need to configure through the Remoting Services portion of the .NET Framework Configuration Console.

Managing Individual Applications

To add a new application to the console, right-click the **Applications** item and select **Add** from the pop-up menu. The console displays a list of recently executed applications, from which you can select an application to add. You can also select any other application if the one you want isn't displayed on the list. For each application you add, you can do the following:

- **Modify the application's properties**—This includes publisher policy, a private folder path used to locate additional assemblies, and so forth. Your developers will need to help you configure these properties if they should change from the defaults.
- **View the application's dependencies**—This is a list of all assemblies used within the application. This feature can be useful when you're installing an application written by a third party or a poorly documented application because it helps you track down the assemblies the application needs to run properly.
- **Manage Remoting Services for this particular application**—Applications that use Remoting Services need additional configuration information here, which your developers should be able to provide to you.
- **Fix the application**—This great tool examines the application and looks for problems with its dependencies. The tool can even modify the application's configuration file to fix certain problems. This tool is useful when installing a poorly documented application to check for dependency issues that can otherwise be difficult to track down.

You can also configure a private set of configured assemblies for the application, enabling you to create a custom configuration that affects only this particular application, rather than a generic configuration that affects all applications on the server.

Web Services Support

Web Services, as we've already described, are essentially reusable software applications that are accessible through Internet technologies, such as the HTTP protocol. For example, suppose that one of the developers at your company's headquarters creates a Web service that provides access to your company's customer database. All your company's other developers can immediately take advantage of this service by incorporating it into other applications. No other developer will ever again need to write code to access the customer database because he can simply use the existing Web service. One important enabling technology behind Web services is XML, and more specifically the SOAP protocol. *SOAP* stands for Simple Object Access Protocol, and it's simply a protocol that enables one application to use another application's services across the Web (or any other TCP/IP-based network). Another important standard is the Web Services Description Language (WSDL), which is a standard for describing how Web services work and what specific capabilities a service offers. Developer tools such as Visual Studio enable developers to create Web services and export their capabilities in WSDL; other developers can import the WSDL into their own applications to use Web services with little additional coding.

Of course, keeping track of all these WSDL files can be cumbersome, so Windows Server also includes UDDI. When you install UDDI, it attaches itself to IIS and can install a copy of the Microsoft Database Engine (MSDE), a scaled-down version of Microsoft SQL Server 2000. UDDI essentially stores WSDL information in SQL Server and provides an HTTP-accessible means of adding and retrieving WSDL information. Visual Studio .NET includes built-in UDDI support, allowing it to import and export WSDL to and from UDDI directly. That's plenty interesting if you're a developer, but even administrators need to be aware of UDDI and the impact it can have on software developers. Specifically, administrators need to install UDDI, which is an optional component of Windows Server. Administrators also need to decide whether UDDI will use an existing SQL Server or if it should install its own copy of the MSDE for storage purposes. Finally, administrators are responsible for troubleshooting and maintaining UDDI. One key troubleshooting tool is UDDI logging, which administrators configure from within the UDDI Console. As shown in Figure 9.7, you can select a variety of logging levels that provide progressively higher levels of detail.

Web Services offers a significant benefit to administrators: easy deployment. When developers create Web services with the .NET Framework, and most especially with ASP.NET, they allow administrators to easily deploy and manage applications. For example, suppose a developer writes a new ASP.NET application and deploys it to a test server. When testing is finished, you need to deploy it to any number of Web servers. With older ASP applications, that could be pretty complex and involve Registry keys, DLL registration, and much more. Under ASP.NET, you basically just copy the files from one server to another. The .NET Framework itself takes care of the rest, recompiling assemblies as necessary on-the-fly. When developers update the application, you just copy the new files. There's no need to unregister DLLs, uninstall applications, and reinstall everything; a simple file copy is all that's needed for most ASP.NET applications.

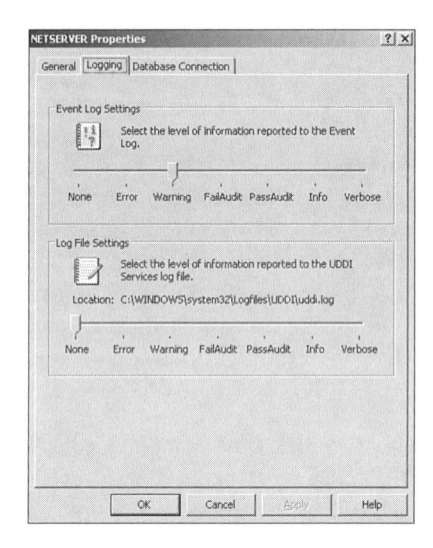

Figure 9.7 The UDDI Console is installed along with UDDI itself, which is an optional component of Windows Server.

Other Development Platform Enhancements

Windows Server also includes Enterprise Services, the latest version of Microsoft's COM and COM+ technologies. Enterprise Servers enables developers to more easily create distributed, enterprise-class applications by making many complex tasks—such as transaction handling, application security, and so forth—available directly from the operating system. Enterprise Services provides several enhancements that are, frankly, only of interest to serious developers. Although it's nice to know that these services exist, they don't really have much impact on an administrator, other than as an explanation for why your developers are so interested in getting Windows Server up and running. If you're interested in reading more about the Enterprise Services features, visit msdn.Microsoft.com/library. In the left menu, drill down to Component Development, Enterprise Services, Technical Articles, Windows Server 2003 and Enterprise Services.

One tremendously important development enhancement is part of the .NET Framework: ASP.NET. ASP.NET is the newest version of Microsoft's Active Server Pages (ASP) technology, which helped make IIS one of the most popular commercial Web servers available. ASP.NET was designed from scratch to address many of the problems that became apparent as ASP was adopted in larger environments.

Other Development Platform Enhancements

> For more information on how ASP and ASP.NET work, and why you should care, visit www.samspublishing.com and enter this book's ISBN number (no hyphens or parentheses) in the Search field; then click the book's cover image to access the book details page. Click the Web Resources link in the More Information section, and locate article ID# **A010901**.

Windows Server even offers improvements in some of the development technologies that were already present in older versions of Windows:

- The .NET Framework is, of course, included with Windows Server, so you don't have to worry about deploying it separately like you did with Windows 2000.
- The .NET Framework's runtime security works along with software restriction group policies, giving you powerful tools to manage the software that runs on your servers.
- Microsoft's Message Queue Service (MSMQ) supports SOAP as a native protocol, making MSMQ more accessible to developers of Web services.
- Under Windows Server 2003, legacy COM+ applications can be converted to a Web service by selecting a check box. This powerful capability relies on Windows Server 2003's native Web services support and enables companies to more easily move their existing applications into a Web services environment.
- ASP.NET, which works with IIS 5.0 in Windows 2000, is integrated more tightly with IIS 6.0 in Windows Server 2003, providing full process model integration for more reliable applications.
- Windows Server 2003's inclusion of Network Load Balancing (NLB) in all editions (as opposed to only including NLB in the Advanced Server and Datacenter Server editions of Windows 2000) provides better support for scalable applications and Web farms.

Your developers will probably be eager for Windows Server 2003 to be rolled into production, so they can start taking advantage of these new features.

10

NETWORKING, REMOTE ACCESS, AND COMMUNICATIONS

In This Chapter

- Learning to use IPv6, **page 160**.
- Making your network more secure, **page 164**.
- Leveraging Universal Plug and Play, **page 168**.
- Taking advantage of Routing and Remote Access, **page 170**.

What's New

Windows Server 2003 introduces a whole new array of networking and communications technologies. In keeping with the traditions of networking and communications, most of these new technologies are referred to by incomprehensible acronyms: UPnP, SIPS, BITS, and so forth. In this chapter, however, we'll lift the veil of mystery and show you how these new technologies will make an impact on your network.

Perhaps the most important new networking technology in Windows Server 2003 is IPv6. You're no doubt familiar with TCP/IP, but you're most likely familiar only with IPv4, the version of the IP protocol that has been around since the explosive growth of the Internet in the early 1990s. Although that explosive growth made IP familiar to millions of people, it also presented some significant challenges. Most importantly, everyone realized that the IPv4 protocol's addressing scheme wasn't designed to support the number of computers that are now on the Internet. As a result, the number of available IP addresses has been rapidly decreasing over the past few years, requiring many Internet service providers (ISPs) to severely ration the IP addresses they issue and requiring networking innovators to create many new technologies to work around the lack of available addresses. IPv6 is designed to fix all that, with an enormous new addressing space and, of course, new concepts to remember.

Windows Server 2003 also includes all the networking improvements originally introduced in Windows XP Professional, such as improved wireless support, new networking diagnostic tools, and much more. Many of these features are more suitable for a client operating system such as Windows XP Professional than for a server, but you might find applications for them in your environment. Some of the most important new Windows Server 2003 networking technologies include

- **Support for the IPSec network security protocol over Network Address Translation (NAT)**—This is a capability that improves the security of virtual private networks (VPNs) and other communications. Windows Server 2003 also supports IPSec with the included Network Load Balancing (NLB) service, allowing farms of Windows Server 2003 computers to receive IPSec traffic.
- **Support for Point-to-Point over Ethernet (PPPoE)**—This allows Windows Server 2003 to connect directly to many broadband service providers, especially cable and xDSL providers, without the need for additional software. PPPoE is a popular protocol in the broadband market because it enables providers to dynamically provide IP addressing information to clients over a high-speed Ethernet connection.
- **Enhancements to the Internet Authentication Service (IAS), Windows's bundled RADIUS-compatible authentication service.**

IPv6 Overview

The initial goal of IPv6 was simply to address the problem of IP address depletion that has become common with the older, familiar IPv4 protocol suite. As you'll see in a bit, IPv6 addresses that problem with a massive new addressing scheme that should provide ample addresses far into the future. However, once underway, the developers of IPv6 also decided to address some other problems that new and innovative uses of the Internet were making apparent, including broadcast and multicast support, security, addressing boundaries, and more. In this section, we'll provide you with an overview of how IPv6 works in general and some specifics about the IPv6 implementation in Windows Server 2003.

> **Note** If you're interested in reading the official documents that describe how IPv6 works, visit www.faqs.org/rfcs and enter one of these RFC numbers: 791, 1918, 2460, 3041, and 3056. Each of these Request for Comments (RFC) documents describes a specific portion of the overall IPv6 suite. You can also learn more about Microsoft's IPv6 plans at www.microsoft.com/ipv6.

If you can't wait for the day when IPv6 becomes an everyday reality, don't hold your breath. Although the IT industry in general has committed to moving to IPv6, doing so is going to make the Year 2000 crisis look like a walk in the park. Nearly every single network device in the world, from desktop computers to servers, from routers to Web-capable cell phones, and many more, will have to be upgraded to support IPv6. Certainly, the process is well underway, with major vendors such as Microsoft and Cisco including IPv6 support in their new products. Additionally, IPv6 provides backward-compatibility with IPv4, enabling older devices to function while the transition is underway. Even so, the move to IPv6 remains slow (the protocol has existed for more than five years already), and it will likely be a few more years before you can forget everything you know about IPv4.

IPv6 Tutorial

Perhaps the easiest place to begin a discussion on IPv6 is with addressing. Rather than the four-octet, dotted-decimal IP addresses you're accustomed to, such as 192.168.0.52, IPv6 uses hexadecimal addresses like this: 21DA:00D3:0000:2F3B:02AA:00FF:FE28:9C5A. For simplification, you can remove any leading 0s for any segment of the address, resulting in something similar to this: 21DA:D3:0:2F3B:2AA:FF:FF228:9C5A. IPv6 addresses are roughly four times longer than IPv4 addresses, and, whereas IPv4 addresses provide for 4.2 billion possible addresses, IPv6 can support 3.4×10^{38} addresses (that's like a trillion quadrillion quadrillion addresses, or about a million quadrillion addresses for every square meter of the earth's surface). Just as IPv4 addresses were divided into classes (Class A, Class B, and so forth), IPv6 addresses are also divided. For example, approximately 1/256 of the IPv6 address space is reserved for multicast addresses, another 1/1024 is reserved for local site unicast addresses, and so forth. About 15% of the address space is available for unicast, or single-host, addresses. Because so much of the address space is reserved for particular uses, and because IPv6 allows addresses to be compressed, or expressed in shorthand, so that 0s aren't displayed, you might find yourself working with addresses such as FF02::02, which is a shortened version of FF02:0:0:0:0:0:0:2. Basically, you just leave out all the contiguous 0s and include a double colon in their place, compressing the address down to a much more manageable size. You can remove only one contiguous series of 0s, meaning compressed addresses such as FF02::5::2 aren't legal.

> **Note** Even compressed IPv6 addresses are long and complex, which means that you'll rely even more heavily on name resolution services like DNS to translate easliy remembered names into IPv6 addresses. IPv6-compliant DNS software supports AAAA records for hostname registration and an IP6.INT domain for reverse (name-to-address) lookups.

In IPv4, you use a *subnet mask* to specify which portion of an IP address is the host address and which portion is the network address. IPv6 doesn't use subnet masks. Instead, it relies on a prefix to specify which portion of the address is the network's ID number. Prefixes are identical to the Classless Interdomain Routing (CIDR) notation you might already use for subnet masks. For example, 21DA:D3:0:2F3B::/64 specifies a 64-bit mask, which represents a particular subnet on a network.

IPv6 supports three distinct types of addresses:

- **Unicast**—Represents a single network interface, which might be a network adapter in a computer.
- **Multicast**—Identifies multiple interfaces. Packets sent to a multicast address are delivered to all interfaces, or network adapters, that subscribe to the multicast address. Multicasts are most often used to distribute videoconferencing audio and video streams.
- **Anycast**—Similar to a multicast, except that the data is delivered only to the nearest interface using the address, rather than to all interfaces using the address. Whereas multicast is used for one-to-many conversations, anycast is used for one-to-"one of many" conversations.

Notice that IPv6 does not define a broadcast address, like IPv4 does. Under IPv6, all broadcasts are conducted as multicasts. The IPv6 specification includes special multicast addresses to which all IPv6 interfaces must subscribe, enabling subnet-specific broadcasts, site-wide broadcasts, and so forth. IPv6 does define a couple of special addresses. The *unspecified address*, used in routing calculations, is simply ::, or 0:0:0:0:0:0:0:0, which is equivalent to IPv4's 0.0.0.0 address. IPv6's loopback address is ::1, which is equivalent to IPv4's 127.0.0.1 loopback address.

To provide backward-compatibility with IPv4, IPv6 specifies compatibility addresses. For example, 0:0:0:0:0:0:192.168.0.2 supports the IPv4 address 192.168.0.2 and also can be expressed as ::192.168.0.2. When these compatibility addresses are used, the computer encapsulates all IPv6 header information into an IPv4 packet, allowing the IPv6 packet to be carried by an older IPv4 network. Compatibility addresses are used by computers that support both IPv6 and IPv4.

For an IPv6 computer to address an IPv4-only computer, it must used *mapped addresses*, such as 0:0:0:0:0:FFFF:192.168.10.5, or simply ::FFFF:192.168.10.5. This internal IPv6 representation of an IPv4 address tells the computer that, when sending packets to that destination, it must fall back to the pure IPv4 protocol and not attempt to send IPv6 packets.

Interestingly, computers on an IPv6 network usually have multiple addresses, even if they have only a single network adapter. These addresses include

- **A link-local unicast address**—It allows the computer to communicate with other hosts on the same network subnet. This is a nonroutable address and is similar to the Automatic IP Addressing (APIPA) addresses, in the 169.254.0.0 range, that IPv4 defines. Windows Server 2003's IPv6 stack automatically creates a unique link-local address for each network adapter in the computer.
- **A site-local unicast address**—It is similar to the private IP address ranges (such as 192.168.0.0) used in IPv4. This address is routable only within a private network and cannot be used on the global Internet. Different private networks can reuse the same site-local addresses.

- **A global unicast address**—It is similar to a public IP address under IPv4. These addresses are routable across the entire Internet.

The purpose of these different addresses is to help conserve address space and to make routers' jobs easier. A major problem with IPv4 is that the simple volume of IP traffic makes it tough for routers to keep up because they must analyze a great deal of traffic simply to see whether that traffic needs to be routed. IPv6's use of specific classes of address, some of which are routable and some of which aren't, helps routers perform their tasks more efficiently. Also, computers won't necessarily have one of each type of address. For example, a computer within a large enterprise network might have a link-local and site-local address but no global address. Instead, only the network's boundary devices—such as firewalls—would use global addresses, performing the IPv6 version of NAT to provide Internet access to internal clients.

There's plenty more to the IPv6 protocol, of course, including complex new packet headers, routing tables, and so on. For details, connect to `www.microsoft.com/ipv6`, where you'll find several detailed technical documents regarding IPv6.

IPv6 in Windows Server 2003

Windows Server 2003 contains the first production version of Microsoft's IPv6 stack (Windows XP includes a similar, prerelease version of the stack). The stack contains all the features to operate on a pure IPv6 network or a combined IPv4/IPv6 network, including

- **6to4 tunneling**—Allows IPv6 hosts to communicate with one another over an older, IPv4 network.
- **PortProxy-enabled communications for applications that cannot select a specific IP stack**—PortProxy provides proxying from IPv4 to IPv6 and vice versa, as well as proxying from IPv4 to IPv4 and from IPv6 to IPv6. This capability is critical for computers that need to access services provided by a computer offering a different version of the IP stack. You can configure PortProxy by using the `netsh interface portproxy` command from a command line.
- **Dynamic registration of IPv6-compatible host ("AAAA") records**—Both the DNS Client service and the DNS Server included with Windows Server 2003 support this.

   ➤ For more information on changes to DNS in Windows Server 2003, **see** "WINS, DHCP, and DNS," **p. 126**.

- **IPSec now supports IPv6 in several configurations**—Plus, Windows Server 2003 includes a new tool, `IPsec6.exe`, which enables you to manually configure security policies, associations, and encryption keys for IPv6.
- **Windows's native Remote Procedure Call (RPC) protocol uses Windows Sockets**—This has been updated to support both IPv4 and IPv6 connections.

- **Internet Explorer, Telnet, FTP, IIS 6.0, file and print sharing, Windows Media Services, and Network Monitor**—These are all included with Windows Server 2003, and they all fully support IPv6.
- **Windows Server 2003 supports IPv6 routing through the use of the `netsh interface ipv6 route` command**—This command enables you to configure a Windows Server 2003 computer with static IPv6 routes, thus allowing the computer to act as a rudimentary IPv6 router.

To install and configure the IPv6 stack on Windows Server 2003, follow these steps:

1. Open the properties for the network connection you want to use IPv6.
2. Click the **Install** button and select **Protocol** from the list.
3. Select **Microsoft TCP/IP Version 6** from the protocol list, and click **OK**.

Unlike the IPv4 stack, which includes a complete GUI for configuring IP addresses and other information, IPv6 is configured entirely from the command line by using the `netsh interface ipv6` command. For example, `netsh interface ipv6 add address "Internal" AEB0::2` adds the address `AEB0::2` to the network interface named Internal. Other commands enable you to add DNS server information, interfaces, routes, prefix policies, 6to4 tunnel settings, and so forth. Of course, configuring IPv6 settings from a command line is definitely a step backward, when everyone has become used to automatic configuration through DHCP. There is a specification for DHCPv6—the IPv6 update to DHCP—which provides full automatic configuration. Unfortunately, Windows Server 2003 does not include a DHCPv6-compatible DHCP service, nor does Windows Server 2003's IPv6 stack include DHCPv6 support. By default, Windows Server 2003's IPv6 stack creates a unique local-link address automatically (similar to APIPA in IPv4), removing a minor piece of manual configuration effort. Also, all IPv6 hosts listen for advertisement messages sent by IPv6 routers and use those messages to configure their default router, the location of a DHCPv6 server (assuming one exists and the stack supports its use), and other information. On a network with multiple IPv6 subnets, you'll likely have to perform some manual configuration, especially if your routers aren't configured to send IPv6 router advertisements.

> **Tip** If you're planning to move to IPv6, it makes the most sense to migrate your network boundary devices—routers, firewalls, and the like—first. Those devices play a key role in IPv6 host configuration, replacing some of the functions performed by DHCP in an IPv4 network.

IPSec Improvements

First introduced in Windows 2000, IPSec has undergone a number of improvements to make it more usable and more secure. One of the major drawbacks of IPSec in Windows 2000, for example, is the fact that IPSec/L2TP VPN tunnels cannot traverse a NAT device. This requires administrators to use their Internet firewalls (which usually perform NAT for network clients) as the endpoint of all L2TP/IPSec VPNs or to use the somewhat-weaker PPTP protocol for VPNs because PPTP could pass through NAT under certain circumstances. Windows Server 2003, however, extends the IPSec protocol to comply with new Internet Engineering Task Force (IETF) drafts that provide support for passing IPSec/L2TP tunnels through NAT devices. This new capability enables completely secure VPNs to originate behind NAT devices (most often firewalls) and to be directed to destinations behind NAT devices, creating more secure point-to-point tunnels of encrypted data.

Similarly, the Enterprise and Datacenter editions also provide NLB support for IPSec/L2TP tunnels, allowing you to create a farm of multiple VPN endpoint servers by using Windows Server 2003's bundled NLB software. This capability means that you can now create clusters of VPN servers to handle incoming user VPN connections; these clusters can be fault tolerant and will balance the incoming workload between themselves. If a user establishes a connection with a particular server and that server fails, another server in the cluster will be capable of adopting the connection and provide uninterrupted services to the user.

Another common problem with IPSec policies under Windows 2000 is that they have to be configured with specific IP addresses, making it impossible to create policies for servers that use DHCP to obtain dynamic IP addresses. In Windows Server 2003, source and destination addresses can be set to a specific IP address or be set to the DHCP server, DNS server, default gateway, or WINS server, enabling policies to automatically adjust to computers with dynamic IP addresses. Figure 10.1 shows the new configuration dialog box, including the new dynamic addresses. You can use the new dynamic policies to, for example, ensure packet encryption between any DNS or WINS server. This new capability is supported only by Windows Server 2003; these dynamic addresses are ignored by Windows 2000 and Windows XP computers, which can result in inconsistent application of your IPSec policies within your domain.

The IP Security Policies snap-in can now map computer encryption certificates to computer accounts in Active Directory, which is the same SChannel certificate mapping IIS and other PKI-enabled applications already use. After they're mapped, you can set up access controls using the settings for network logon rights. For example, an administrator can restrict access to a particular computer to other computers from a specific domain, computers with a certificate from a particular certification authority (CA), a specific group of computers, or a single computer. Only computers running Windows Server 2003 have this capability; computers running Windows XP or Windows 2000 ignore this extension to IPSec policy.

Finally, Windows Server 2003 includes support for 2,048-bit Diffie-Hellman key exchange, as described in the Internet draft, "More MODP Diffie-Hellman Groups for IKE." The practical upshot of this support is stronger encryption keys. The IP Security Policies snap-in provides the interface to configure this new setting for both local and domain-based IPSec policy. This support is provided only in Windows Server 2003; Windows 2000 and Windows XP computers ignore this setting. Figure 10.2 shows the new Diffie-Hellman group, which you can add as an active Internet Key Exchange (IKE) method by using the IP Security Policies snap-in.

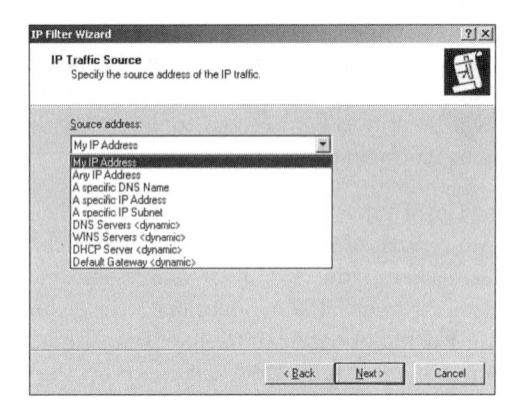

Figure 10.1 Dynamic addressing supports more complex and dynamic IPSec policies.

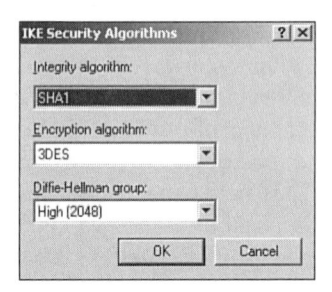

Figure 10.2 2,048-bit encryption is roughly twice as strong as the strongest encryption previously available in Windows.

New Tools

As shown in Figure 10.3, Windows Server 2003 also sports an all-new IPSec Monitor snap-in, providing a better administrative interface for monitoring IPSec policies and security associations. Windows Server 2003 also include the IP Security Policies console, which enables you to actually configure and manage IPSec policies, manage filter lists and actions, and so forth. The IP Security Policies snap-in is included in the Local Security Policy console, which is listed in the Start menu's Administrative Tools folder.

IPSec Improvements **167**

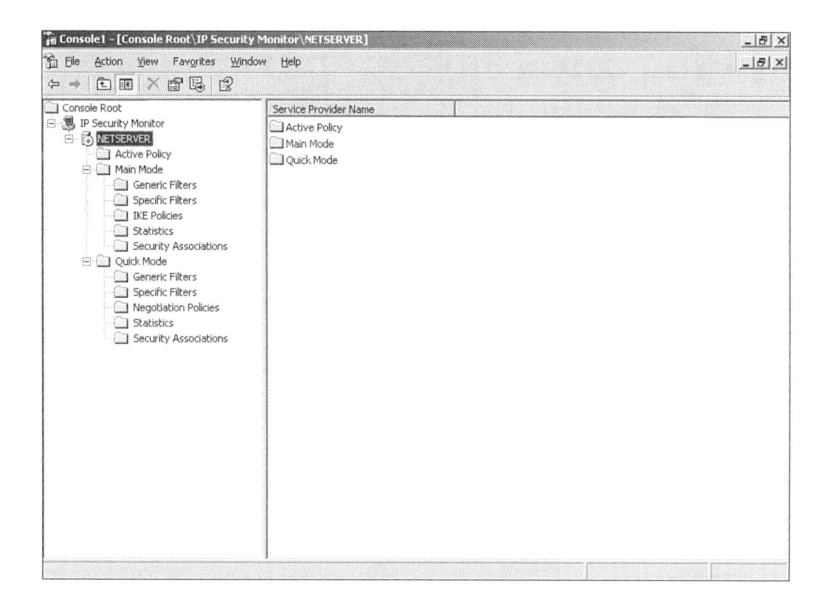

Figure 10.3 The new IP Security Monitor provides a tool for monitoring active IPSec policies.

To use the new snap-in, do the following:

1. Select **Run** from the Start menu.
2. Type mmc and press **Enter**.
3. From the File menu, select **Add/Remove Snap-in**.
4. Click **Add**.
5. Locate the **IP Security Monitor** in the list and double-click it.
6. Close all dialog boxes, and you'll be ready to work with the IP Security Monitor.

Tip | You can use the IP Security Monitor to monitor remote computers, too. Just right-click **IP Security Monitor** and select **Connect** from the pop-up menu. You can monitor the IPSec policies on any computer you're an administrator of.

The Windows 2000 Server Resource Kit includes Ipsecpol.exe, a command-line tool for administering IPSec policies. Windows Server 2003 replaces this tool by bundling IPSec administration into the Netsh.exe command-line tool. You can now use Netsh.exe to configure main-mode policies, quick-mode policies, settings, rules, and other parameters. Just open a command-line window and run netsh -c ipsec to enter configuration mode.

Universal Plug and Play Support

First introduced in Windows XP, Universal Plug and Play (UPnP) promises to change a lot about the way we use computers. You're already familiar with basic Plug and Play (PnP), which enables Windows to automatically recognize and use hardware devices such as modems, printers, monitors, and more. UPnP extends the PnP concept to include network devices, allowing Windows to discover and use devices present on your network. One of the best current examples of UPnP in action is Windows's own Internet Connection Sharing (ICS) service. ICS provides UPnP discovery information, enabling UPnP clients to discover the presence of the gateway and request services from it. Hardware gateways, such as a cable or xDSL modem, could function similarly (and, in fact, UPnP-compatible gateways are now becoming available to purchase), allowing your client computers to automatically discover and take advantage of the gateway's capabilities.

> **Note** A number of companies are participating in UPnP development. Read more at www.upnp.org.

Future applications of UPnP will likely eliminate the need to connect devices directly to your computer. Instead, devices will connect to your network, where they will be accessible to all networked computers. For example, a new printer could be plugged directly into your network. Client computers would immediately detect the new printer's presence, query the printer for its capabilities (whether it supports color, the paper sizes it can handle, and so forth), and set up an icon for the printer. Instantly, you could begin using the printer without any further configuration.

Traditionally, unconnected devices could use UPnP for new levels of technology integration. Your home stereo receiver, for example, could connect to your network, exposing its power, tuning, and volume controls to your client computers and enabling you to control the receiver from any desktop or laptop on your home network. Your DVD player could perform similar functions, streaming video from DVDs to any network-attached computer for a completely distributed home entertainment system. Other applications might include controllable lights, sprinklers, and other appliances. Although all devices must be connected to the network to operate, bear in mind that wireless networking, such as 802.11b or Bluetooth, are becoming less expensive and more common every day.

On a corporate network, UPnP offers better centralized management of networked devices. UPnP's protocols include authentication and security provisions, ensuring that only designated administrators can control UPnP devices. Windows Server 2003's UPnP support makes it ready to support UPnP devices as they are released; with the UPnP support also included in Windows XP, such devices will now start hitting the marketplace in force.

New Networking Services

Windows Server 2003 now includes the Internet Connection Firewall (ICF), an entry-level firewall designed to protect specified network adapters from unauthorized network traffic. This feature is most frequently used in small environments, in conjunction with ICS. The combination of ICF and ICS provides small offices with the capability to share a single Internet connection through Windows Server 2003, while also providing protection from Internet-based hackers. Note that ICF is not available in the 64-bit edition of Enterprise Edition or in any edition of Datacenter Edition. As shown in Figure 10.4, ICF can be enabled by simply selecting a check box in the network connection's properties dialog box.

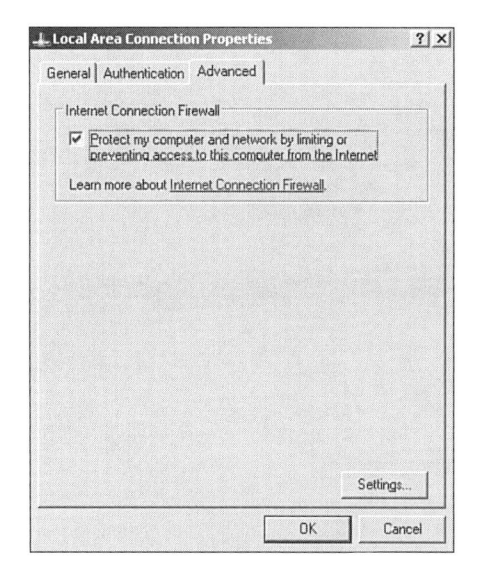

Figure 10.4 ICF can be used to protect any network connection on a server.

By default, ICF allows all outgoing traffic to pass through the firewall, and allows all replies to outgoing traffic to enter the network. This behavior accommodates the most common use of ICF, which is to protect an internal network from the Internet. You can also configure ICF to permit specific types of traffic, allowing ICF to protect an internal Web or mail server, if desired. Figure 10.5 shows the Advanced Settings dialog box, which you access by clicking the Settings button in the network connection's Properties dialog box.

The Advanced Settings dialog box includes three tabs:

- **Services**—This tab enables you to specify the network protocols, such as HTTP or FTP, that ICF should allow into your network from the outside. The list includes several common protocols, and you can add your own to accommodate specific applications available on your network.

- **Security Logging**—This tab allows you to enable ICFG logging and select a location for the log file. You can configure ICF to log all successful connections and dropped connections, providing a comprehensive log of firewall activity.
- **ICMP**—This tab allows you to configure the Internet Control Message Protocol (ICMP) traffic that ICF will allow to enter your network. ICMP is the protocol behind common troubleshooting tools such as ping, and blocking ICMP traffic prevents outsiders from gaining information about your internal network's infrastructure. However, you might need to temporarily enable ICMP traffic to troubleshoot connectivity problems.

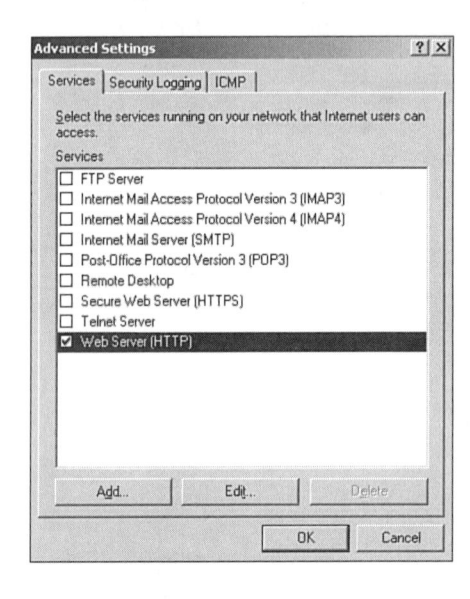

Figure 10.5 This dialog box allows you to configure incoming traffic and ICF logging.

Caution | ICF is worth what you pay for it, which isn't much. Don't confuse ICF for more powerful and robust firewall solutions such as Checkpoint Firewall1 or Microsoft's own Internet Security and Acceleration Server. If you need to protect a medium- to large-size network, need the highest possible network throughput, or need powerful intrusion detection capabilities or other enterprise-class features, don't rely on ICF.

RRAS Enhancements

The Routing and Remote Access Service (RRAS) included in Windows Server 2003 provides several functions that enable Windows to accept VPN connections, accept dial-up connections, act as a network router, provide Internet connectivity to an entire network (including NAT), and much more. Additionally, RRAS's snap-in has received a minor facelift for Windows Server 2003, making the service easier to configure and manage.

As always, RRAS includes robust remote access policies to control access to the server's connectivity features, static routing capability, dynamic routing protocols, a variety of remote access authentication protocols, and so forth.

> To learn more about RRAS and how it works, visit www.samspublishing.com and enter this book's ISBN number (no hyphens or parentheses) in the Search field; then click the book's cover image to access the book details page. Click the Web Resources link in the More Information section, and locate article ID# **A011001**.

You can also configure RRAS as a NAT/firewall server by using the new Manage Your Server application, shown in Figure 10.6. This capability lets administrators configure their servers' operations from a single application and reduces the complexity of many basic configuration tasks. The Manage Your Server application also provides buttons that open the traditional management consoles, providing a central location for new administrators to locate Windows Server 2003's various management tools.

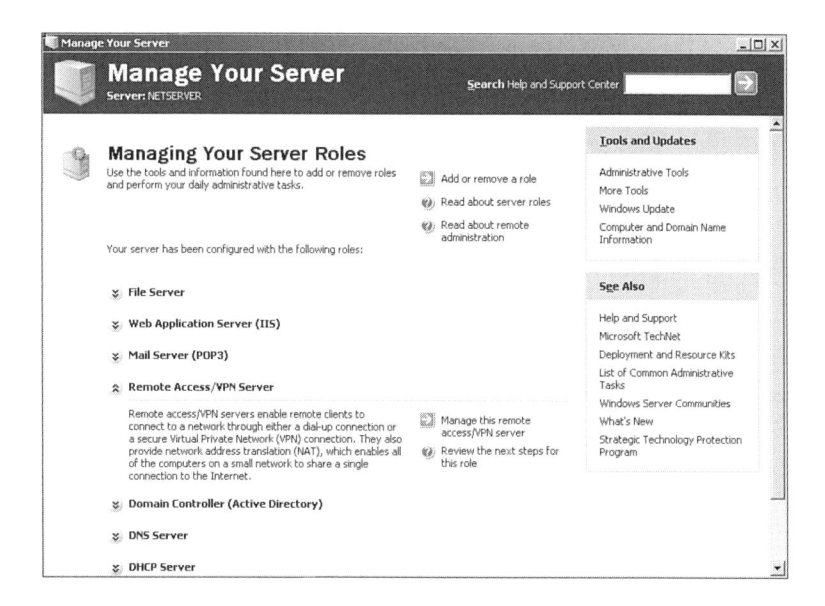

Figure 10.6 Manage Your Server enables you to configure a server for new roles, automatically adding new services (such as RRAS) and software as required.

Some of RRAS's other significant improvements include

- **Better EAP-TLS configuration**—A new dialog box allows you to more easily configure smart card and other certificate properties for RRAS authentication parameters. You can now configure multiple RADIUS servers and multiple root certification authorities, providing better integration with multiple networks or very large networks.

- **RRAS includes a new NetBIOS over TCP/IP proxy**—This provides remote access clients with name resolution capabilities without having to use a discreet DNS or WINS server. Using the proxy, RRAS can receive name resolution requests from the client, resolve those requests internally, and pass the response back to the client—all without the need to deploy a WINS or DNS server on the network. This new feature is especially useful to small businesses that would otherwise not require a DNS or WINS server.

- **Demand-dial connections can now use PPPoE in addition to regular modems and Ethernet connections**—This enables RRAS to automatically create network connections over broadband services, such as cable modems or xDSL modems. This feature lets you easily establish VPNs over a cable or xDSL connection or utilize RRAS's NAT and firewall capabilities to share a single cable or xDSL connection with an entire small network. Figure 10.7 shows a new demand-dial interface being created to use a PPPoE interface.

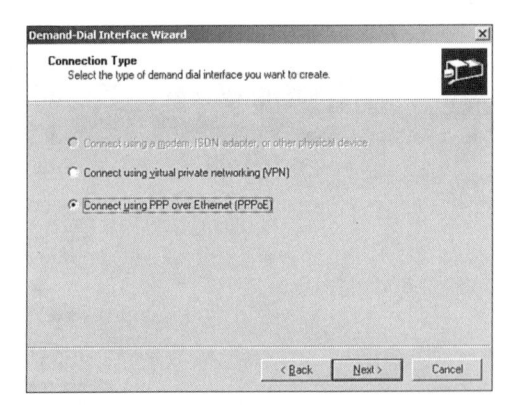

Figure 10.7 PPPoE connections are generally used with xDSL or cable modem providers.

A major new functional improvement in RRAS is the NAT/Basic Firewall feature. This feature combines the ICS and ICF features into a single interface, allowing you to designate a particular network interface as a shared Internet connection and provide basic firewall capabilities for it. Unlike the basic ICS feature, NAT/Basic Firewall provides you with full control over RRAS's DHCP allocator, enabling you to customize the IP addresses RRAS provides to network clients. To create a new NAT/Basic Firewall interface, right-click **Nat/Basic Firewall** in the RRAS snap-in and select **New Interface** from the pop-up menu. You'll see a configuration dialog box similar to the one shown in Figure 10.8, which enables you to configure the interface as a shared connection, a shared connection with firewall capabilities, or a basic firewall. Although these capabilities aren't new to Windows, having them available from a single, unified interface with such easy administration is definitely a major improvement.

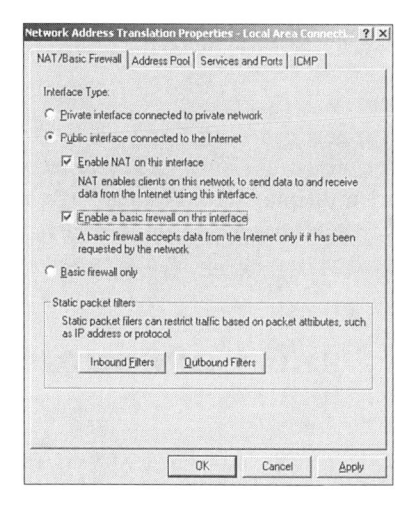

Figure 10.8 The new NAT/Basic Firewall interface makes configuring shared Internet connections for smaller offices easy.

RRAS also includes a number of VPN-specific enhancements. In Windows 2000, VPN servers dynamically register the names and IP addresses for all network interfaces with a DNS server. This creates problems when internal clients attempt to access server resources because they can receive the server's external IP address in a DNS query. Additionally, Windows 2000 enables NetBIOS on all network interfaces, which presents potential security problems if the server's external interface is connected to an unsecured network. In Windows Server 2003, the default registration behavior is changed, so dynamic DNS registration is disabled for both internal and external interfaces, and NetBIOS is disabled for the external interface. This new behavior requires you to manually create DNS host entries for your VPN servers but gives you full control over the IP address internal clients receive when they query the server's name. The new behavior also improves security by automatically disabling NetBIOS on the external interface.

> To learn more about VPNs and how they work, visit www.samspublishing.com and enter this book's ISBN number (no hyphens or parentheses) in the Search field; then click the book's cover image to access the book details page. Click the Web Resources link in the More Information section, and locate article ID# **A011002**.

Another improvement isn't specifically targeted at VPNs, but rather at all demand-dial connections, including client-to-server VPN connections. In Windows 2000, RRAS could bridge from its external interface—including dial-up connections—only to its internal interface, which connects to the corporate network. In the case of an Internet-connected server, RRAS could not provide both corporate network and Internet access to demand-dial clients. In Windows Server 2003, however, RRAS has been extended so that its internal interface can be added as a private interface to the NAT service included in RRAS. The practical effect of this change is that RRAS can provide NAT services for both internal clients and demand-dial clients, including VPN clients.

One "disimprovement" for VPN support comes in Windows Server 2003 – Web Edition, which can support only one VPN connection using either L2TP/IPSec or PPTP. All other editions of Windows Server 2003 can support multiple simultaneous VPN connections. The intent of this change is to allow Windows Server 2003, Web Edition to accept a VPN connection for administrative purposes, but to otherwise function solely as a Web server.

Other Networking and Communications Improvements

One of the coolest new networking features is the Networking tab on the Windows Task Manager. As shown in Figure 10.9, this new tab displays a real-time graphical chart of network utilization, as well as summary statistics for all network interfaces in the computer. You can use the new tab to easily see which network adapters in your servers are working the hardest, spot initial signs of over utilization, and so forth.

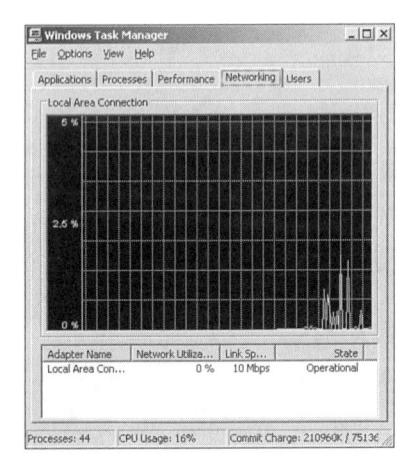

Figure 10.9 The new Networking tab is just one of the additions to the Windows Server 2003 Task Manager.

Windows Server 2003 includes several networking enhancements that were originally introduced in Windows XP. Remember, Windows XP is the client equivalent of Windows Server 2003, so a great deal of feature parity exists between the two operating systems, despite their dissimilar names and user interfaces. The major enhancements are discussed next.

Network Location Awareness

Windows Server 2003 is capable of notifying applications when network settings change. Some built-in services, such as Internet Connection Sharing, disable themselves when the computer is moved to a different network. This behavior ensures that applications function only when attached to the network for which they are configured and provides a more seamless experience on computers that are frequently moved between different networks.

New Group Policies

These new policies, which are applicable to Windows Server 2003 and Windows XP computers, allow administrators to designate specific users as members of the Network Configuration Operators Group. Members of this group can modify their local TCP/IP properties, giving advanced users the flexibility to manually configure the network connections. You can also use the new group policies to block the local Administrators group of a computer from modifying ICS, ICF, network bridging, and general network settings, providing better control of computer configurations.

Native Support for PPPoE

This new support eliminates the need for third-party software when connecting Windows Server 2003 to PPPoE connections, which are most often broadband cable or xDSL connections. By including PPPoE support in Windows Server 2003, Microsoft hopes to improve the stability and reliability of these broadband connections, which previously had to rely on poorly written software provided by ISPs. Native PPPoE support also makes leveraging other native features, such as ICS and ICF, with broadband connections easier.

Network Bridging

Network bridging allows Windows Server 2003 to act as a bridge between dissimilar network architectures. For example, a small office might support both a wired network and a wireless network. By attaching a Windows Server 2003 computer to both networks and bridging the connections, Windows Server 2003 can join the two networks to create a single logical network. Any native network connection can be bridged, including Ethernet, wireless, phone line, and IEEE-1394 (FireWire). To bridge two connections, simply select them both in the Connections Manager window, right-click, and select **Bridge Connections** from the pop-up menu.

IEEE-1394 (FireWire) Support

This new feature allows Windows Server 2003 to treat IEEE-1394 connections as network connections. Although this feature is often more useful on client computers (support is also included in Windows XP), IEEE-1394 networking support can be invaluable during server migration or consolidation. IEEE-1394 provides a fast, 400Mbps connection, enabling extremely fast file copy operations from one computer to another. This high-speed connectivity is ideal when moving large quantities of files from one server to another during a migration or consolidation and can, in many cases, be the fastest way to move those files.

Automatic Network Configuration

Automatic configuration kicks in whenever a Windows Server 2003 computer is configured to obtain IP addressing information via DHCP but cannot contact a DHCP server. By default, Windows Server 2003 automatically generates an APIPA address in the 169.254.0.0/16 range, without a DNS server, default gateway, or other information. You can also manually configure alternative IP configuration settings to be used when a DHCP server is unavailable. Although this feature is most useful for client computers running Windows XP, you need to be aware of this feature's operation. For example, if you find that a server is using a `169.254.x.x` IP address, you know that it was unable to contact your DHCP server.

A New Netstat Tool

The new Netstat tool can display active TCP connections, along with the process ID (PID) of the process handling the connection. This enormously useful new feature can enable you to track down IP ports that aren't supposed to be open, troubleshoot connectivity problems, and much more. Simply run Netstat and, as shown in Figure 10.10, the output will include process IDs for each open connection.

Figure 10.10 Given the output from Netstat, you can use the Task Manager to look up PIDs and determine the names of the related processes.

Native Support for xDSL

Built-in native support for xDSL recognizes the growing popularity of xDSL connections for branch offices and other business applications. The new support, referred to as *permanent virtual circuit encapsulation*, includes an intermediate device driver that appears to the operating system as an Ethernet interface but actually uses a DSL/Asynchronous Transfer Mode (ATM) permanent virtual circuit (PVC) to carry TCP/IP frames. This is a common implementation used by many xDSL carriers and enables Windows Server 2003 to support TCP/IP over PPP over ATM and TCP/IP over PPPoE, using vendor-supplied DSL/ATM miniport drivers. The practical advantage of all this is that future xDSL implementations will be of dispensing with specialized DSL modems and will rely on less expensive add-in cards, which will connect Windows Server 2003 directly to the DSL network.

Wireless Improvements

Windows Server 2003 also sports a host of wireless networking improvements. Many of these improvements are better used on client computers than on servers because servers tend to be connected to high-speed wired networks. However, smaller environments can use wireless-connected servers and can benefit from these enhancements:

- **Support for 802.1X**—This is a standard for wireless port-based network access control that provides better network security.
- **Wireless Zero Configuration**—Allows Windows Server 2003 to automatically configure supported wireless network adapters, select a wireless network connection, and automatically switch to ad-hoc networking mode when an infrastructure network is unavailable.
- **Better roaming support**—This includes the ability to automatically request DHCP information when associating with a new wireless network, reauthenticating automatically when necessary, and so forth.
- **Group policy support for wireless network policies**—Allows centralized configuration of wireless networking policies. These policies can include preferred networks, privacy settings, and 802.1X settings. These settings can be applied along with other group policies to members of a site, a domain, or an organizational unit (OU) through Active Directory. Figure 10.11 shows the new policies in the Group Policy snap-in.

Missing Protocols

Finally, a few older networking protocols were removed from Windows Server 2003: The Direct Link Control (DLC) protocol, which was primarily used to connect to older Hewlett-Packard JetDirect network print servers, and the NetBEUI protocol. Note that NetBIOS still exists; NetBIOS is a session-level protocol. NetBEUI was a nonroutable, nonconfigurable transport protocol. The 64-bit editions of Windows Server 2003 also remove support for IrDA, an infrared communications protocol; IPX/SPX (and all IPX/SPX-dependent services); and the Open Shortest Path First (OSPF) routing protocol.

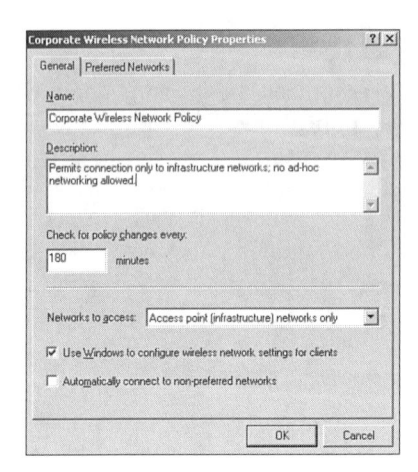

Figure 10.11 Wireless group policies provide centralized configuration capabilities for increasingly popular wireless networks.

Additionally, Microsoft has removed support for RPC over NetBEUI, RPC over NetBIOS over TCP/IP, RPC over NetBIOS over IPX, RPC over IPX, and RPC over MSMQ. The 64-bit editions also eliminate RPC over SPX and RPC over AppleTalk.

11

TERMINAL SERVICES

In This Chapter

- Remotely Control Servers across the Enterprise, **page 180**.
- Managing Terminal Services, **page 186**.
- Terminal Services client features and performance, **page 190**.
- Terminal Server Clusters or Farms, **page 194**.

What's New

Terminal services in Windows Server 2003 provide significant new features designed for improved manageability, usability, performance, security, and scalability. With all the changes, it might seem like the terminal services model has been completely redone. In reality, the model is very much the same. It still has a terminal services client component and a terminal services server component. Also, the server component still has two possible modes—remote administration and application server mode—just like in Windows 2000.

The terminal services client component has been renamed and is now called Remote Desktop Connection, just like in Windows XP. The biggest change that makes terminal services look different is the server-side component. The former remote administration mode is now called Remote Desktop for Administration and is treated separately from the Terminal Server application mode component. Although Remote Desktop for Administration and

Terminal Server appear to be two separate things, they are in reality two facets of the same technology, like in Windows 2000. The difference is in the way they appear and how they are installed.

> **Note** The Remote Desktop Connection client actually has the same filename as the previous terminal services client (`mstsc.exe`).

With the new name comes several new features for both administrators and end users alike. There are new methods for administration (Group Policy, WMI, and ADSI), and the terminal services client is now the Remote Desktop Connection application and uses a new version of the Remote Desktop Protocol (RDP 5.1). The updated protocol provides several client enhancements for usability and performance, such as access to local resources and customization settings for low-bandwidth environments, which brings it up-to-date to rival Citrix's Metaframe client and the ICA protocol. There are also a number of new security features, such as easier management of accessibility permissions, client encryption policies, and support for stronger encryption to help administrators secure their terminal services environments. To top it all off, the new Terminal Server Session Directory enhances scalability by fixing problems with running terminal server clusters or farms.

Terminal Services Overview

What is terminal services? Terminal services is simply a technology for providing access to remote servers via a graphical interface. Terminal services allows multiple users to simultaneously access a given machine—the terminal server. Each user connects to the terminal server via a terminal services client and gets his own environment as if he were the only user. All processing is performed on the terminal server. Applications run from the server and only the screen shots and keyboard/mouse input pass between the client and the server. This transfer between the terminal services client and the terminal server is handled by the Remote Desktop Protocol (RDP). RDP controls the session between client and server and determines which features are available. Terminal services is ideal for remote administration because you can access a server as if you were physically there. Terminal services is also ideal for centralizing applications. By simply installing an application on a terminal server, you can make it immediately available to your entire enterprise. You don't have to deal with complicated deployments to the various clients. Additionally, because all the processing is performed on the terminal server, terminal services is ideal for making applications available to users across low-bandwidth connections or with low-end hardware clients.

Remote Desktop for Administration

Remote Desktop for Administration is the former Terminal Services Remote Administration Mode, with a few improvements, of course. With Windows 2000, Terminal Services is integrated into the operating system as an optional service. It can be installed using Add/Remove

Programs, Add/Remove Windows Components, and when installed, the administrator is prompted for the terminal server mode. The two choices are Remote Administration Mode and Application Server Mode. Application Server Mode is designed for installing the server to be used in the role of a traditional terminal server or Winframe/Metaframe server. In this role, applications are to be installed on the box for use by remote users; making these applications available to remote users is the primary purpose of the box. Traditionally, Citrix Metaframe has offered several additional features that make it more worthwhile as an enterprise application hosting solution than Microsoft's terminal server.

> For a comparison of terminal services and Citrix Metaframe, visit www.samspublishing.com and enter this book's ISBN number (no hyphens or parenthesis) in the Search field; then click the book cover image to access the book details page. Click the Web Resources link in the More Information section, and locate article ID# **A011101**.

Windows 2000 Remote Administration Mode

Remote Administration Mode was something new for terminal services introduced in Windows 2000. Installing Terminal Services in Remote Administration Mode allows up to two (free) concurrent connections. Plus, when using terminal server in this mode, you don't have to worry about keeping track of licenses, as you do in Application Server Mode and previous versions of terminal server.

> For information on terminal services licensing for Application Server Mode, visit www.samspublishing.com and enter this book's ISBN number (no hyphens or parenthesis) in the Search field; then click the book cover image to access the book details page. Click the Web Resources link in the More Information section, and locate article ID# **A011102**.

The purpose of Remote Administration Mode is to allow system administrators to remotely access Windows 2000 servers. By installing Terminal Services in Remote Administration Mode, administrators can get much of the same functionality as with third-party applications such as pcAnywhere—namely access to the server desktop via a graphical interface, right out of the box. This provides for a lower total cost of ownership for managing remote servers. No longer do you have to be physically at the server to perform various types of maintenance, nor do you have to buy expensive third-party software. (Management likes this because it improves the bottom line, but poor administrators no longer have an excuse to fly out to Hawaii for server maintenance—at least not as often.)

Windows Server 2003 Terminal Services Modes

Window Server 2003 no longer has a Terminal Services Remote Administration Mode. The so-called Remote Administration Mode and Application Server Mode are now treated as two separate entities and are installed differently. Under the hood, they are both still technically terminal services—they just have different names now and are installed differently. The former Remote Administration Mode is now called Remote Desktop for Administration. Windows 2003 Server comes preinstalled with Remote Desktop for Administration (although it is disabled). There is still an optional Windows component for installing terminal services, but it is now called Terminal Server. Installation of this service converts the Remote Desktop for Administration installation into a full-blown Terminal Server (Application Server Mode) installation; uninstalling Terminal Server returns the system to the Remote Desktop for Administration mode. Once again, Remote Desktop for Administration is always installed. It can be enabled simply by selecting **Allow Users to Connect Remotely to This Computer** in the Remote Desktop section on the Remote tab of the System Properties screen, as shown in Figure 11.1. To highlight this distinction, Windows Server 2003, Web Edition does not have Terminal Server (it cannot be an application server); however, it does have Remote Desktop for Administration, so it can be accessed remotely via a terminal services client.

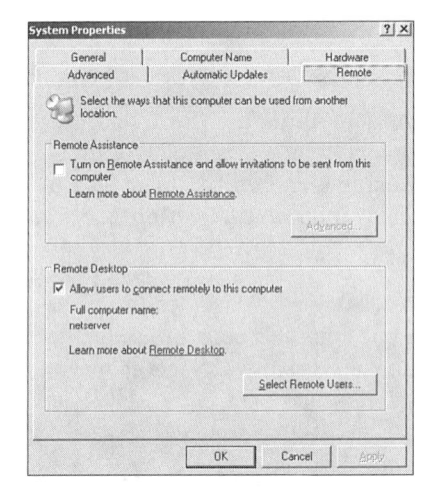

Figure 11.1 Enable Remote Desktop for Administration from the Remote tab of the System Properties dialog box.

When Remote Desktop for Administration is enabled, a security message pops up warning that local accounts might not have passwords and that a port on the firewall might need to be opened to allow communication. This is just an informational message to remind you that enabling Remote Desktop for Administration is a potential security risk because it allows direct access to your machine across the network.

Note | The whole point of Remote Desktop is to allow you to log on to the machine from a remote location, so you should ensure that the user accounts that are granted access are secure. If the client and server are on opposite sides of a firewall, you also need to open the port used by RDP for the Remote Desktop sessions to work. By default this port is TCP 3389. However, for security purposes, the server can be

> reconfigured to listen to a different port (Q306759) and the client can then be configured to connect via that port (Q304304). If this is the case, you will need to know the port used to be able to open it on the firewall.

In addition to selecting the check box to enable Remote Desktop, you must also designate who is permitted to use Remote Desktop for Administration. By default, the Administrator account is the only one that has access. To grant additional users (domain or local) permissions to be allowed to connect to the server via Remote Desktop for Administration, click the **Select Remote Users** button and then simply add the user or group accounts as appropriate. This adds the users on this list to a local group called Remote Desktop Users, which has permissions to log on to the terminal server.

New Client(s)

Windows Server 2003 has two installed clients that can be used for connecting to Remote Desktop for Administration (or Terminal Server). The Remote Desktop Connection application is found by selecting **Start**, **All Programs**, **Accessories**, **Communications**—just like in Windows XP. This is the terminal services client application, and it is used for connecting to a single Terminal Server/Remote Desktop for Administration machine. In fact, Remote Desktop Connection is the same terminal services client application Windows XP uses. This client uses the RDP 5.1 protocol, which provides several enhancements over the previous terminal services. (See "Remote Desktop Protocol 5.1," later in this chapter, for more information.)

The other client installed by default is the Remote Desktops MMC, which is installed under Administrative Tools. Although it too uses the RDP 5.1 protocol, the interface limits the configurable options. This console can be particularly useful for enterprise administrators because it has a tree pane view of remote desktop connections, which enables an administrator to create several connections in the left pane and then connect and view them in the right pane. It makes switching between sessions and keeping track of multiple sessions much easier. These connections can also be configured to automatically connect (and even log on, provided the terminal server allows it) when selected. Both clients also have the capability to connect to the server console session. This can be accomplished with the Remote Desktops MMC simply by selecting the **Connect to Console** check box, as shown in Figure 11.2. You can also connect to the console session via the Remote Desktop Connection application by launching `mstsc.exe /console` from a command line. The console session is a special session that shows what's actually displayed on the server's monitor (although the physical monitor gets locked when the console session is accessed remotely). With Terminal Server installed (thus putting it in Application Server Mode), applications must be installed via the server console session so that they can be made available for all user sessions.

184 Chapter 11 Terminal Services

Note | Certain functions cannot be performed from the console session. For example, using Terminal Services Manager to Connect to or remote control another session can be performed only when connected to the terminal server via a client session, not when connected via console.

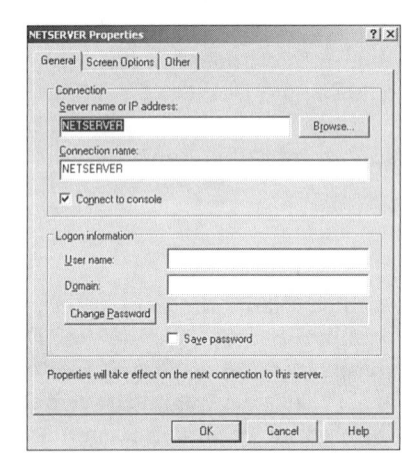

Figure 11.2 Connecting to the terminal server console session using the Remote Desktops console.

Another benefit of the Remote Desktop MMC console is that it is an MMC snap-in. Just like any other MMC snap-in, it can be used to create customized administrative consoles.

If you're not familiar with the MMC and would like a quick tutorial, visit www.samspublishing.com and enter this book's ISBN number (no hyphens or parenthesis) in the Search field; then click the book cover image to access the book details page. Click the Web Resources link in the More Information section, and locate article ID# **A011301**.

Either client can be used for connecting to Windows Server 2003 Remote Desktop for Administration or Terminal Server sessions. In fact, the RDP 5.1 protocol is backward-compatible to previous versions, so these clients can be used to connect to Windows 2000 (RDP 5.0) or even NT Terminal Server 4.0 (RDP 4.0). Of course, you won't get the new features of the RDP 5.1 protocol when connecting to these down-level servers. Similarly, previous versions of the terminal services client can connect to Windows Server 2003 Remote Desktop for Administration or Terminal Server sessions.

Although down-level clients can't get the features of the new RDP 5.1 protocol when connecting to a Windows 2000 or NT 4 terminal server, they can get the new features when connecting to Windows Server 2003 by installing the Remote Desktop Connection client application. This client can be installed on the Windows 9x platform (Windows 95, 98 Special Edition, and Millennium) as well as Windows NT 4 and Windows 2000. To install it and thereby gain the new features, simply run the Remote Desktop Connection installation program from the Windows XP CD (`\Support\Tools\msrdpcli.exe`) or download it from `http://www.microsoft.com/windowsxp/remotedesktop`. A version for Windows CE is available in the Windows CE .NET Platform Builder, and there is even a version available for the Macintosh (`http://www.microsoft.com/mac/DOWNLOAD/MISC/RDC.asp`). With this Remote Desktop Connection client, you can have a Windows "window" on a Macintosh (although some might consider this blasphemous).

One particularly nice feature of the new Remote Desktop client is Full Screen mode, which enables you to use the full screen when connected to a terminal server. Windows 2000 terminal server client sessions show as a window that cannot be maximized. With the Remote Desktop Client, you can expand to full screen, so it feels like you are actually on the box. Additionally, you can configure how control keys (except Ctrl+Alt+Del) function: on the client, on the server, or in Full Screen mode only. With these settings, you can get the same look and feel as if you were on the server—even the keys behave the same (except Ctrl+Alt+Del, of course).

Full Screen Mode

An option on the client configuration displays the Connection bar when in Full Screen mode. This puts a little note-style bar at the top of the screen to let you know you're in a terminal server session, as opposed to the local system. I recommend pinning the bar (by selecting the push pin icon) so the Connection bar won't disappear. This serves two purposes: First, it lets you know at a glance that you're connected to a terminal server, and secondly, it tells you to which server you are connected.

You can connect using Full Screen mode in Windows 2000; a separate Terminal Services Connection Manager allows configuration of terminal services client connections, similar to the Remote Desktops MMC console in Windows Server 2003. You can configure these client connections for Full Screen mode. However, you cannot configure the control key functionality, and you also don't get the connection bar. Additionally, you have to manually configure each connection to use Full Screen mode because it is not the default. In Windows Server 2003, however, Full Screen mode is the default screen resolution setting and is configurable on the default Remote Desktop Connection client.

The last terminal services client, the Remote Desktop Web Client, allows connections to a terminal server via a Web browser, as shown in Figure 11.3. The name is somewhat deceptive because you don't actually install a client. Remote Desktop Web Client is installed on an IIS server and enables machines with IE 5 or better to connect to terminal server sessions. To allow Remote Desktop Web Clients to connect to your terminal server, simply install the Remote Desktop Web Connection component on the server. This component is installed just like any other component, by selecting Add or Remove Programs, Add/Remove Windows Components. After the Windows Components Wizard screen displays, select **Web Application Server** and click the **Details** button. On the Web Application Server screen, select **Internet**

Information Services (IIS) and click the **Details** button. Next, select **World Wide Web Service** and click the **Details** button. Finally, select **Remote Desktop Web Connection**, click **OK** three times, and then click **Next**.

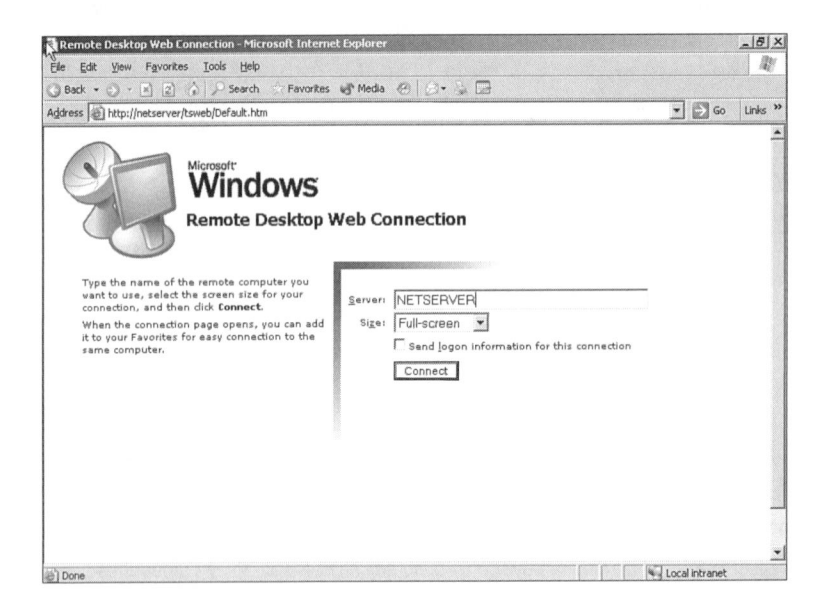

Figure 11.3 Log on to a remote computer using Remote Desktop Web Client.

The Remote Desktop Web Client opens in a browser window, which is obviously different from the normal Remote Desktop Connection Client. However, if you choose to log on in Full Screen mode, the view is just like that of the Remote Desktop client.

New Administration

In addition to a new name and a new client, terminal services in Windows Server 2003 provides new features for administration. Terminal services settings can be configured with the usual Terminal Services Configuration MMC snap-in and administered with the Terminal Services Manager MMC snap-in. Plus, these settings have now been exposed so they can be configured with Windows Management Instrumentation (WMI) through scripts, the WMIC command line, or Active Directory Services Interface (ADSI). Probably the most useful enhancement is the addition of a number of group policy settings for configuring these terminal services settings, as shown in Figure 11.4.

Figure 11.4 shows the settings under the Computer Configuration section of Group Policy. In addition, a few group policy settings can be configured under the User Configuration section.

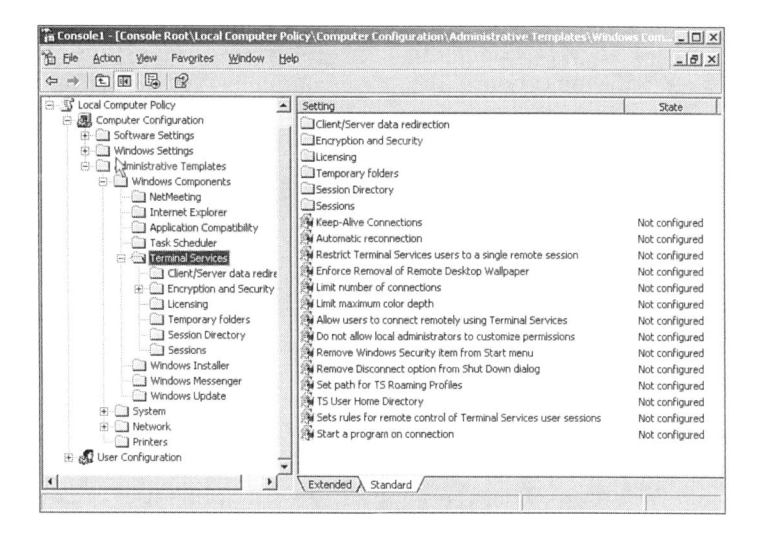

Figure 11.4 Group policy settings for configuring Terminal Services.

A lot of the new terminal services group policy settings are available simply for centrally managing settings previously available in Windows 2000. These settings can still be managed via Terminal Services Configuration (for per-server settings) or Active Directory Users and Computers (for per-users settings). Because many administrators are already familiar with the Windows 2000 settings and enumerating all the available group policy settings is too lengthy, we will concentrate here on the new settings. Just remember that for almost every setting you could configure manually in Windows 2000, you can now configure it with group policy. I will point out a couple of notable exceptions.

General Terminal Services Policies

The new settings in the main Terminal Services policy section include the following:

- **Keep-Alive Connections**—Maintains persistent terminal server connections. By default, this is off. In certain cases, if a client loses connection to the terminal server, the server might not detect it, so the connection might stay in an active state. When the client attempts to reconnect, the terminal server will treat it as a new connection. The user would then have a fresh sign-on (assuming she is allowed more than one connection), and it would appear as though what she was previously working on is gone. This is particularly annoying in Remote Desktop for Administration because now the user is using both available connections and preventing anyone else from getting in. Enabling Keep-Alive Connections adds more overhead on the Terminal Server because it is more actively monitoring the link state, but it prevents the scenario mentioned here.

- **Automatic Reconnection**—Designates whether to allow clients to automatically attempt to reconnect dropped sessions.

- **Restrict Terminal Services Users to a Single Remote Session**—Just as it says, users are allowed only one connection to the terminal server, which prevents a user from leaving a bunch of disconnected sessions and wasting terminal server resources.
- **Limit Maximum Color Depth**—Allows control of the number of colors available to all clients. This is generally used to improve performance. Higher color depths require more data to be transferred across the session and put more of a burden on the terminal server.
- **Do Not Allow Local Administrators to Customize Permissions**—Disables modification of the security tab in Terminal Services Configuration. This prevents modification of the discretionary access control list (DACL) that specifies which users/groups have which levels of access to the server. Access can still be granted and revoked by modifying the membership of the groups specified on the DACL; the DACL itself just can't be modified (read-only). In other words, an administrator could look at the list to see which group has access and then add or remove a user from that group (assuming he has access to modify the group). This is essentially an enforcement of Microsoft's recommendation of assigning permissions to resources based on groups and then managing those permissions by adding and removing users to and from those groups.
- **Remove Windows Security Item from Start Menu**—Just as it sounds, the Windows Security item is basically like pressing Ctrl+Alt+Del (because pressing Ctrl+Alt+Del in a terminal server session affects your client machine, not the actual terminal server session). This is one way to prevent users from shutting down or restarting the entire server.
- **Remove Disconnect Option from Shut Down Dialog**—This feature is set up to try to force users to log off rather than disconnecting. This is an attempt at preventing users from leaving disconnected sessions active on the terminal server. Even with this setting, users can still disconnect without logging off by simply closing the Remote Desktop Window. However, if they do that, they will at least be prompted with a reminder that their sessions will still be active.

Client/Server Data Redirection

The settings in this new section determine the types of resources that are allowed to be redirected to the client:

- **Allow Time Zone Redirection**—Changes the session time zone to be the time zone on the client instead of the server (if different). Personally, I like to keep the time zone of the server so I know what the local time is for the box on which I am working.
- **Do Not Allow Smart Card Device Redirection**—Essentially prevents using a smart card to connect to the terminal server. By default, this is disabled, so you can use a smart card to log on to the server by inserting the card in your local card reader (redirected so the server can view it). If this smart card redirection is disabled then to use a smart card to log on, you would have to put the smart card in a card reader physically attached to the terminal server, which kind of defeats the purpose.

Encryption and Security

These settings are covered later in this chapter in the section "Security Enhancements."

Licensing

These settings are used to configure the behavior of a terminal services license server:

- **License Server Security Group**—Allows control over to which terminal servers a terminal services license servers will issue licenses. Enabling this setting creates a Terminal Services Computers local groups. The terminal server license server will issue licenses only to those terminal servers that are a member of this group.
- **Prevent License Upgrade**—Prevents the terminal services license server from issuing Windows .NET Client Access Licenses (CALs) to clients attempting to connect to Windows 2000 terminal servers.

Session Directory

These settings are covered later in this chapter in the section "Terminal Server Session Directory."

Special Settings

The following settings cannot be configured via group policy:

- **Permission Compatibility - Full Security or Relaxed Security**—This setting determines the terminal services compatibility level and is configured when Terminal Server is installed. Full Security increases the security of the terminal server by restricting user access to various Registry keys.
- **NIC for Session Directory to Use for Redirection**—Tells the Session Directory which IP address to use for client connections. Because this is server specific, it has to be configured on a per-server basis using Terminal Services Configuration.
- **Enable TS per NIC**—Tellsthe server which NIC to listen to for terminal server requests. Because this is server specific, it has to be configured on a per-server basis using Terminal Services Configuration.

In addition to being able to centrally manage terminal server settings with group policy, Windows Server 2003 server provides interfaces for configuration with WMI and ADSI. By querying and manipulating the appropriate objects, the previously listed settings can be configured in batch files or scripts. For more information on WMI or ADSI scripting, see www.microsoft.com/technet/scriptcenter.

All these new management interfaces make configuring terminal services and managing them centrally much easier. They can also be used for managing Remote Desktop settings on

Windows XP. This is particularly useful for implementing Remote Desktop for Administration throughout your organization.

Remote Desktop Protocol 5.1

The Remote Desktop Protocol is the communication protocol used by terminal services and remote desktop. The protocol determines what is sent between client and server. At a bare minimum, it passes the video display from the server to the client and the keyboard and mouse inputs from the client to the server. Previous versions of the RDP protocol (RDP 4.0 in Windows NT 4 Terminal Server and RDP 5.0 in Windows 2000) were limited in functionality as to the type of traffic it could pass. This usually meant that corporations purchased the Citrix Metaframe add-on to gain the additional functionality and performance. Windows Server 2003 uses version 5.1 of the RDP protocol, which provides several new features and enhancements.

Local Resource Redirection

One of the new features is the capability to redirect client resources to the remote terminal server. Windows 2000 allows mapping of the local client's printer to the terminal server (provided the appropriate printer driver is installed). This is still supported in Windows Server 2003, but the new protocol supports remapping of other resources—local drives, COM ports, and printers. For example, a client (CLIENT1) with a C: drive (COM1) and LPT1 can connect to a terminal server (NETSERVER) and have those resources available from the remote system, as shown in Figure 11.5 (provided the appropriate options are selected on the client and the terminal server allows it).

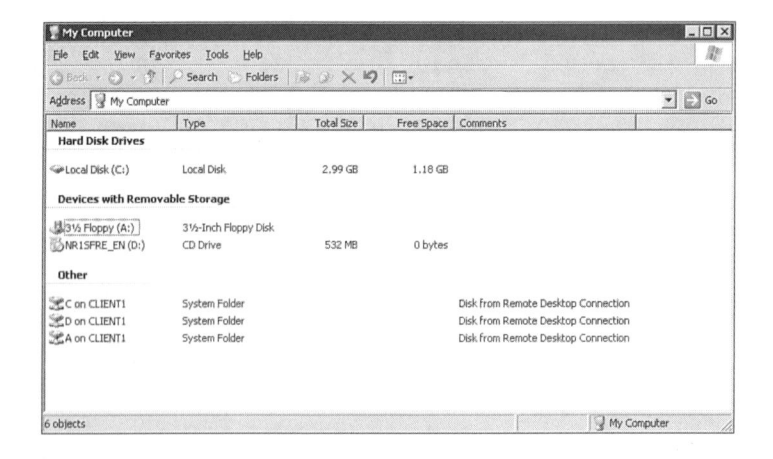

Figure 11.5 Access local resources from the remote terminal server.

> **Note** Because making local drives available to a remote machine is a potential security risk, a warning message is displayed if this option is selected.

In addition to allowing the remapping of other local resources, the mapping of printer drivers has been enhanced. Now it not only provides for detection and automatic installation of local printers if the print driver is installed, but also attempts to locate near-miss printer drivers. Therefore, it attempts to install a compatible driver even if the exact driver for the local printer is not installed on the remote machine. Additionally, you can put the drivers you want it to use in a particular directory and tell it to use that directory by specifying the trusted driver path Registry setting.

The following are some additional improvements to the client experience provided by the RDP 5.1 protocol. Each of these options can be configured in the Remote Desktop Connection clients. Some of these options can also be enabled or disabled or configured with default settings via group policy:

- **Sound Card Redirection**—With this option, you can choose to Bring To This Computer. This redirects the sound from the server to the local machine and enables you to run applications with sound on the server and hear them. The other options are to Leave At Remote Computer and Do Not Play.
- **Enhanced Color and Resolution**—Now supports up to true (24-bit) color and the maximum resolution supported by client video(640×480 to 1600×1200). Additionally, the client automatically detects the color and resolution supported by the local computer and attempts to size appropriately. As mentioned previously, a Full Screen mode is available that gives the look and feel of being at the remote computer.
- **Shared Clipboard**—This server-side configurable option enables clients to cut and copy items on the local system and paste them in the terminal server session, or vice versa. For example, you could be working in a document on the terminal server, copy a paragraph, and then paste it in a document on your local system. For that matter, you could even cut or copy the entire document file itself and paste it to the local system. This, coupled with the ability to access your local drives (via drive redirection), makes working on remote systems much easier because you still have access to local resources.
- **Enhanced Performance in Low Bandwidth Environments**—Additional options are available in RDP 5.1 and are configurable in the Remote Desktop Connection application for improving performance, particularly over low-bandwidth connections. These are configured via the Experiences tab of the Remote Desktop Connection client, as shown in Figure 11.6.

> **Caution** Enabling each of these options generates more network traffic between the client and the remote systems, which degrades perceived performance.

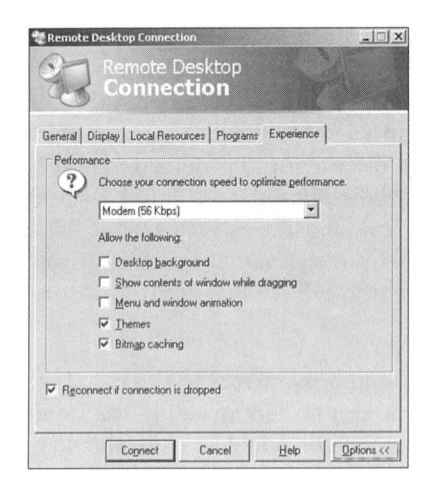

Figure 11.6 Configure Experience settings for low-bandwidth environments.

To help the user choose the appropriate settings based on the connection speed, there are default recommended settings for certain environments: Modem (56Kbps), Broadband (128Kbps–1.5Mbps), and LAN (10Mbps or higher), or you can create your own (Custom). For example, the Modem (56Kbps) setting enables Themes and Bitmap Caching but disables all the rest.

Is RDP Ready for Prime Time?

So, is RDP 5.1 good enough to rival the Citrix Metaframe protocol, Independent Computing Architecture (ICA)? Certainly. But will it completely replace ICA in all implementations? Probably not. RDP 5.1 now provides most of the commonly used features that made ICA superior to RDP. There are still some features that Metaframe provides that might be of benefit, such as support for protocols other than TCP/IP, the capability to directly dial in to the application server without connecting to a network first, and so on. The determination of whether to use Citrix Metaframe (and the ICA protocol) or stick with terminal services is a judgment call as to whether the extra cost is worth the extra features. Generally, for simple remote administration of your servers, the Remote Desktop for Administration and the RDP 5.1 protocol are usually more than adequate. For terminal server application servers, on the other hand, serious thought needs to be given to how they will be used before a determination can be made. Currently, no Metaframe add-on to Windows Server 2003 is available. But then, as of this writing, Windows Server 2003 hasn't been released yet either. Look for Citrix to make a Metaframe add-on soon after Windows Server 2003 is released. Then you can make your final determination.

Security Enhancements

In Windows 2000, to give a user access to connect to a terminal server, you must modify the permissions on the RDP Connection Configuration of each terminal. This usually means creating a group (or groups) and granting them the appropriate access on each and every terminal server. In Windows Server 2003, this is already done for you. By default, a local group called Remote Desktop Users has User Access and Guest Access permissions to the terminal server. By simply adding users or groups to this local group, you can grant users access to log on to the terminal server. Of course, you can still manually modify the individual server configuration settings to get more granular control. To get further centralized control, you can manage the membership of the Remote Desktop Users group using the Restricted Groups group policy at the domain level.

As with Windows 2000, when installing terminal services (Application Server Mode), you are given the option for compatibility level. This adjusts the permissions on Registry keys, system files, and so on. With Windows 2000, the choice is between Permissions Compatible with Windows 2000 Users and Permissions Compatible with Terminal Server 4.0 Users. With Windows 2003, the choice is between Full Security or Relaxed Security. It is, of course, recommended that you use the Windows .NET compatibility mode to provide a more secure environment.

By default, Windows Server 2003 terminal servers attempt to encrypt client sessions with 128-bit (RC4) bidirectional encryption. Whether the terminal server will respond to clients that don't support 128-bit encryption can be configured with the Set Client Connection Encryption Level group policy setting. After it's enabled, the options are Client Compatible or High Level. High Level accepts connections only from clients that support 128-bit encryption; Client Compatible allows connections with whatever encryption algorithm the client supports. By specifying 128-bit security, you can ensure that the communications between client and terminal server are secure.

In addition to configuring the encryption level the terminal server will use, you can also use group policy to configure the RPC session security. The RPC Security Policy\Secure Server (Require Security) group policy settings allows RPC connections only with trusted clients and only over authenticated and encrypted sessions. This prevents unauthorized machines (outside your organization) from even establishing a connection.

Additionally, you can configure the server (via group policy or the Terminal Server Connection Configuration) to always prompt clients for a password on connection. This is available in Windows 2000 (but not as a group policy) and prevents users from being able to connect to the terminal server via passwords stored in the client settings. This therefore helps to secure the terminal services environment by forcing users to type in a password to authenticate.

The RDP 5.1 protocol adds another enhancement to make authentication to the terminal server more secure: smart card redirection support. This feature enables the terminal server to use the local machine's smart card reader. By redirecting the local smart card reader to the terminal server, a remote user can log on to the terminal server by inserting a smart card (in the local card reader) and typing in the PIN. The smart card reader verifies that the PIN matches the PIN stored on the card and then transmits the digital certificate for the user ID to be authenticated against the domain. This is a more secure form of authentication because the user's ID and password are never transmitted on the network and the physical card must be inserted.

Another new security feature for terminal server is the ability to use Software Restriction Policies. Although not specifically a terminal server enhancement, the new Software Restriction Policies section of group policy can be used to protect the terminal server environment. Software Restriction Policies can be used to specify whether certain file types are allowed to run, as well as to specify certain levels of permissions for various Registry keys.

Note | Software Restriction Policies replaces AppSec, the Application Security tool from NT 4.0 Terminal Server or the Windows 2000 Resource Kit.

▶ For more information on Software Restriction Policies, **see** "New Group Policies," **p. 93**.

Terminal Server Session Directory

Windows Server 2003 provides enhancements to terminal services to scale it for the enterprise. A new feature available in Enterprise Server and Datacenter Server is called Terminal Server Session Directory, and it provides the capabilities to use network load balancing or other third-party load balancing services. This enables the creation of terminal server clusters, or *farms*. The network load balancing service provides a virtual network interface card (NIC) that is shared among up to 32 cluster members. This provides TCP/IP load balancing across all machines in the cluster. When a request comes in to the virtual NIC (the cluster NIC), it is directed to any of the servers in the cluster (presumably the least busy).

▶ For more information on network load-balanced clusters, **see** Chapter 12, "Clustering," **p. 199**.

The Problem with Clustering Terminal Servers

The problem with load balancing terminal servers is how to handle disconnected sessions. If a user drops a terminal server connection (either voluntarily or involuntarily) without logging off, the session remains active on the terminal server as a disconnected session. The disconnected session is still active, and any applications continue to run. When the user attempts to connect to the terminal server again, she is reconnected to her disconnected session. It essentially is as if the user simply walked away from the console for a while and came back. She is still logged on, and any applications she was running are still running. This is particularly useful for kicking off long-running applications or reports. The user logs on, kicks it off, and then comes back a couple hours later to obtain the results.

In a load-balanced cluster, if a user disconnects from one terminal server, that session is still active on the server. When she attempts to reconnect to the cluster, her request is load-balanced among all available servers again. Thus there is no guarantee that she will be routed back to the server with her disconnected session. Depending on the number of servers in the cluster, the probability could be as low as 1 in 32. The net result is that she would connect to a different server, establish a new session, log on to the new server, and get a fresh console as if she were logging on for the first time. This can be disconcerting for the user, especially if she had been running an application in the previously disconnected session. Not only would it probably cause her to panic, but she might take action (such as rerunning the application or report) that could interfere with what's going on in the other session (remember it is still running). At the very least, it wastes resources because now two sessions are running—one on the original server and one on the new server. If the user disconnects and then reconnects, she could start a session on another cluster member, and another, and so on. The Terminal Servers Session Directory is designed to prevent this problem.

The Solution

Terminal Server Session Directory is simply a database that resides on a server. It could be any server, not necessarily a member of the cluster. In fact, it is recommended that the session directory be located on a highly available server outside the load-balanced cluster, so all members of the cluster can easily access it. The Session Directory server does not need to be a Windows Server 2003 Enterprise or Datacenter Edition—it can be a Standard server, although the cluster members (terminal servers) that will be querying the Session Directory database do need to be Enterprise or Datacenter servers. Figure 11.7 shows a typical terminal server cluster configuration with multiple clusters accessing a single Session Directory server. The Session Directory server itself could be a Microsoft Cluster Server (MSCS) cluster, in which case you would need Enterprise Edition or Datacenter Edition.

The database on the Session Directory server maintains a list of disconnected user sessions and the terminal servers to which they are connected. When a client attempts to connect to a terminal server that is a member of a load-balanced Session Directory-enabled cluster, the Terminal Services Connection Manager queries the Session Directory the cluster is configured to use to determine whether any disconnected sessions exist for the user. If so, it routes the logon to the terminal server with the disconnected session and updates the Session Directory database; if not, the logon request is load balanced as usual.

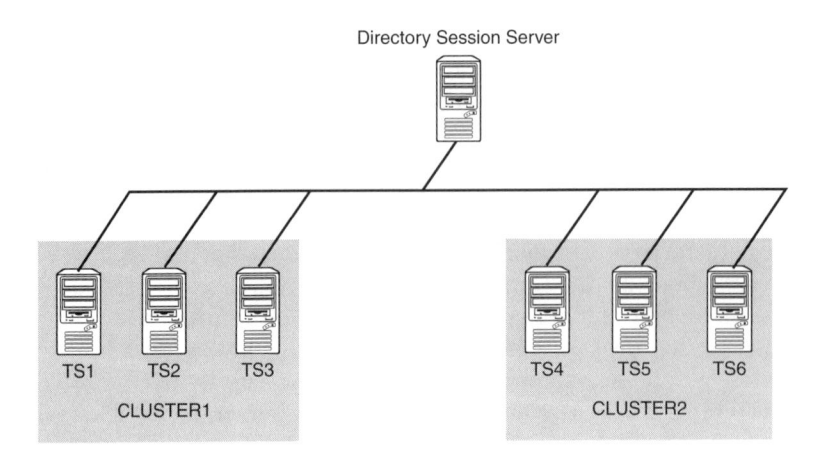

Figure 11.7 The Terminal Server Session Directory architecture.

Installing the Session Directory server itself is fairly straightforward. Simply start the Session Directory service on the Windows Server 2003 that you want to maintain the database. You should also set the service startup to automatic (the default is disabled), so it will restart whenever the computer is rebooted. When the Session Directory service starts, it looks for a local group called Session Directory Computers. If the group doesn't exist, it creates it. This group is used to grant access to the session directory, so you should add the computer accounts of all the terminal servers that will use this computer for their session directory to the Session Directory Computers group.

The terminal servers themselves also need to be configured to use Session Directory to tell them to use the Session Directory and provide cluster naming information. The terminal servers are configured to use Session Directory by any of the management methods mentioned earlier in this chapter (group policy, WMI [either script or WMIC command line], or the Terminal Services Configuration console). As shown previously, configuration with group policy provides more centralized control and is the recommended method. Several settings must be configured; in group policy, they are found by selecting **Computer Configuration Settings**, **Windows Components**, **Terminal Services**, **Session Directory**. They are as follows:

- **Join Session Directory**—Tells the terminal server to use a Session Directory.
- **Session Directory Server**—Tells the terminal server which Session Directory server to use.
- **Session Directory Cluster Name**—Associates the terminal server with a particular terminal server cluster. Session Directory maintains connection information based on the terminal server clusters. This enables a single Session Directory server to support multiple load-balanced terminal server clusters.

- **Terminal Server IP Address Redirection**—Determines how the client actually connects to the terminal servers in the cluster. If enabled (the default), you should still configure the particular NIC (IP address) for client redirections on the individual terminal servers.

Terminal Server IP Address Redirection

The purpose of Terminal Server IP Address Redirection needs further explanation. When a client attempts to connect to a terminal server cluster, the normal process is as follows:

1. A client connects to the IP address of the cluster; let's call it CLUSTER1.
2. This request is load balanced and directed to the IP address of one of the terminal servers in the cluster; let's call it TS1. The client then logs on directly to TS1. The user disconnects from TS1.
3. Later, the user tries to reconnect to CLUSTER1.
4. The request is load balanced, but this time it is directed to TS3.
5. The client logs on directly to TS3, which (because it is configured to use a Session Directory) sends a query to the Session Directory server to see whether a previous connection exists. One does (the one on TS1), so the Session Directory responds and tells TS3 to redirect the client's logon request to TS1.
6. The user's session is redirected to TS1, he is logged on directly to TS1, and he picks up his disconnected session.

Note that throughout this process, the client was logging on directly to the terminal server in question (TS1 or TS3). The load balancing was simply providing the IP address with which he should connect. In certain load-balance solutions or scenarios, the client might not be able to directly connect to the terminal server IP address. In this case, the client must connect to the terminal servers using the virtual NIC of the cluster. The way this is accomplished is through the use of tokens: When the terminal server queries the Session Directory and a disconnected session exists, that information is passed to the client via a *token*. The client then presents the token to the virtual NIC of the cluster and gets routed to the appropriate server (through the virtual NIC). To use this method, the terminal servers and the load-balancing technology need to support the passing of tokens (Windows Server 2003 and the Remote Desktop for Connection client, of course, do), and you need to disable the Terminal Server IP Address Redirection setting.

Terminal Server Session Directory makes operating terminal servers in a clustered configuration more viable. This improvement, combined with the capability to centralize administration with group policy and the enhancements to the underlying communications protocol (RDP), make the new terminal services in Windows Server 2003 more attractive for enterprise

198 Chapter 11 Terminal Services

deployments. These are just some of the many improvements in Windows Server 2003 for scaling Windows for larger organizations. As you'll see in the next chapter, Microsoft has further enhanced its clustering offerings.

1. Initial request.
2. Load balanced to TS1.
3. Subsequent request (after disconnect).
4. Load balanced to TS3.
5. Query Session Directory. Determines that session on TS1 is active.
6. Subsequent requests to TS1.

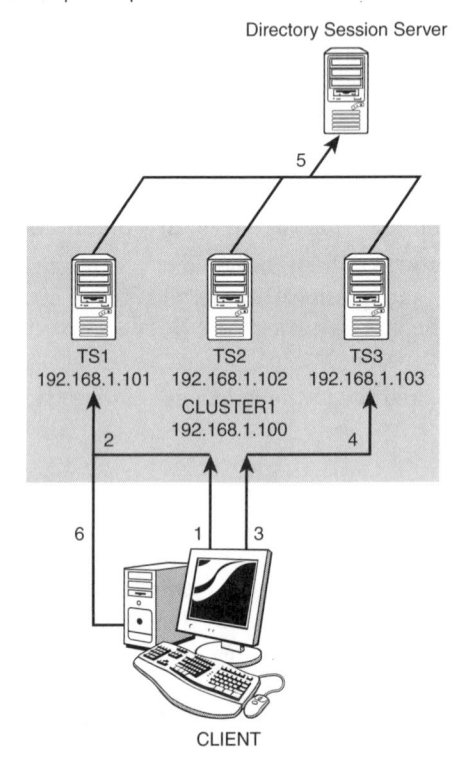

Figure 11.8 An example of Terminal Server IP address redirection.

12

CLUSTERING

In This Chapter

- Understanding clustering terminology, **page 200**.
- The new Cluster Service, **page 201**.
- Using Network Load Balancing, **page 207**.
- Clustering Windows components, **page 213**.

What's New

Windows Server 2003 doesn't introduce many new clustering concepts, but it does extend clustering capabilities throughout most of the Windows Server 2003 family. New clusterable applications and services are also available, making creating high-availability network services easier.

One of the most important changes to clustering is that the Cluster Service is now available on three of the four Windows Server 2003 editions: Standard, Enterprise, and Datacenter. Cluster Service clusters can also contain up to eight nodes, double the number of Windows 2000. Note that Standard Edition supports only two-node clusters.

Windows's other major clustering technology, Network Load Balancing (NLB), is now available in four editions of Windows Server 2003, not just Enterprise (formerly Advanced) and Datacenter, as was the case in Windows 2000. Network Load Balancing is a crucial technology for deploying scalable, high-workload Web sites and .NET Web Services, so it's easy to understand why Microsoft chose to include the technology in all editions.

Both of these clustering technologies have been available in prior versions of Windows. However, some of the details of their operation, as well as how they're managed, have been updated for Windows Server 2003. We'll cover both technologies in this chapter, including detailed, step-by-step instructions for using them.

Clustering Terminology

Unfortunately, Microsoft hasn't brought any new logic to how its cluster technologies are named. To avoid mass confusion, you must realize that Microsoft offers two distinct clustering technologies. Each is designed for a different purpose, each is more or less incompatible with the other, and the two have nothing in common—yet they're both called *clustering*. They are

- **Cluster Service**—This clustering is designed for high availability. Essentially, between two and eight servers function entirely on their own but are also capable of taking on the tasks of another server in the cluster should one fail. This behavior is similar to how most offices work: Joe and Bob normally have their own job tasks. However, when Joe goes on vacation, Bob gets to wear both hats and perform Joe's job tasks along with his own. In Windows terms, Joe and Bob are *nodes* in a Cluster Service cluster.
- **Network Load Balancing**—This clustering is designed for high availability and scalability. Each server in the cluster—up to 32 are possible—is completely independent but performs the exact same work as the other servers. Work is more or less evenly distributed between them. In office terminology, this is similar to a customer service call center. Each call center employee can handle the same tasks, and the phone system directs incoming calls to the next available representative.

You'll find the Cluster Service most often used to cluster enterprise back-end servers, such as Exchange Server computers or SQL Server computers. Generally, companies build so-called *active-active* clusters, in which each computer is an independent, fully functional server. Should one server fail, however, another server in the cluster picks up the failed server's work. You can also create *active-passive* clusters, in which one server performs useful work and the other simply waits for the active server to fail. At that point, the passive server seizes control and becomes active, performing useful work.

NLB, on the other hand, is most often used in Web server applications. Large groups, or *farms*, of Web servers are configured to use NLB. Each server in the farm (or cluster) can perform the same work, and incoming user requests are distributed to the server that's least busy at the time. If the farm becomes overworked, new servers can be added at any time. NLB provides high availability because, if a server in the farm fails, other servers are already performing the same work. Therefore, users are able to continue working with the farm, if not with a particular server.

Cluster Service

The Cluster Service is a special piece of software that runs on Windows Server 2003 and manages the relationships between the servers in the cluster, which are referred to as *nodes*. You don't manually install Cluster Service like you did in prior versions of Windows; you simply use the Cluster Administrator console to create a new cluster. We'll walk through that procedure later in this chapter.

Windows Server 2003 clusters are a bit picky about who they'll allow in a cluster. If you've built the first cluster node on Windows Server 2003, Enterprise Edition, all other nodes that are running Windows Server 2003 must also be running Enterprise Edition. The same restriction applies to the Standard and Datacenter editions; the edition of the first cluster node sets the edition that all other Windows Server 2003 nodes must follow. However, you can have clusters that have a mix of nodes running Windows Server 2003 and Windows 2000 Server.

You can build the following three types of clusters:

- **Single node**—In this type of cluster, only one node exists. Essentially, all clusters start out this way: You create the first node and then add more nodes. However, clusters with only one node don't have any failover capabilities, which defeats the purpose of clustering. The only practical use for a single-node cluster is to experiment with the Cluster Service in a lab or classroom.
- **Single quorum device**—The *quorum,* as we explain in the next section, is a special resource the cluster uses to store the cluster configuration. The quorum is accessible to all nodes in this type of cluster, generally through an external drive array physically attached to each cluster member.
- **Majority node set**—A new type of cluster for Windows Server 2003, this stores the quorum across the nodes, and the nodes might not be physically attached to one another. This type of clustering enables you to create geographically dispersed clusters, but setting them up is very complex because Windows is incredibly picky about little implementation details. Microsoft recommends that you use this type of cluster only if it is provided preconfigured from a server manufacturer, and we tend to concur.

Tip | Most major server computer manufacturers offer preconfigured cluster packages you can buy. These are far and away the best way to get a cluster into your environment because manually setting up your server hardware to support a cluster can be a difficult, time-consuming task. If you decide to build a cluster from scratch, make absolutely certain that your hardware is on Microsoft's special Cluster Hardware Compatibility List (ask the hardware manufacturer about this), and make sure you have the hardware manufacturer's specific directions for setting up a cluster with its equipment.

The next section discusses some of the basic concepts you'll need to start building your own clusters.

Cluster Service Concepts

Imagine you have a single server you want to make into a SQL Server computer. You can simply install Windows and then install SQL Server. Suppose that, for reasons of your own, you install Windows on one hard drive and install SQL Server onto a completely separate RAID array. Now imagine that you make that RAID array an external array, connected to the computer by a small computer system interface (SCSI) cable or by fibre channel. This shouldn't be that hard to imagine; most database servers are set up in this fashion.

Conceptually, all you need to do now to build a cluster is attach a second server to the external drive array. You'll install Windows and SQL Server on that server, too. However, SQL Server's services will remain stopped, and the two servers will communicate via a special service, sending a *heartbeat* signal to one another. If the first server stops sending the heartbeat, the second server knows that something has gone wrong. It immediately seizes control of the external drive array, starts the SQL Server services, and takes over where its failed companion left off.

Clustering Details

Even though this example omits a few crucial details, it's essentially how an active-passive cluster operates. Active-active clusters are more difficult to conceptualize. Imagine that you have two servers, each running SQL Server and each connected to two external drive arrays. One server owns a single external drive array and stores the SQL Server databases there. If one server fails, the other one detects it and seizes control of its external drive array (now owning two drive arrays total). The second server starts a second copy of SQL Server and takes over where the failed server left off. Now, the remaining server is effectively two SQL Server computers, all running in one box.

> For details on how the Cluster Service operates and handles failovers, visit www.samspublishing.com and enter this book's ISBN number (no hyphens or parenthesis) in the Search field; then click the book cover image to access the book details page. Click the Web Resources link in the More Information section, and locate article ID# **A011201**.

Each cluster, then, is comprised of a variety of resources, which can include the following:

- **One or more IP addresses**—These are addresses users and client computers use to communicate with the cluster. Each cluster node has its own private IP addresses, as well, which nobody really uses.

- **One or more computer names**—As with IP addresses, these belong to the cluster and not to any one cluster node. Users and client computers communicate with these names, and not with the nodes' private computer names.

- **A quorum resource**—This resource contains all the information about the cluster's resources, which node owns each resource, and so forth.

- **Logical drives**—These represent shared drive arrays, which can be external SCSI arrays or fibre channel arrays.
- **Application services**—This might be the DHCP service, SQL Server, or any other clustered application.

Each resource can be owned by only one node at a time. Each resource does, however, have a list of all nodes that could possibly own the resource. When the node that owns a resource fails, the resource's other possible owners detect the failure and one of them takes ownership of the resource. Administrators can also manually transfer resource ownership from one node to another. This enables you to transfer workload off of one node, letting you shut down the node for maintenance without interrupting your users' work.

Resources can have dependencies. For example, most clustered applications require TCP/IP (other network protocols aren't supported under clustering), so a node can't own an application resource unless the node already owns the shared TCP/IP address the application requires. To keep dependencies easy to manage, Windows lets you organize resources into groups. Resource groups can be transferred from node to node as a single unit, so you don't have to worry about forgetting a dependency when transferring ownership of an application to another node.

Creating a New Cluster

To create a new cluster, first make sure your hardware is ready. Then, launch Cluster Administrator on any Windows Server 2003 computer and follow these steps:

Caution | These steps assume that your hardware and device drivers are already properly configured for, and compatible with, clustering. Don't assume that the hardware drivers normally used in Windows Server 2003 will support clustering because that's often not the case. Contact your hardware manufacturer's support division for detailed instructions on how to build a cluster and for the correct device drivers.

1. If your cluster nodes have a shared storage device, such as an external SCSI drive array, power down all nodes except the first one.
2. In Cluster Administrator, select **File**, **New**, **Cluster**.
3. Enter the domain in which the first cluster node exists and its name. This step is necessary to identify the first node because you don't have to perform this process on the first node—you can perform it on any computer capable of running Cluster Administrator.
4. Enter a name for the cluster; this name must not conflict with any other NetBIOS names on your network.
5. Provide an IP address to be used by the cluster. The cluster can't use DHCP to obtain an address, so be sure the address you provide isn't in use on your network and won't be issued by a DHCP server to another computer.

Note You must specify an IP address that's in the same range as the first node's private IP address. Otherwise, the wizard won't be capable of determining the correct subnet mask and you'll see an error message prompting you to enter a different IP address.

6. Enter the credentials the Cluster Service should use, as shown in Figure 12.1. This account will be granted local Administrator privileges on the node.

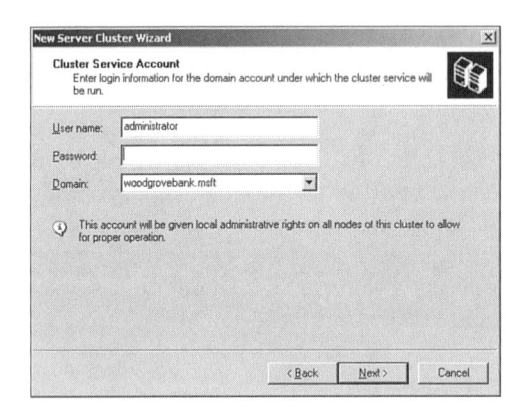

Figure 12.1 The account you provide cannot use a blank password.

Tip For smooth operation of your new cluster, use a domain user account for the Cluster Service. All nodes in the cluster should specify the same account.

7. Wait for the wizard to install and configure the Cluster Service.

After your first cluster node is fully functional, you can add more nodes to the cluster. Simply right-click the cluster in Cluster Administrator. Then, from the pop-up menu, select **New**, **Node**.

Cluster Administrator

You'll use Cluster Administrator to manage your clusters. With it, you can add and remove cluster resources and resource groups, add and remove nodes, and transfer resource ownership from one node to another.

To add a new resource group, just right-click a cluster and select **New** from the pop-up menu; then select **Group**. Enter the name and details for the new group, and you're ready to go. To add a new resource to an existing group, right-click the group and select **New**; then select **Resource** from the pop-up menu. You'll see a dialog box similar to the one in Figure 12.2, which allows you to specify the type of resource you want to add.

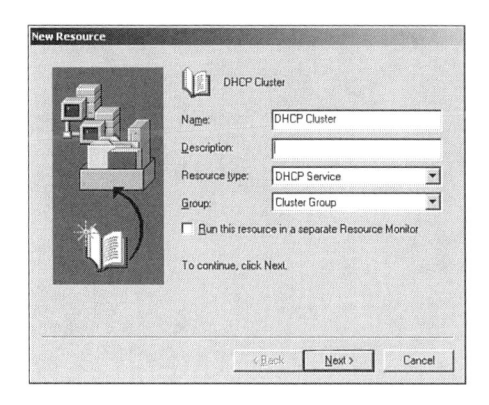

Figure 12.2 You can add any type of new resource from this dialog box.

In the New Resource dialog box, you'll specify the following:

- A name for the new resource.
- A brief description of the resource. This is especially useful when you have multiple resources of the same type because it enables other administrators to more easily figure out which is which.
- The resource type, which can include clusterable Windows services, file shares, and so forth. We'll discuss those in the next section.
- A group to which the new resource will belong.

After clicking Next, you can specify the nodes that are allowed to own the resources. For example, the DHCP Service resource can be owned only by nodes that have the DHCP Service already installed, so you use that condition to limit the potential owners for a DHCP Service resource. After specifying the potential owners, click **Next**.

Last, you'll specify any resources on which your new resource depends. As shown in Figure 12.3, you can choose from all existing resources as possible dependencies, and you typically must specify at least one resource of the Storage type. That's because most resources, especially applications and services, have to store their data somewhere. In a cluster, that data must be on a cluster-owned (shared) storage location, making the application or service dependent on the availability of that storage location.

Tip | Generally, your resource should be in the same resource group as any resources on which it depends. That way, the entire group can be transferred from node to node as a single unit.

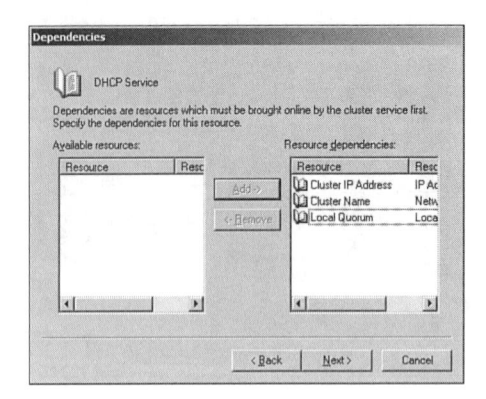

Figure 12.3 Specify only the resources necessary for your new resource to run properly.

Transferring resources from one node to another is easy. If you want to perform a transfer that tests your resources' capability to fail over from one node to another, simply right-click a resource group and select **Initiate Failure** from the pop-up menu. The resource will immediately fail and transfer to another possible owner.

> Tip: Be sure that all resources have at least two nodes as possible owners. Otherwise, a failed resource won't be capable of transferring to another node.

Note that resources have their own properties that affect their behaviors. To access these properties, right-click a resource and select **Properties** from the pop-up menu. The Properties dialog box enables you to change the resource's name, description, and list of possible owners; you can also change the resource's dependencies. As shown in Figure 12.4, you can also configure advanced properties. For example, you can configure the Cluster Service to automatically try to restart a service any time it stops, and you can configure how often the Cluster Service checks a service to see whether it's responding.

Resource groups have properties, too, which you can access by right-clicking the group and selecting Properties from the pop-up menu. Group properties include *failover* and *failback* policies, which are defined as follows:

- **Failover policy**—Determines how many times a group is allowed to fail from node to node within a given time period. The default is 10 times in 6 hours. If the failovers exceed this threshold, the Cluster Service assumes the group is not working correctly and takes it offline. You must manually restore the group to service after correcting its problems.
- **Failback policy**—Disabled by default, this allows the Cluster Service to move a group back to its original cluster node. You can either allow an immediate failback, in which case the group returns to its original node (referred to as the *preferred node*) as soon as that node becomes available or specify that failback occur only during certain hours.

Specifying hours for failback allows the group to remain where it is until a relatively idle period when users won't be affected by the failback.

Cluster Administrator includes a comprehensive help file that can provide step-by-step instructions for other cluster operations.

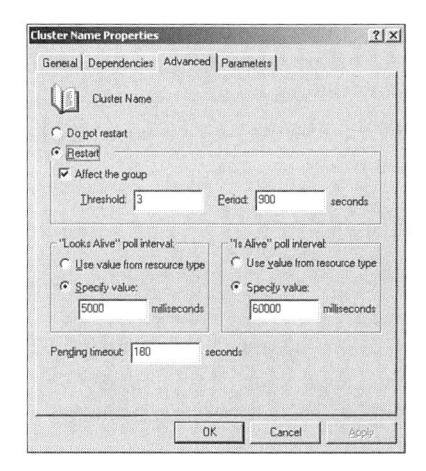

Figure 12.4 The default values for the advanced properties are sufficient in most environments.

Network Load Balancing

Network Load Balancing used to be included in the Advanced (now named Enterprise) and Datacenter versions of Windows. With Windows Server 2003, NLB is available in all editions.

Note | NLB is also available in Microsoft Application Center 2000. The version of NLB included in Application Center is different from the one in Windows Server 2003, and that version is managed very differently.

NLB Concepts

In NLB, each cluster member is a separate, individual computer connected to the other cluster members only by a network. Cluster members don't share storage space as in a Cluster Service cluster.

User requests are sent to one or more IP addresses that are shared by all cluster members. All cluster members receive all requests sent to the cluster, but only one cluster member responds to each request. NLB determines which member will respond based on a set of internal rules and request affinity. The NLB service on each cluster member constantly communicates with the NLB services on the other cluster members, exchanging information about how busy each cluster member is from moment to moment. That workload information factors into NLB's decision about which member will handle incoming requests. NLB uses the following rules to make that decision:

- Any members that are offline or haven't recently responded to other cluster members are removed from consideration.
- If the request has been received by a known client and affinity is enabled, the server with affinity for the client handles it.
- If the request is from a new client or affinity is disabled, the least-busy member with the highest priority handles the request.

You configure many of these properties, including priority and affinity, when you set up a new cluster.

> For details on how NLB operates and distributes requests between cluster members, visit www.samspublishing.com and enter this book's ISBN number (no hyphens or parenthesis) in the Search field; then click the book cover image to access the book details page. Click the Web Resources link in the More Information section, and locate article ID# **A011202**.

Creating a New NLB Cluster

To create a new NLB cluster, open the Network Load Balancing Manager console. Then follow these steps:

1. From the Cluster menu, select **New**.
2. As shown in Figure 12.5, enter an IP address, a subnet mask, and a name for the new cluster. You can also choose to enable or disable remote control for the cluster and configure the cluster for Unicast or Multicast mode.

> Caution | Remote control is disabled by default and doesn't prevent you from managing remote cluster members by using NLB Manager. NLB's remote control feature is a serious security risk and should generally be left disabled.

> For more information on Unicast and Multicast modes, visit www.samspublishing.com and enter this book's ISBN number (no hyphens or parenthesis) in the Search field; then click the book cover image to access the book details page. Click the Web Resources link in the More Information section, and locate article ID# **A011203**.

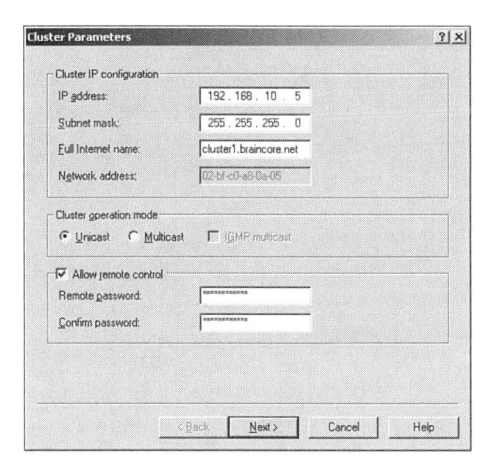

Figure 12.5 Configure the cluster's basic properties and IP address.

3. If the cluster will use any additional IP addresses, enter them as shown in Figure 12.6. Web servers with multiple Web sites, for example, often use multiple IP addresses that you'll need to identify here.

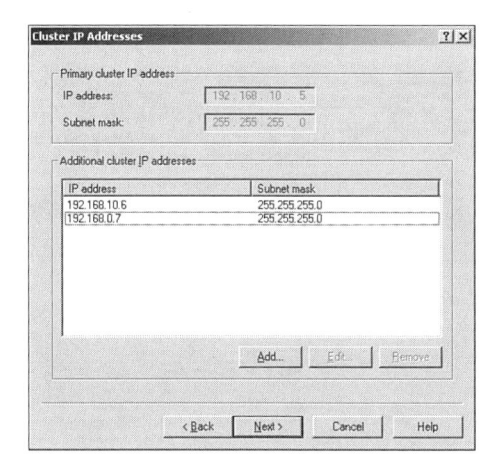

Figure 12.6 All IP addresses must be static; NLB doesn't use DHCP to acquire addresses.

4. Specify port rules and affinity modes. By default, NLB enables itself for all TCP and UDB ports and sets Single Client affinity mode. Figure 12.7 shows the defaults, and we'll discuss changing them in the next section.

210 Chapter 12 Clustering

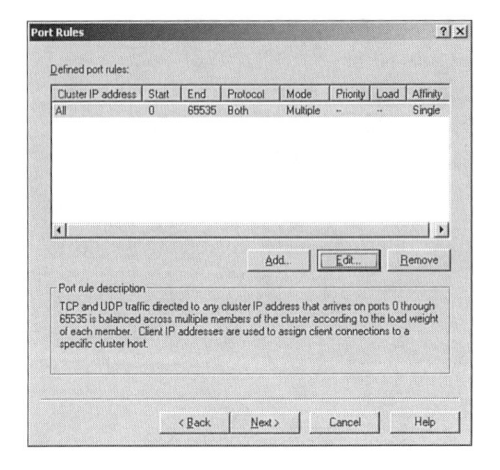

Figure 12.7 Web servers typically use these default settings.

5. Select the network interface NLB will use. In servers with multiple network adapters, NLB typically runs on only one adapter.
6. Wait as NLB configures itself on the new cluster member. Be sure to check the log messages, shown in Figure 12.8, for any errors that might occur.

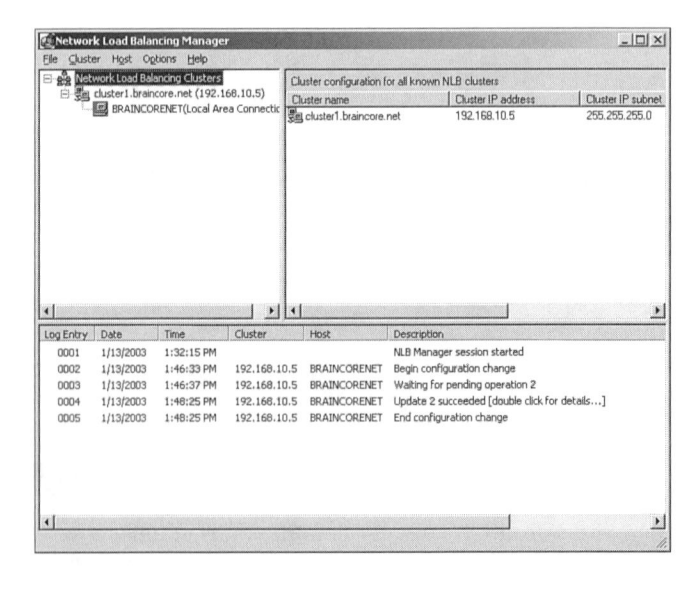

Figure 12.8 NLB displays a running status of its progress as it configures the new member and cluster.

You're done, and you're ready to add new members to your new cluster. Simply right-click the cluster itself and select **Add Host to Cluster** from the pop-up menu.

Configuring NLB Port Rules and Affinity

You can decide to which TCP and UDP ports NLB will respond. This enables your cluster members to run a clustered application, such as a Web server on TCP port 80, and to run non-clustered applications that NLB ignores. You can also configure each port range with a different affinity setting.

To control a cluster's ports, right-click the cluster and select **Control Ports** from the pop-up menu. For each configured port range, you can do the following:

- Enable or disable the range by clicking the appropriate buttons. Disabled ranges are ignored by NLB.
- Drain the range by clicking the Drain button. Draining instructs NLB to refuse new connections but to allow cluster members to finish any work for connections they've already accepted. This is a great way to take a cluster offline.

You can also edit the port settings. To do so, right-click the cluster and select **Properties** from the pop-up menu. Then, select the **Port Rules** tab. Click the appropriate button to add, edit, or remove any existing port ranges. When you add or edit a range, you'll see a dialog box similar to the one in Figure 12.9.

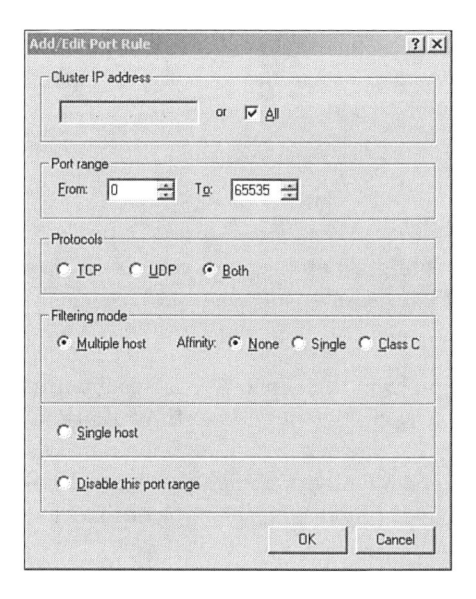

Figure 12.9 Each cluster can support multiple port ranges, as long as they don't overlap.

Port ranges have the following properties:

- **Affinity setting**—This controls how NLB load balances incoming requests to this port range. Available options are
  - **None**—In this mode, all incoming requests are load balanced across the cluster. This is appropriate when cluster members aren't maintaining any information between user requests or when the information is being maintained in a back-end database server accessible to all cluster members.
  - **Single**—In this mode, requests from new IP addresses are load balanced normally. From then on, the same server handles all requests from a given IP address. If servers are maintaining state information locally, this is a good setting for an intranet. However, Internet clients might seem to be coming from multiple IP addresses because of their service providers' network address translations, so this affinity mode won't work.
  - **Class C**—In this mode, each range of 253 IP addresses in a Class C range is handled by a single cluster member. This mode largely defeats load balancing, but it ensures that Internet users will always connect to the server that's maintaining their state information locally.
- **A port range**—This is expressed as a starting port number and an ending port number. Port numbers in this range are handled by NLB and use the affinity mode designated.
- **A protocol**—This can be TCP, UDP, or both. It specifies to which IP protocol the port range applies.

Tip | For best performance, use no affinity in your port ranges. If your application developers inform you that the application running under NLB stores state information locally, select Single affinity mode for an intranet or Class C for Internet applications.

Using NLB Manager

NLB Manager enables you to configure and control your NLB clusters. Most importantly, it allows you to set the status of your cluster members, taking them offline for maintenance if necessary.

A valuable option in NLB Manager is the capability to specify alternative login credentials. Normally, the console uses your regular login credentials to attempt to connect to NLB clusters for management. However, your workstation login credentials might not have administrative privileges on the NLB cluster members, which results in NLB Manager being incapable of connecting. To specify alternative credentials, select **Credentials** from the Options menu. Then, provide the correct domain, username, and password that NLB Manager should use to connect to NLB clusters.

Clusterable Services

Windows Server 2003 includes a number of applications and services that can be clustered using either the Cluster Service or NLB. They are as follows:

- **Internet Information Services (IIS)**—Supported by both the Cluster Service and NLB. Using NLB makes the most sense because you can have up to 32 independent servers in an NLB cluster. NLB provides both failover and load balancing, whereas the Cluster Service can provide only failover.
- **DHCP Service**—Supportedonly by the Cluster Service.
- **Distributed file system (DFS) roots**—Even though NLB could technically load balance between DFS roots, there's usually little need to do so. The Cluster Service provides failover for the DFS root, which is what enterprises are usually interested in.
- **Distributed Transaction Coordinator**—Supported only by the Cluster Service.
- **File shares**—Technically, you could provide load balancing of file servers by using NLB. However, it's unsafe to do so because no provision exists for synchronizing copies for changes and so forth. The Cluster Service provides failover for file shares, and DFS allows you to load balance and synchronize file shares across multiple servers.
- **Message Queuing**—Supportedonly by the Cluster Service.
- **Printer spools**—Supported only by the Cluster Service. Theoretically, you could use NLB to provide load balancing between identical print queues on separate servers, but the queues would still be competing for the same physical print devices, so there would be little point in doing so.
- **Volume Shadow Copy Service Tasks**—Supported only by the Cluster Service.
- **WINS Service (WINS)**—Supported by the Cluster Service. You could potentially use NLB to provide load balancing between WINS servers, provided the servers were configured as replication partners. However, WINS typically isn't used so heavily that load balancing would be useful.

Of course, NLB can potentially support any TCP/IP-based application, and the Cluster Service can support TCP/IP-based applications that meet certain requirements. For more details, consult Windows Server 2003's online Help and Support Center.

▶ For more information on DHCP, DFS, file sharing, print sharing, and WINS, **see** Chapter 8, "Network Services," **p. 125**.

▶ For more information on IIS, **see** Chapter 7, "Internet Information Services," **p. 101**.

13

MANAGEMENT

In This Chapter

- Taking advantage of other management improvements, **page 216**.
- Building headless servers, **page 220**.
- Accessing Windows Management Instrumentation, **page 225**.
- Using new command-line tools, **page 227**.

What's New

A large number of Windows Server 2003's most visible changes are in the area of server management. An entirely new Group Policy Management Console, for example, makes it easier to manage enterprise-wide group policy configuration, automate that configuration, and more. A wide array of new command-line tools makes management more efficient and easier to automate through batch files and other means. Windows Server 2003 even includes command-line utilities that enable you to directly work with Windows Management Instrumentation (WMI), Windows's universal management foundation. Unix administrators working with Windows Server will especially appreciate the new command-line tools, which allow a much higher degree of server management without using less-efficient graphical user interfaces (GUIs).

One of the coolest new management features is Windows Server 2003's built-in support for *headless servers*. Today, most Windows-based data centers are filled with racks of servers, and key components in those racks include a monitor, keyboard, mouse, and some type of keyboard-monitor-mouse switch. Most server hardware requires a keyboard, at least, for the server to boot properly, and you can't completely manage most servers without at least a keyboard and monitor because power on self test (POST) and BIOS configuration screens aren't available over remote connections. Headless servers, however, can be completely managed without an attached keyboard, monitor, or mouse. In the "Headless Servers" section of this chapter, I explain Microsoft's hardware specification for headless servers and show you how to configure and manage them in your environment.

General Management Changes

Windows Server 2003 has a large number of relatively minor, but very important, changes in the management category. We consider many of these changes to be minor only because they build on previous functionality or implement functionality first available in Windows XP; the impact of these changes on your environment can by anything but minor.

Security Templates

Security templates were introduced in Windows 2000 and provide a means of consistently applying security settings across all the computers in your organization. Security templates can be deployed via group policy, enabling you to configure account policies, local security policies, event log settings, system services settings, Registry entries, file system permissions, and the membership of restricted groups. In fact, about the only things you can't configure in a security template are IPSec and public key policies.

Windows Server 2003 introduces some new predefined security templates, so you can deploy specific security scenarios without having to custom-build your own security templates. Windows Server 2003 installs these templates to your system root folder (`\Windows` by default), under the `Security\Templates` subfolder. Some of the predefined templates are included with Windows 2000 Server, as well; for completeness, we'll list them all and their effects on Windows Server 2003:

- `Setup security.inf`—This template is applied by Windows Server 2003 Setup and creates the initial security settings for a new installation of the operating system. The template's exact effects differ between an upgrade from a prior version and a clean install, and you can reapply the template, preferably by using the `Secedit` tool, to restore the default settings.

> **Caution** `Setup security.inf` is huge because it contains all the security settings needed on a new installation of Windows Server 2003. "Huge" in this case means that you should under no circumstances apply this template through group policy. If you do, you'll see some seriously slow performance and group policy struggles to deal with such a massive group of settings.

- `DC security.inf`—This template is applied when a server is promoted to a domain controller. This template includes several file permission settings, so reapply it with caution because it can overwrite custom security settings you've applied to your server.
- `Compatws.inf`—This template lowers system security somewhat in favor of compatibility with older applications. Older applications, for example, can require the built-in Users group to have write permissions to areas of the Registry. Under older versions of Windows, the Users group had those permissions; under the more-secure Windows Server 2003, it doesn't. This template restores older-version security to enable older applications to run without modification. You should use this template only if absolutely necessary because it does, after all, lower system security. Never apply this template to a domain controller because it will negatively affect domain controller security and operations.
- `Secure*.inf`—This is actually two templates: `Securews.inf` is intended for client computers and member servers, and `Securedc.inf` is intended for domain controllers. These templates raise system security from the default as much as possible while maintaining a high level of application compatibility. These templates configure clients to use only NTLMv2 authentication and configure servers to refuse older LAN Manager authentication. From an authentication standpoint, these templates can be safely used in any environment running Windows NT Server 4.0, Service Pack 4, or higher. Note that Windows 9x computers can use NTLMv2 authentication only if they have Microsoft's Directory Services Client Pack installed; without it, they will be unable to authenticate in an environment using `Securedc.inf`.
- `Hisec*.inf`—These templates impose stronger security than the `Secure*.inf` templates. `Hisecdc.inf` configures domain controllers to refuse all LAN Manager and NTLM authentication, and `Hisecws.inf` forces clients to use only NTLMv2. The `Hisec*.inf` templates also require data encryption between clients and file servers and stronger encryption between domain controllers and domain members. These templates are safe only in environments that are running Windows 2000 or higher operating systems or Windows 9x clients with the Directory Services Client Pack installed. The `Hisec*.inf` templates also remove all members from clients' Power Users group and ensure that only the Domain Admins group and the local Administrator account are members of computers' local Administrators group. This behavior can create problems with older applications expecting users to have additional security privileges.
- `Rootsec.inf`—This template defines the root permissions for Windows Server 2003, which are the permissions on the root of the system drive (usually `C:\`). You can use this template to reapply the default root permissions, if necessary, or you can modify the template to apply the same root permissions to other volumes. The template does not overwrite explicit permissions on child folders; it simply changes the root permissions and enables them to propagate to child folders that inherit permissions.
- `Notssid.inf`—The default file and Registry permissions on Windows Server 2003 grant permissions to the special Terminal Server Security Identifier (SID), which is used when Terminal Services is running in application compatibility mode. If you're not using

Terminal Services, however, you can apply `Notssid.inf` to remove the Terminal Server SID from all files and Registry entries. Alternatively, you can run Terminal Services in Full Security mode, which does not utilize the special Terminal Server SID.

> **Note** Some of these template names might look familiar because many of them are included in Windows 2000. However, the templates included with Windows Server 2003 configure a different range of settings, and in many cases configure different settings, so you'll need to analyze them all over again before you start using them.

So, how can you apply these templates? Just as in Windows 2000, you can use the Security Configuration and Analysis snap-in to the Microsoft Management Console (MMC), or you can use the command-line tool `Secedit.exe`.

If you're not familiar with the MMC and would like a quick tutorial, log on to www.samspublishing.com and enter this book's ISBN number (no hyphens or parentheses) in the Search field; then click the book's cover image to access the book details page. Click the Web Resources link in the More Information section, and locate article ID# **A011301**. If you'd like a quick tutorial on `Secedit.exe`, enter ID# **A011302**.

Software Restrictions

Windows Server 2003 includes a full set of software restriction policies, which enable you to control the software that runs on your servers. You can configure these policies within a server's local security policy, or you can use group policy to deploy a consistent software restriction policy set to all your servers and client computers. Software restriction policies consists of some basic components:

- **One or more security levels**—By default, two levels are included: Disallowed and Unrestricted. You can set one of these to be the default (Unrestricted starts out as the default), and it will be applied to all software that doesn't have a specific policy defined.
- **A basic enforcement policy**—By default, it allows all software except DLL files and other libraries to execute for all users.
- **A designated file types policy**—Defines specific file types that are considered to be executable code, such as EXE, COM, BAT, VBS, and so forth. The default list is quite comprehensive, including just about every bit of executable code Microsoft could think of.
- **A trusted publishers list**—Defines who can select software publishers to trust. By default, end users are given this capability. Software restrictions will allow software from a trusted publisher to run, provided the software is digitally signed with the publisher's certificate.

- **Additional rules**—This is where you can define your own specific software restrictions. Windows Server 2003 supports four types of rules:
    - **Certificate rules**—Enable you to identify software by a digital certificate used to sign the software and decide which security level will be applied to the software.
    - **Hash rules**—Enable you to identify software through a checksum method. You need to identify a specific file, and then Windows will perform a mathematical operation on the file to generate a hash, or *checksum*. You then decide which security level will apply to software that meets the hash. The purpose of the hash is to uniquely identify software regardless of its name. For example, if you want to ensure that Notepad.exe will execute, no matter what filename it actually uses, you would create a hash rule. Hash rules are most often used to stop software from being run because the hash detects the software even if a user attempts to rename it.
    - **Internet zone rules**—Enable you to define a security level for specific Internet zones.
    - **Path rules**—Enable you to define a security level for a specific file according to its exact path. Note that a user can almost always move the file to a different location, rendering the path rule inoperative.

Figure 13.1 shows a new hash rule that assigns the Unrestricted security level to all files matching the hash for Notepad.exe. If you defined the Disallowed security level as your default, you would need to define a rule such as this one for all the software you want your users to be able to run.

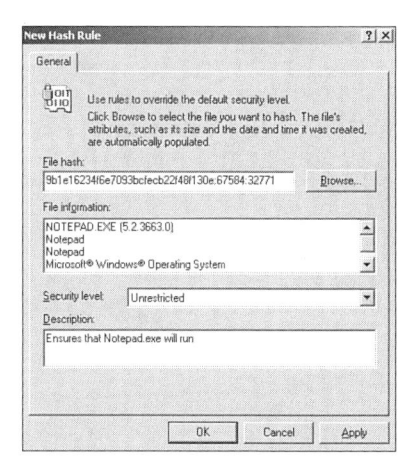

Figure 13.1   This rule associates Notepad.exe with a specific security level.

Keep in mind that, because software restriction policies can be deployed through group policy, you can define multiple, different sets of restrictions. For example, one set might apply to domain controllers only and include severe restrictions on the software that can run, helping to prevent viruses and other unauthorized software. Users' computers might have a less restrictive set of policies applied, which might prevent only specific unauthorized software, such as Napster-style applications, from running. Software restrictions can also be configured in either or both of the Computer or User Configuration sections of a group policy object (GPO), enabling you to get very specific and even assign restrictions to particular users—provided those users are organized into organizational units (OUs) within Active Directory.

Software Deployment

Microsoft's IntelliMirror technologies are alive and well in Windows Server 2003, with only minor changes to support new Windows Server 2003 and Windows XP deployment options. One important new change is in the software deployment user interface. This interface now includes an option to allow 32-bit packages to be deployed to 64-bit computers. Because both Windows XP and Windows Server 2003 are available in 64-bit editions, this option enables you to deploy 32-bit applications (which will run in 32-bit compatibility mode) or prevent 32-bit applications from being published or assigned to 64-bit clients.

> **Note** Microsoft's white papers on IntelliMirror stress its suitability for "simple" software deployments and take care to point out the availability of Microsoft Systems Management Server (SMS) for more complex deployment needs. If you're evaluating SMS for use in your environment, do so with great care: SMS is a complex product with important planning requirements. You also might want to look into the next version of SMS, which will integrate more fully with Active Directory and other Windows Server 2003 technologies.

Some of the most useful changes to IntelliMirror are actually changes to group policy, such as the new Resultant Set of Policies display, the new Group Policy Management Console, and so forth. These changes all contribute to IntelliMirror management and troubleshooting, as well as general group policy administration.

> ▶ If you'd like to know more about changes to group policy in Windows Server 2003, **see** Chapter 6, "Group Policy Changes," **p. 81**.

Headless Servers

Headless servers are definitely one of the coolest new features in Windows Server 2003, and they can make data center management much more efficient. Windows 2000 already offers a great solution for remote administration in Terminal Services, but Windows Server 2003 goes one step further by always including Terminal Services, in at least remote administration mode, in every install of Windows Server 2003. However, remote administration isn't the complete solution for headless servers.

> We've always been advocates of remote administration because it can help improve server uptime. For more details on this philosophy and how other operating systems rely on remote administration, visit www.samspublishing.com and enter this book's ISBN number (no hyphens or parentheses) in the Search field; then click the book's cover image to access the book details page. Click the Web Resources link in the More Information section, and locate article ID# **A011303**.

After Windows is up and running, Terminal Services becomes the perfect remote administration interface. But what about before Windows is up and running, or if Windows crashes? Terminal Services isn't available then, and plenty of configuration and maintenance tasks need to be performed, including BIOS configuration, POST screen analysis, and so on. Several server manufacturer utilities run outside Windows and aren't accessible remotely through Terminal Services. A special combination of software and hardware is necessary for truly headless servers.

> **Tip** Looking for information on headless servers in Windows Server 2003's help files? Look for *remotely administered servers* and *Emergency Management Services*; *headless* isn't a term Microsoft felt was appropriate for the official product documentation. You will, however, see *headless* in many Microsoft white papers available on the Windows Server 2003 Web site.

Headless Hardware

Microsoft's specification for headless server hardware is contained within the company's Server Appliance Kit (SAK) because the industry tends to refer to headless servers as *server appliances*. The name implies exactly what they are: Boxes that plug into your network and function without the usual computer trappings of a mouse, keyboard, or monitor. Microsoft's SAK even includes a utility named Saprep.exe, which allows server manufacturers to disable VGA, keyboard, and mouse devices so they can't be used even if they're attached to the computer. Windows Server 2003 includes a special null VGA driver that's installed by Saprep.exe. The *null driver* enables the operating system to generate video images normally and simply discards the image data instead of feeding it to a display adapter card.

Servers also have to support specific hardware features for headless operation. Specifically, the hardware needs to allow administrators to perform the following tasks without the benefit of local input or display devices:

- Power the system on or off.
- Modify the BIOS or view POST screens.
- Select an operating system to start, or set startup options (such as Safe Mode).
- Utilize preoperating system utilities.

- Analyze STOP errors (the popularly named blue screens of death).
- Reset the system.

Most of these features are implemented through special *out of bandwidth management (OOB)* techniques, such as connecting special remote control devices to the server's serial port. The server's hardware and firmware must be capable of directing screen output to the serial port, where the remote control device can make it available to administrators running specialized client software. Microsoft includes such serial port support in its boot code, startup menu, STOP screen displays, and a special text-mode management console, all of which are a part of Windows Emergency Management Services (EMS), which is described in the next section.

By default, Windows expects serial ports to be set to 9,600 baud, 1 stop bit, no parity, and 8 data bits and to use hardware flow control. Essentially, Windows implements a VT100+ compatible terminal output, which is the standard for remote management on most Unix systems, providing a good deal of management client compatibility between Windows and Unix. Server firmware must permit text screens to be redirected to the serial port, as well, so that BIOS screens, POST screens, and other preoperating system screens can be viewed remotely.

> **Note** Interestingly, Microsoft's interest in headless servers comes at a time when hardware vendors are starting to eliminate legacy hardware, such as serial ports, from their designs. Oops! To accommodate this change, Windows Server 2003 supports not only built-in serial ports, but also add-on serial ports installed in a PCI expansion slot. Headless server operation is not supported over newer connectivity options such as USB ports.

Server manufacturers are also welcome to implement specific remote-control hardware directly within the server. For example, some manufacturers are installing hardware that appears as a serial port to Windows and the server's firmware but is externally exposed as an Ethernet connection. This enables the server to be assigned an IP address for OOB management and connected to a dedicated management network. Administrators can then connect directly to the remote management system from their workstations. This technique has been used in the past in proprietary solutions such as Hewlett-Packard's (formerly Compaq) Remote InSight add-in adapters and its companion software drivers, but it is now universally supported by Windows, provided the correct hardware is installed in the computer.

Microsoft defines a number of other specifications for the OOB hardware:

- **The hardware must appear to Windows as a standard serial port using standard UART interface chipsets.**
- **The OOB hardware must be statically mapped and not require (or allow) Plug and Play configuration**—This is because the Windows EMS software doesn't include Plug and Play functionality. This requirement eliminates last-generation hardware, which allows the BIOS to dynamically remap serial port addresses.

- **The OOB hardware must be available at all times**—This is because EMS executes without the benefit of a Windows Hardware Abstraction Layer (HAL).
- **Windows will access the hardware directly, not through Windows's I/O manager**—No device drivers or other software will be permitted access to the serial port at any time, even when Windows is up and running perfectly.
- **The OOB hardware should be powered independently and must not be turned off at any time.**

We have some other recommendations for headless servers that aren't specifically required by Microsoft. For example, you should purchase only servers that implement a PXE-compliant network adapter and include BIOS settings that enable the computer to boot from the network. This feature makes the server compatible with Windows's Remote Installation Services (RIS), enabling you to install an operating system on the server without having a mouse, keyboard, or monitor attached. Also look for Uninterruptible Power Supplies (UPSs) that communicate via serial port, instead of USB, because USB communications require Windows to be running, making the UPS unmanageable in an emergency when Windows won't start.

Headless Software

We've already touched on EMS, the bits of Windows software that make headless servers possible. EMS is used mainly for OOB management; normal, or *in-band* management, is performed using tools such as the MMC and Terminal Services' remote administration mode. EMS kicks in during several system states:

- While the operating system is loading, EMS redirects text output to the server's OOB management hardware.
- When the operating system is running the text-mode portion of Windows Setup, EMS redirects screen displays to the OOB hardware. EMS can also redirect the graphical portion of Setup.
- When the operating system displays a STOP error, EMS redirects that output to the OOB hardware for administrator analysis.

Note that EMS doesn't provide any redirection when Windows completely crashes; if Windows goes, so does EMS. In that case, all you can do is reset the server. Some server manufacturers include the capability to reset servers through their OOB connections, particularly manufacturers who implement those connections as network interfaces. Specialized management software enables you to send a remote restart signal to the OOB hardware, which can then physically reset the computer, allowing it to restart Windows. Again, this is similar to the functionality provided by proprietary remote administration solutions such as HP's Remote InSight boards.

224 Chapter 13 Management

EMS isn't a single piece of software; rather, it's a service built into many Windows components:

- Ntloader and its equivalent for 64-bit systems
- Setup loader
- Text-mode Setup
- Recovery Console
- RIS loader
- STOP displays

> For more information on 64-bit systems and how Windows operates on them, **see** Chapter 15, "64-bit Windows," **p. 253**.

Note | EMS is designed to redirect output to both the OOB hardware and any video card installed in the server. This behavior enables you to attach a monitor, assuming your server contains a video adapter, for management purposes, if desired.

EMS also includes two new components designed specifically for emergency management: The Special Administration Console (SAC) and !Special Administration Console (!SAC). SAC is the primary command-line environment for EMS and is available very early in the Windows Server 2003 boot process. You can use SAC to manage the server when Windows is running normally, during startup, during safe mode, and during the graphical portion of Windows Setup. SAC is always available after the Windows Server 2003 kernel is loaded and running. SAC is not a full-fledged Windows command line; it provides limited functionality, which includes

- Restarting or shutting down the server.
- Viewing running processes and end processes.
- Viewing and modifying the server's IP address.
- Generating STOP errors to force the creation of a memory dump file.
- Accessing a regular Windows command-line prompt. Simply enter the `cmd` command and use the Esc+Tab key combination to switch between the command-line window and the SAC window. SAC-launched command lines can run any text-based tools but cannot launch graphical tools such as Notepad. Additionally, you must provide domain or local user credentials before SAC will launch the command line, and any commands you launch will be under that user context.
- While viewing the graphical portion of Windows Setup, SAC enables you to press the Esc+Tab key combination to switch between the SAC window and the Setup log files, which enables you to troubleshoot Setup problems more easily.

The oddly named !SAC also accepts commands through the server's OOB hardware and is completely separate from SAC and the Windows command line. !SAC is available only after EMS determines that the server has failed or if SAC fails to load or function properly. !SAC enables you to redirect STOP message text and restart the computer if SAC is unavailable. Essentially, !SAC is a last-ditch attempt by Windows to provide remote access to your server so you can get it running again.

Remember that EMS isn't the be-all and end-all of remote management. Your server's firmware must provide OOB redirection for you to

- Remotely view POST screens
- Remotely edit the server BIOS
- Start a RIS-based setup (which also requires a PXE-compatible network adapter)
- Remotely respond to the `Press any Key to Boot from CD` prompt that Windows Setup CDs display when the system starts and the CD is inserted

SAC isn't available until Windows's kernel is loaded, and EMS itself doesn't start working until `Ntloader` executes. On 64-bit systems, the server's firmware must also redirect the boot menu because that menu is constructed by the server's firmware, and not by the Windows startup software.

New Command-Line Tools

Windows Server 2003 boasts more than 60 new command-line tools, which should satisfy the demands of all the administrators—including ourselves—who've been screaming for better command-line support for years. Why the emphasis on command-line administration of an operating system named "Windows?" Command-line tools are easier to use remotely through low-bandwidth, low-overhead interfaces such as Telnet. Command-line tools are also the enabling tools behind automated administration because the tools can be used in batch files to automate repetitive tasks. Most of the new command-line tools even provide a special /S parameter, which forces the tool to run against a remote server. That's a huge benefit for centralized administration.

WMI Command-Line Tool

One exciting new tool is the WMI command line. WMI is based on the Common Information Model (CIM) and defines a hierarchical namespace for managing Windows-based systems. You can use WMI to do everything from querying free drive space to restarting the computer. WMI even includes extensions into Active Directory, making it a complete management solution. Unfortunately, until now, WMI was accessible only to developers working in a language such as Visual Basic or VBScript; the command-line tool makes WMI accessible to all administrators. The tool also provides aliases to the WMI namespace, which enables mere mortals to keep track of the exceedingly complex WMI classes and attributes. That said, WMI is still not a tool for the faint of heart, although it provides exceptionally flexible access for administrators who want to write scripts to help manage their environments.

The command-line tool Wmic can run in interactive mode. Simply type `Wmic` from a command-line prompt to start the tool. You can also run the tool in noninteractive mode by supplying command-line parameters that tell it what you want it to do. Enter `Wmic /?` to see the usual command-line help menu.

> **Tip** The command-line tool isn't installed by default; the first time you run it, Windows Server 2003 installs it for you. If you plan to use the tool on your servers, take the time to execute it at least once to get it properly installed.

Figure 13.2 shows an example of Wmic output. The input command was `Wmic Sysdriver`, which asks the tool to query information about all system drivers and their statuses (started or not). The alias Sysdriver maps to the `Win32_SysDriver` portion of the WMI namespace. This is a WMI query; other Wmic commands enable you to change the state of the system, such as setting a driver to disabled or stopping it.

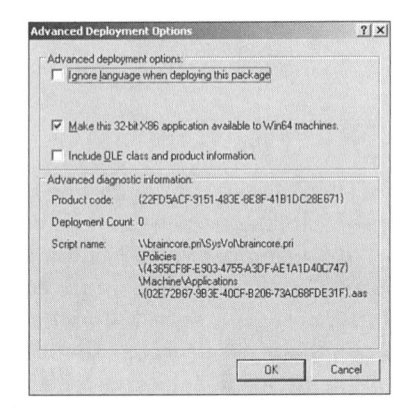

Figure 13.2 In interactive mode, Wmic remains running after each command so that you can run additional commands.

With such power, you might be wondering how secure WMI is. WMI includes limited security capabilities, essentially giving all members of the local Administrators group full control over WMI and all other users read-only permissions on their local computers. Domain administrators are usually members of the local Administrators group, allowing them to remotely manage WMI on any computer in the domain. You can change permissions only by adding users to the Administrators group or by authorizing them in WMI itself, a fairly complicated process. For more information on WMI security, consult Windows Server 2003's Help and Support Center.

> **Caution** WMI exists not only on Windows Server 2003, but also on Windows 2000, Windows NT, and Windows 9x systems. Windows 9x systems grant full control over WMI to all local users, although you can set permissions for remote WMI usage. Also note that WMI checks security only when you initially connect to it; if you change permissions while a user is still connected, your changes do not take effect until the user disconnects. Also, WMI security is service-wide, affecting all WMI access, not just access through Wmic.

Other New Command-Line Tools

Ready for a rundown of Windows Server 2003's new tools? Table 13.1 lists them in alphabetical order.

Table 13.1 Windows Server's New Tools

Name	Description
Adprep	Prepares Windows 2000 domains and forests for an upgrade to Windows Server 2003 by extending the Active Directory scheme to include new classes and attributes.
Bootcfg	Enables you to modify the `Boot.ini` file.
Choice	Enables your batch files to display a menu of choices and to control the batch files' operation based on the choice selected. Choice enables you to create multipurpose batch files without hard coding difficult-to-remember command-line parameters.
Clip	Redirects command-line output to the Windows clipboard, enabling you to paste the output into other applications, such as Notepad.
Defrag	Provides complete control over Windows's built-in disk defragmentation tool.
Diskpart	Manages disks, partitions, and volumes. Especially useful for creating batch files that configure new computers to meet corporate standards.
Dsadd	Adds computers, contacts, groups, OUs, or users to a directory, such as Active Directory.
Dsget	The companion to Dsadd, this tool displays attributes of directory objects.
Dsmod	Modifies existing directory objects in a directory such as Active Directory.
Dsmove	Moves directory objects to a new location, provided the move can be accomplished by contacting a single domain controller. Also renames objects without moving them.
Dsrm	Removes objects from a directory.
Eventcreate	Creates custom events in one of Windows's various event logs. Useful for logging events from within a batch file to track success or failure.
Eventquery	Lists events from a particular event log.

Table 13.1 Continued

Name	Description
Freedisk	Enables you to create batch files that check for free disk space before performing an operation.
Fsutil	Manages reparse points, sparse files, volume mounting, and volume extensions.
Getmac	Retrieves the MAC addresses of network adapters.
Gpresult	Displays the resultant set of policies (RSoP) for a user or computer that is applying group policy objects.
Inuse	Replaces locked operating system files.
Iisback	Creates and manages backup copies of the IIS metabase and schema. Fantastic for quickly backup up the metabase of remote IIS computers to a centralized backup repository.
Iiscnfg	Imports and exports portions of the IIS metabase. This is a great tool for consistently configuring IIS machines: Back up portions of the metabase from a master machine, and import them to the others.
Iisftp	Manages FTP sites on IIS servers.
Iisftpdr	Manages virtual directories under IIS FTP sites.
Iisvdir	Manages virtual directories under IIS Web sites.
Iisweb	Manages Web sites on IIS servers.
Logman	Manages and schedules performance counter and event trace log collections on remote servers.
Nlb	Manages network load balancing (NLB). Also, Nlbmgr provides similar control for entire NLB clusters.
Openfiles	Displays and disconnects open files.
Pagefileconfig	Configures the system paging file.
Perfmon	Opens System Monitor configured with the settings from a Windows NT 4.0 Performance Monitor settings file.
Prncnfg	Configures printers.
Prndrvr	Manages the printer drivers installed on a server.
Prnjobs	Manages the jobs associated with a printer.
Prnmngr	Manages printer connections.
Prnport	Manages TCP/IP printer ports.
Prnqctl	Prints test pages, pauses and resumes printers, and clears printer queues.
Relog	Extracts performance counters from performance counter logs into various text formats or into SQL Server databases.
Rss	Enables Remote Storage.
Sc	Manages service information and tests and debugs service software.

Table 13.1 Continued

Name	Description
Schtasks	Command-line interface to the Task Scheduler. Replaces the At command, which is also included in Windows Server 2003.
Setx	Sets local or remote environment variables.
Shutdown	Shuts down the local or a remote computer. This utility was always a Resource Kit favorite and is now in the base operating system.
Systeminfo	Displays basic system information.
Takeown	Takes ownership of files.
Taskkill	Replaces the Resource Kit Kill and Pkill utilities, which end a running process.
Tasklist	Replaces the Plist and Tlist Resource Kit utilities, which list running processes.
Typeperf	Writes performance data to the command-line window in a text format. Incredibly useful from within the SAC because SAC doesn't support graphical applications such as System Monitor.
Waitfor	Synchronizes batch files running on multiple computers.
Whoamii	Lists the current domain name, computer name, username, group names, logon ID, and privileges.
WMIC	WMI command-line interface, which we've discussed in the previous section.

▶ For more information on managing IIS, **see** Chapter 7, "Internet Information Services," **p. 101**.

▶ For more information on NLB, **see** "Network Load Balancing," **p. 207**.

▶ For more information on printing enhancements, **see** "File Sharing," **p. 135**.

Keep in mind that most of these tools support the new /S switch, which enables you to run the tool against a remote Windows Server 2003 computer. Simply add /S *computername* to the command line. Some additional command-line tools, such as Forfiles, have specific uses within batch files; check out Windows Server 2003's Help and Support Center for a complete list of available command-line tools.

14

MAINTENANCE

In This Chapter

- Using Software Update Services, **page 233**.
- Automating administration via scripting **page 246**.
- Backing up your server, **page 249**.
- Using Automated System Recovery **page 250**.

What's New

Maintenance is a curious area for the Windows Server 2003 editions. In some ways, you'll find that the product hasn't changed much from Windows 2000. In other ways, you won't recognize the product because so much has changed. The biggest changes come in areas of totally new or improved functionality, such as Automated System Restore (ASR) and Software Update Services. Other major maintenance tools, such as Windows's built-in backup and restore application, have changed very little.

Hotfix and service pack management is one of the biggest areas of improvement in Windows Server 2003. In previous versions of Windows, hotfixes were usually applied individually, or in batches by using add-on tools such as Microsoft's Qchain.exe. Windows Server 2003 eliminates the need for these services by including hotfix installation and management software right in the core OS. In addition, Microsoft's new Software Update Services

(SUS) provides tools that allow corporations to deploy security hotfixes (now called *security updates*) and service packs directly to other servers and to client computers.

If you've been working with Windows XP, you'll notice that a number of its maintenance features have found their way into Windows Server 2003. ASR, for example, originally appeared in earlier versions of Windows and is fully integrated into Windows Server 2003. Windows XP's expanded Windows Management Instrumentation is also included in Windows Server 2003, providing an excellent interface for VBScript-savvy administrators who want to automate common management tasks.

Hotfix and Service Packs Management

The process of keeping your computers up-to-date with the latest fixes has always been somewhat difficult. Microsoft actually offers different types of fixes, which many administrators choose to deal with in different ways:

- **Hotfixes**—Also called *quick-fix engineering (QFE)* or simply *updates*, these offer fixes for bugs and other anomalous conditions. Generally, these fixes aren't fully regression-tested, which means they haven't been subjected to an extensive beta-testing process to ensure full compatibility with all operating environments. Microsoft usually recommends that you apply a hotfix only if you're experiencing the specific problem the hotfix corrects.

Note Microsoft doesn't usually make hotfixes as easily available as other updates. Hotfixes that correct common problems are often available for download from Microsoft's Web site but aren't often included in Windows Update (which we'll discuss momentarily). Many additional hotfixes are available only from Microsoft's Product Support Services (PSS), after Microsoft determines that the hotfix will correct a problem you're experiencing.

- **Security hotfixes**—Now called *security updates*, these correct specific security flaws in Windows. Because they address security issues, these updates are almost always considered critical and Microsoft recommends that they be deployed to all your computers as rapidly as possible. These updates are generally available from Windows Update (and are, in fact, listed in the "Critical Updates" section of Windows Update). Deploying these fixes has been a major nightmare for most organizations: Unfortunately, Microsoft has had to release a lot of these for Windows 2000 and Windows XP, and hasn't—until recently—offered great tools to make the deployment process easy and automatic.

- **Service packs**—These are collections of hotfixes, security updates, new features, and other product improvements that are released periodically. Service packs go through a complete beta-testing process, making them more stable than individual hotfixes. Service packs are cumulative, which means they contain all fixes from prior service packs, hotfixes, and security updates.

> **Service Packs: Not Just For Fixes, Anymore**
>
> At one time, Microsoft planned to include only fixes in service packs, saving new product features for some other type of update. The idea was to ensure that organizations could deploy a service pack without affecting the functionality of their existing servers. Unfortunately, that plan never came to fruition, and almost every new service pack for Windows 2000 has contained at least minor new functionality. By including new functionality in service packs, Microsoft effectively changes the version of Windows running on your servers after the service pack is applied, which means you'll need to think of a service pack more as a minor version upgrade and not just a collection of bug fixes. As with any other version upgrade, you should pilot the service pack in a lab environment to ensure its compatibility with your production environment prior to full deployment.

Managing these updates involves two distinct tasks: Deploying updates and inventorying updates. Windows Server 2003 includes tools that assist with both tasks.

Note
: Windows Server 2003 doesn't include any tools for easy enterprise-wide deployment or inventory of updates. The tools we cover here are included with the product and are suitable for smaller networks. However, these tools don't scale especially well, making them less suitable for larger networks. Microsoft Systems Management Server (SMS) is Microsoft's recommended solution for software management in the enterprise; if you're working in a large environment and find that Windows Server 2003's built-in tools aren't meeting your needs, you should evaluate SMS to see whether it can help.

Software Update Services

You can think of SUS as a corporate internal version of Windows Update, Microsoft's Web-based application for software update management. In fact, SUS was originally named Windows Corporate Update, reflecting its Windows Update origins.

> To learn more about Windows Update and how it works, visit www.samspublishing.com and enter this book's ISBN number (no hyphens or parentheses) in the Search field; then click the book's cover image to access the book details page. Click the Web Resources link in the More Information section, and locate article ID# **A011402**.

Windows Update enables users to easily check for updates to their operating systems, download the updates, and install them automatically. Unfortunately, Windows Update has several major drawbacks in a corporate environment:

- **Most updates require users to be administrators of their computers**—That was fine on Windows 98 (where Windows Update debuted), which had no concept for administrative privileges. However, in Windows 2000 and Windows XP, administrative privileges aren't usually provided to end users, making Windows Update less useful.

- **Windows Update provides a one-on-one update service**—This means each computer must connect to the Windows Update Web site individually to retrieve updates. In organizations with hundreds or thousands of computers, this technique is inefficient and unreliable. It's mainly a waste of Internet bandwidth because each computer must individually download the same updates.
- **Windows Update isn't automatic**—Windows XP did introduce a new feature called Automatic Updates (which was released for Windows 2000 in Service Pack 3); this feature automatically checks for updates, downloads them, and asks for permission to apply them.

Windows Update also includes the Windows Update Catalog, which allows administrators to access the entire update library. Using the Catalog, administrators can download individual updates for any operating system. Unfortunately, there is no tool to easily distribute the downloaded updates.

SUS is designed to fix all of that. Essentially, SUS is your very own version of Windows Update, which you install on one or more servers within your environment. Each SUS server can be configured to download updates from Windows Update (which serves as the central worldwide source for updates) or from another SUS server. Client computers and other servers running the Automatic Updates client (also referred to as the *SUS client*) can be directed to a SUS server for their updates. This architecture allows you to create your own internal, distributed update infrastructure, such as the one shown in Figure 14.1.

SUS is available as a free download from Microsoft's Web site. It can be installed on any Windows 2000 Server or Windows Server 2003 computer, except domain controllers. During the installation, you specify where you want downloaded updates to be saved, as shown in Figure 14.2. Updates can be saved to a local folder, or they can be retained on the Windows Update server. Generally, you'll store updates locally; if you leave them on Windows Update, each client will have to use your Internet bandwidth to download its updates.

Caution | Unlike Windows Update, which offers updates only for the operating system of a single computer, SUS downloads all available updates for all operating systems. That's a lot of updates, and you'll need to ensure that your SUS server has ample disk space—at least 20GB—to store current updates while allowing room for future updates.

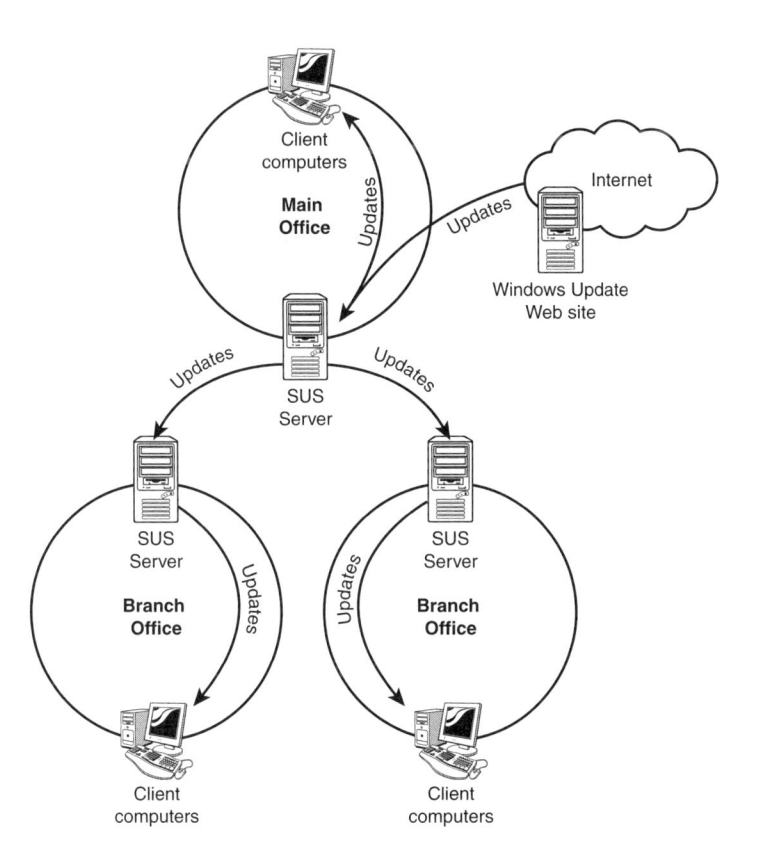

Figure 14.1 A SUS infrastructure utilizes your network resources more efficiently than Windows Update.

After you install SUS, you configure its synchronization schedule. To do so, click the **Synchronize** item in the left menu bar and then click the **Schedule** button. The dialog box shown in Figure 14.3 appears, allowing you to tell SUS when to download recent updates from the Windows Update servers. We recommend a weekly synchronization during idle hours, such as Sunday mornings at 3 a.m.

236 Chapter 14 Maintenance

Figure 14.2 Saving updates to a local folder can take quite a bit of space, so make sure your server has plenty to spare.

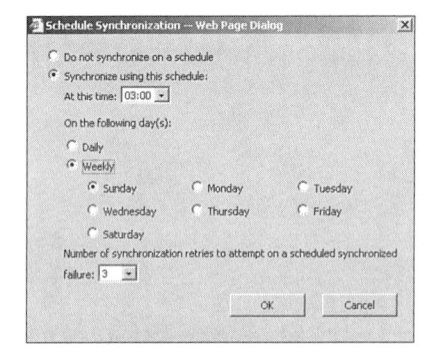

Figure 14.3 Your initial synchronization can take several hours because SUS has a few years' worth of updates to download.

Keep in mind that you can change SUS's operating options at any time by clicking the Options menu item. As shown in Figure 14.4, you can choose to store updates locally, automatically approve new versions of updates, and select the languages supported in your environment. (You'll read more about automatically approving new versions of updates a little later.) Language support is useful in large, multinational corporations because it allows SUS to maintain updates in multiple languages, supporting all of a corporation's users.

Because your first SUS synchronization can take several hours, you might want to start it manually, so that you can keep an eye on it as it downloads the available updates. Simply click the **Synchronize** button to start the synchronization process and, as shown in Figure 14.5,

SUS will display progress bars indicating how it's doing. As we've mentioned, your first synchronization will include every available update for the products SUS supports: Internet Explorer 5.0x, Internet Explorer 5.5x, Internet Explorer 6.x, Windows 2000, Windows XP, and Windows Server 2003.

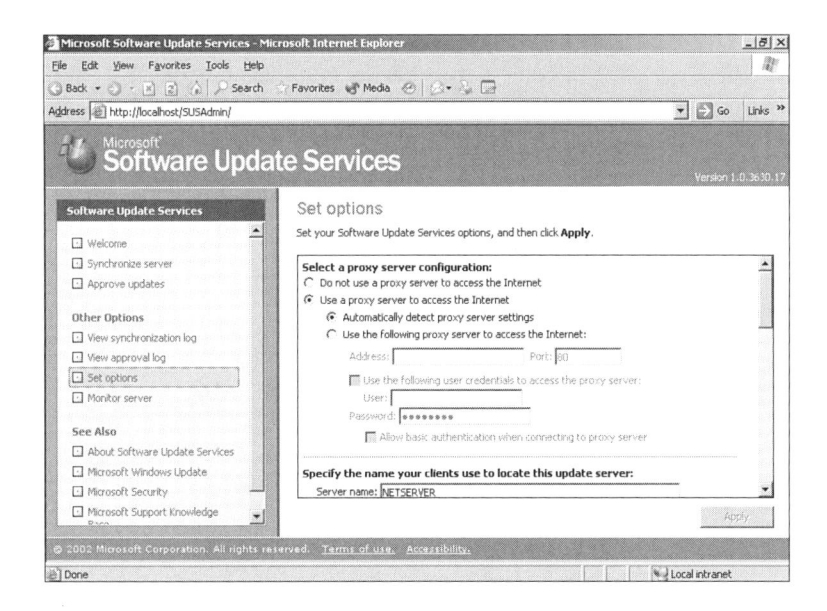

Figure 14.4 Changes to SUS options take effect immediately.

Note | Before Windows Server 2003 was released, more than 1,200 updates were available to Windows 2000 and Windows XP, so expect your first synchronization to take quite some time, no matter how fast your Internet connection is.

Microsoft recognizes that not all organizations will want to deploy every single update to their computers. For example, one of the updates available for Windows XP is the Windows Movie Maker, which probably isn't a major line-of-business application for most companies. To give administrators maximum control, SUS doesn't make any of its updates available to your network until you approve them. To approve updates, click the **Approve Updates** menu item. You'll see a list of all updates, as shown in Figure 14.6.

238 Chapter 14 Maintenance

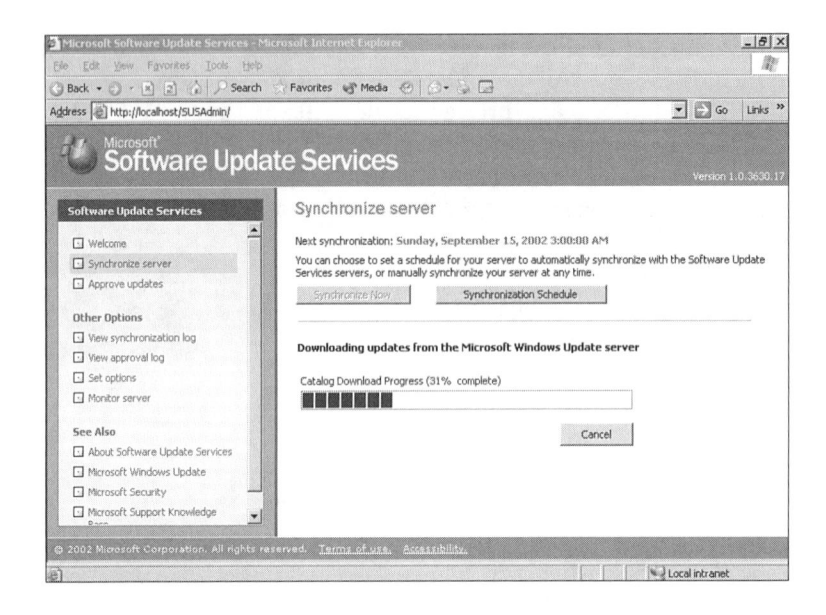

Figure 14.5 Your first synchronization will include well over 1,200 updates.

The list of updates includes several pieces of valuable information:

- The name of the update and the date on which it was released.
- The size of the update.
- Whether the installation of the update requires a reboot.
- The operating systems to which the update applies. Note that SUS doesn't support Windows NT or Windows 9x operating systems; only Windows 2000 and higher are supported.
- The language of the update. If you're downloading multiple languages, you'll find each update listed multiple times—once for each language you support.
- A brief description of the update. A Details link pops up a new window with a more complete description of the update.

Note Because SUS is available as a download, Microsoft will probably make minor changes and improvements to it more frequently than it would with features built right into Windows Server 2003. As a result, the version of SUS you're using might differ slightly from the one shown here, but it should operate in substantially the same way that we're describing.

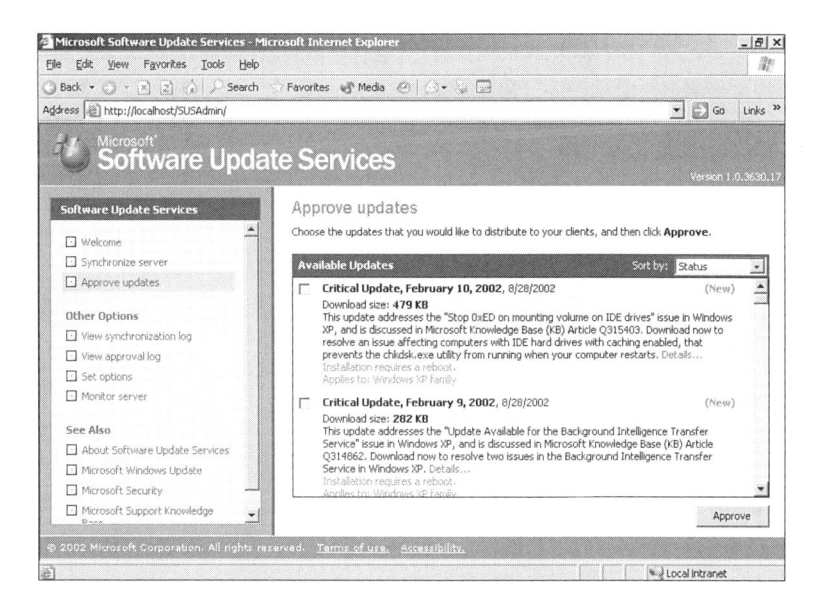

Figure 14.6 Updates must be manually approved one at a time before being made available to your network.

After you approve an update, it becomes available to clients running Automatic Updates. Where do your computers get Automatic Updates? A version of it is included with Windows XP, but that's not the latest version and it isn't SUS compatible. The correct version can come from several places:

- You can manually install the client by using the Windows Installer package you download from the Windows Web site.
- Any Windows XP computers that have been using the built-in Automatic Update have probably already downloaded and installed the new version.
- Windows 2000 Service Pack 3 contains the new version of Automatic Updates.
- Windows XP Service Pack 1 contains the new version of Automatic Updates.
- All editions of Windows Server 2003 ship with the correct version of Automatic Updates.

Administrators can use group policies to centrally configure Automatic Updates within a domain; doing so enables you to create a consistent update configuration for all computers in a domain. You can also manually configure Automatic Updates on each computer. On Windows XP and Windows Server 2003, right-click **My Computer** and select **Properties** from the pop-up menu. Locate the **Automatic Updates** tab, shown in Figure 14.7, and select the desired update option.

Tip | Don't forget to configure Automatic Updates on your SUS servers, too. SUS only downloads updates; it doesn't apply them to the local server. Also, don't let the term *SUS Client* confuse you: This software should be installed on all corporate computers, including servers.

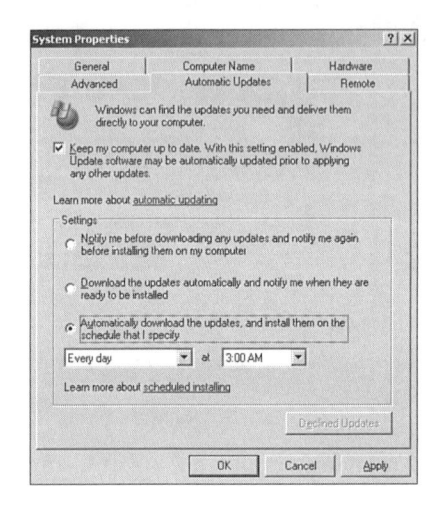

Figure 14.7 The SUS Client (Automatic Updates) appears similarly on Windows XP, Windows 2000, and Windows Server 2003.

It's important to remember that Automatic Updates is configured by default to use only the Windows Update Web site to obtain updates. If you've deployed SUS on your network, you must reconfigure Automatic Updates on your client computers to use your SUS server. This configuration must come from a centralized group policy, which means your computers must all belong to a Windows 2000 or Windows Server 2003 Active Directory domain.

Caution | Note that you can reconfigure Automatic Updates by manually editing the Registry of each client computer, but this method is time-consuming, can be error-prone, and is definitely not recommended.

Automatic Updates uses new group policy settings that aren't included in Windows 2000 domains by default. The new settings are specified in the WUAU.adm file, which is added to the %windir%\inf folder when you install Automatic Updates. To create a group policy object (GPO) that configures Automatic Updates, first install the newest Automatic Updates client on an administrative workstation (any Windows 2000 or Windows XP computer with Active Directory Users and Computers installed). Then, follow these steps:

1. Open Active Directory Users and Computers.
2. Right-click the organizational unit (OU) to which you want to apply your Automatic Updates configuration. You can also right-click the domain to apply the configuration to all computers in your domain.
3. Select **Properties** from the pop-up menu, and select the **Group Policy** tab.
4. Click **New** to create a new policy.
5. Specify a name for the policy, and click **Edit** to open the Group Policy Object Editor.
6. Under Computer Settings, right-click **Administrative Templates**.
7. Select **Add/Remove Templates** from the pop-up menu, and then click **Add**.
8. Specify the WUAU.adm file. If it's not present on your computer, you can copy it from the %windir%\inf folder on any server with SUS installed.
9. Click **Open** to load the template, and click **Close** to close the dialog box.
10. Expand the **Computer Configuration** section, and then expand **Administrative Templates**.
11. Expand **Windows Components**, and then click **Windows Update**.
12. Two policy settings will be shown in the right pane of the console: Configure Automatic Updates and Specify Intranet Windows Update Server Location. Double-click either policy to configure it.
13. Use the Configure Automatic Updates policy to define the behavior of the Automatic Updates client. Generally, you should select the **Auto Download and Schedule the Install** option, which provides the most automatic operation.
14. Use the Specify Intranet Windows Update Server Location policy setting to specify the name of your SUS server.

Tip Because you can specify a different group policy for an OU, or even for each site, you can implement a distributed SUS infrastructure. For example, you might deploy a SUS server to each branch office and use a site-based group policy to configure all computers within that site to use their local SUS servers. All your SUS servers can be configured to pull their updates from a centralized SUS server at your main office, helping to reduce the use of your Internet connection.

The Automatic Updates client runs at all times, even when no user is logged on to the computer. If you've configured the client to automatically download and install updates, its behavior is as follows:

- If no user is logged on, updates are automatically installed. If a restart is required, the computer is automatically restarted.
- If an administrator is logged on, updates are automatically installed. If a restart is required, a warning is displayed before installation begins, giving the administrator time to shut down any critical processes. Administrators can cancel the update, which will remain pending. The update will automatically apply at a later time, even if cancelled.

- If a non-administrative user is logged on, a countdown is displayed before updates are automatically installed. If a restart is required, the computer is automatically restarted. The countdown is designed to give users time to shut down their applications without allowing them to interrupt the update process.

You should be aware of how Automatic Updates functions when configured via group policy, and when other group policies exist that define Windows Update behavior:

- If you've enabled the Remove Access to Use All Windows Update Features policy setting, Automatic Updates continues to function but displays no notices to logged-on users. This policy setting is available only on Windows XP.
- If you've enabled the Remove Links and Access to Windows Update policy setting, Automatic Updates continues to operate if configured to download updates from an intranet SUS server. If you don't enable this policy, users can still manually access Windows Update. We recommend enabling this policy in conjunction with SUS to ensure that users' computers obtain updates only from your SUS server or servers.

After your clients are configured, they'll contact your SUS server according to the schedule you set. If you've configured them to automatically download and install updates and configured your SUS server(s) to automatically download new updates, you'll have an almost hands-off system for managing software updates in your environment. The only regular task you'll need to perform is approving new updates for deployment to your clients.

> **Tip** Microsoft sometimes releases new versions of specific updates. You can configure SUS's options to automatically approve new versions of an update you've already approved, or you can configure it to treat new versions as unique updates that require separate manual approval.

Managing and Monitoring Updates

SUS provides two tools for managing and monitoring updates: the Approval Log and the Monitor Server link. Both are accessible as menu items from the main SUS administration screen. The Approval Log, shown in Figure 14.8, simply lists the approval actions that have been taken on the server. This log enables you to review which updates might have been approved by other administrators, and it can be useful when troubleshooting problems with package deployment. The Monitor Server page, shown in Figure 14.9, displays a summary of updates available from your SUS server broken down by operating system or product. Clicking a product name displays a complete list of packages, including their globally unique identifiers (GUIDs), file sizes, and other information.

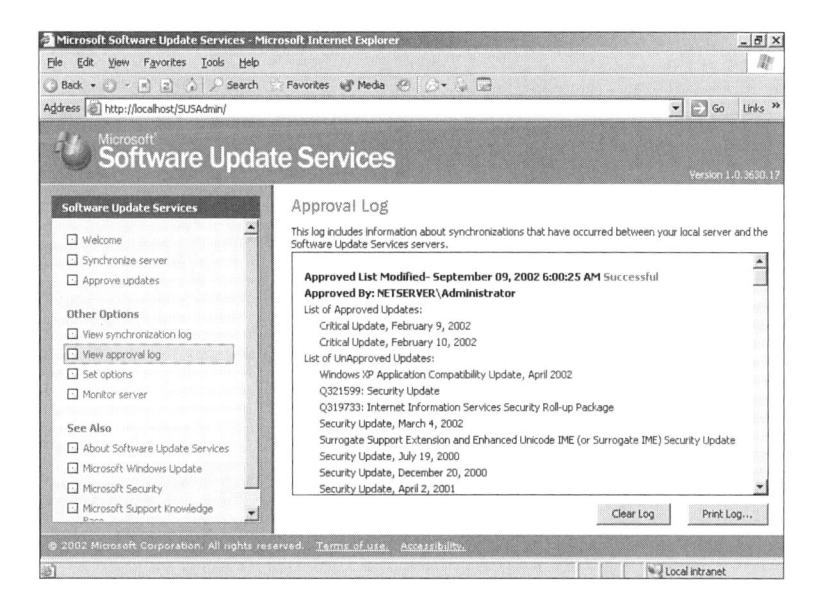

Figure 14.8 A regular review of the Approval Log lets you catch any undesired updates that have been approved by another administrator of your network.

Inventorying Updates

Sadly, Microsoft has provided better free tools for deploying updates than for finding out which ones have already been deployed. Unfortunately, SUS is designed only to make updates available; it can't force client computers to download updates unless they're properly configured, and SUS can't help you determine whether all your clients have successfully downloaded and applied a particular update. Microsoft SMS can do all of these things, but it represents a significant additional investment in both time and money.

The best you can do for free is a downloadable tool from Microsoft called `Hfnetchk.exe`. This tool, combined with an XML-based database, is designed to check for the presence and proper installation of Microsoft security updates. The tool can be run against remote computers, providing a rudimentary centralized update inventory. Unfortunately, the tool is designed for use only with security updates, not other hotfixes, and not for service packs in general (although the tool does properly detect security updates installed as part of a service pack).

Need More Hfnetchk Power?

Hfnetchk is a command-line tool that works with Windows NT 4.0, Windows 2000, IIS 4 and 5, SQL Server 7 and 2000, Internet Explorer 5.01 and later, Windows XP, and Windows Server 2003. Microsoft didn't write Hfnetchk; it's actually a scaled-down version of a commercial tool developed by Shavlik Technologies. Shavlik produces a full

244   **Chapter 14**   Maintenance

(Continued)

GUI-based version of Hfnetchk and a more advanced command-line version; both can be downloaded from www.shavlik.com. Detailed information on Microsoft's version of the tool, including system requirements and download URLs, can be found at http://support.Microsoft.com/default.aspx?scid=kb; en-us;Q303215&sd=tech.

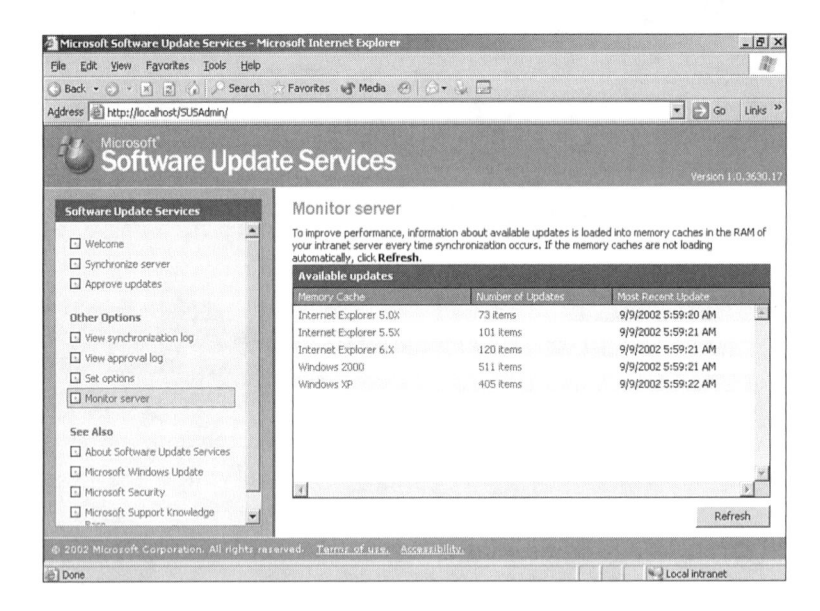

Figure 14.9   The Monitor Server page summarizes the available updates and provides a link to a more detailed list.

After Hfnetchk is installed, you execute it from a command line. For example, running Hfnetchk -v -z -s 1 produces a basic output. The tool is primarily designed to list security updates that are defined in its database but not found on the system that the tool is scanning. The -v switch provides specific details about why an update wasn't found; reasons can range from missing files or Registry keys to incorrect configuration settings on the computer. Hfnetchk always provides a reference to a Microsoft Security Bulletin or Knowledge Base article that provides instructions on how to obtain and properly install each update.

You can have Hfnetchk scan multiple remote computers simultaneously by using the -h switch: hfnetchk -h computer1, computer2, computer3. Alternatively, you can use the -fh switch to point to a text file containing a computer name on each line of the file. For example, hfnetchk -fh computers.txt opens a text file named Computers.txt, looks for one computer name on each line of the file, and scans those computers for security updates.

Other Hfnetchk options include

- `-I ipaddress, ipaddress`—This option specifies IP addresses rather than hostnames and attempts to scan the computer using each IP address provided.
- `-fip`—Works similarly to the `-fh` option, pointing to a text file of IP addresses rather than computer names.
- `-r`—Specifies a range of IP addresses to scan and can be useful when you want to scan an entire subnet.
- `-d`—Specifies an entire Active Directory or Windows NT domain to scan.
- `-n`—Scans all computers on the network. Both this switch and the `-d` switch rely on the Network Neighborhood to obtain a computer list. Unfortunately, Network Neighborhood isn't the most reliable directory of your network, so you might have greater success using an IP address range of a file of computer names.
- `-x`—Specifies the XML database to use during the scan. This can be an XML filename, a compressed XML in a `cab` file, or a URL. If not specified, Hfnetchk defaults to using the `Mssecure.cab` file located on the Microsoft Web site.
- `-s`—Suppresses specific messages. `-s 1` suppresses "Note" messages, whereas `-s 2` suppresses both "Note" and "Warning" messages.
- `-v`—Lists the reason a particular update was not considered installed, which can help you find out exactly how to go about installing it.
- `-f`—Outputs Hfnetchk's results to a file, which may be easier to review than scrolling through the command-line output.
- `-u` and `-p`—Allow you to specify an alternate username and password to use during the scan. For example, you may want to specify a domain user account that has local Administrator privileges on all computers that will be scanned. Don't include this switch if you're using Hfnetchk in a batch file; doing so would expose a powerful user account's password to anyone with access to the batch file.

| Tip | Hfnetchk isn't much, but it's the best you're going to get for free. Microsoft has started a public newsgroup to help with Hfnetchk issues. Connect your newsgroup reader to the `news.Microsoft.com` news server and look for the `Microsoft.public.security.hfnetchk` newsgroup. Additional Knowledge Base articles describing Hfnetchk include Q305385, Q303215, and Q306460. If you're using Internet Explorer, you can access Knowledge Base articles by entering **? mskb *article#*** in the Internet Explorer address bar. |

Microsoft contends that SMS is the ideal method to inventory and manage software updates, including security updates. We feel that this position is unreasonable; asking customers to purchase an entirely separate product to support their base operating systems is asking too much. SUS is a huge step in the right direction, providing in-house automatic updates for service packs and other critical updates. Some equivalent for inventorying updates—and automatically deploying missing ones, perhaps—is necessary, and we hope that Microsoft will provide such a tool in the future at no additional charge.

Administrative Scripting

In recent years, Windows administrators have begun to move away from batch file-based automation to more powerful and flexible administrative scripts written in ActiveX Scripting languages such as Visual Basic Scripting Edition (VBScript).

Batch files have always offered a reasonable degree of flexibility, and with the expanded command-line support in Windows Server 2003, batch files get a new lease on life. However, batch files' functionality is limited to the features provided by command-line utilities and the evaluation of relatively simple logical conditions. Scripts written in VBScript, on the other hand, offer much more flexibility.

> ➤ For more information on Windows Server 2003's new command-line tools, **see** "New Command Line Tools," **p. 225**.

VBScript scripts can be written using Windows Notepad, although experienced script authors prefer tools such as the free Programmer's File Editor (PFE; downloadable from www.download.com), which displays line numbers and has some features better suited for writing scripts. VBScripts can take advantage of almost any operating system feature because VBScripts can use Component Object Model (COM) objects, the basic building blocks of Windows features such as database access, file manipulation, and so forth. VBScript can also fully manipulate Windows Management Instrumentation, querying and modifying operating system and application configuration settings. For example, Listing 14.1 shows a simple script that queries a remote computer for key configuration information, which might help you remotely inventory computers on your network.

Listing 14.1 Using WMI to Query Remote Information

```
Set System = GetObject("winmgmts:{impersonationLevel=impersonate}
➥!//products1/root/cimv2:Win32
ComputerSystem=""PRODUCTS1""")

WScript.Echo System.Caption
WScript.Echo System.PrimaryOwnerName
WScript.Echo System.Domain
WScript.Echo System.SystemType
```

To test this script, type it into Windows Notepad. Save the file with a `vbs` filename extension (be sure to enclose the entire filename in quotes; otherwise, Notepad will add a `txt` extension automatically). Double-click the `vbs` file to run the script.

> **Caution** Some organizations prohibit the use of scripting because it can be an easy vector for computer viruses. Your organization might have removed or disabled `Wscript.exe`, the executable that actually runs the scripts. Your organization also might block `vbs` files. If scripts are somehow disabled in your organization, be sure to consult your company's computer and security policies prior to reenabling scripting on your computer.

So, what does the script in Listing 14.1 do? The first line sets a variable named `System` equal to a WMI query. You'll actually need to modify this query for use in your organization, replacing the two instances of `products1` with the computer name from which you want to query information. After the query executes, the `System` variable becomes a WMI object, with properties such as `PrimaryOwnerName`, `SystemType`, and `Domain`. The remaining lines of the script simply display the values of these properties by using the `Wscript.Echo` command, which displays the values in a pop-up message box.

Scripting can be useful without WMI, too. Listing 14.2 shows a sample VBScript that rotates the log files from IIS, saving old log files to an archive folder and deleting the oldest archived logs.

Listing 14.2 IIS Log File Rotation Script

```
' We'll take yesterday's log and move it to
' an archive folder. We'll delete the log file
' that's 30 days old from the archive

' --------------------------------------------------------
'declare variables
Dim varLogPath, varService, varArchive, varLogFile
Dim varYear, varMonth, varDay
Dim objFS
Dim var30Days

' --------------------------------------------------------
' set up variables
varLogPath = "c:\winnt\system32\logfiles\"
varService = "w3svc2\"
varArchive = "c:\winnt\LogArchive\"

' --------------------------------------------------------
' get yesterday's date
varYesterday = DateAdd( "d", -1, Date() )

' --------------------------------------------------------
```

Listing 14.2 Continued

```
' create a formatted log file name
' for yesterday's log file
' 1. then the 2-digit year
varYear = Right( DatePart( "yyyy", varYesterday), 2)

' 2. Now the month - make sure it's 2 digits!
varMonth = DatePart( "m", varYesterday )
If Len(varMonth) = 1 then
  varMonth = "0" & varMonth
End If

' 3. Now the day - make sure it's 2 digits!
varDay = DatePart( "d", varYesterday )
If Len(varDay) = 1 then
  varDay = "0" & varDay
End If

' 4. Complete the log file name
varLogFile = "ex" & varYear & varMonth & varDay & ".log"

' ........................................................

' Create a file system object
Set objFS = WScript.CreateObject("Scripting.FileSystemObject")

' ........................................................

' Move the file to the archive path
objFS.MoveFile varLogPath & varService & varLogFile, varArchive & varLogFile

' ........................................................

' get date for 30 days ago
var30Days = DateAdd( "d", -30, Date() )

' ........................................................
' create a formatted log file name
' for 30-day-ago log file

' 1. then the 2-digit year
varYear = Right( DatePart( "yyyy", var30Days), 2)

' 2. Now the month - make sure it's 2 digits!
varMonth = DatePart( "m", var30Days )
If Len(varMonth) = 1 then
  varMonth = "0" & varMonth
End If

' 3. Now the day - make sure it's 2 digits!
varDay = DatePart( "d", var30Days )
```

Listing 14.2 Continued

```
If Len(varDay) = 1 then
  varDay = "0" & varDay
End If

' 4. Complete the log file name
varLogFile = "ex" & varYear & varMonth & varDay & ".log"

' .......................................................
' Delete the file from the archive path
objFS.DeleteFile varArchive & varLogFile
```

This script performs some pretty straightforward tasks:

- The script starts by declaring variables, which store values used by the rest of the script.
- The script defines the file paths for the IIS logs, the particular IIS instance, and the archive folder. You'll need to change these definitions to match your environment.
- The next several sections manipulate dates to create log filenames. Keep in mind that IIS log filenames are based on dates.
- The script uses Windows's `FileSystemObject` to manipulate files and folders, moving the current log file to the archive path and then deleting the log file from 30 days ago (if one exists).

This script isn't perfect. As is, for example, it displays an error if the paths you provide aren't correct. But the script is a good example of how VBScript can make administration easier and more automated. You could, for example, use Task Scheduler to configure this script to run every morning, automatically rotating your script files.

> For a quick tutorial in using VBScript for administrative purposes, visit www.samspublishing.com and enter this book's ISBN number (no hyphens or parentheses) in the Search field; then click the book's cover image to access the book details page. Click the Web Resources link in the More Information section, and locate article ID# **A011403**.

Backup and Restore

Windows Server 2003's built-in Windows Backup application hasn't changed much from Windows 2000, which is to say you still need a third-party backup application if you want to manage backups on more than a couple of servers.

Figure 14.10 shows one of Windows Backup's most important features: the capability to back up the server's system state. The system state includes the server's Registry and, on a domain controller, a copy of the Active Directory database. Even if you're not worried about managing backups on your other servers, you must make a backup copy of the system state on your domain controllers; otherwise, you won't have any recovery options in the event of a total Active Directory failure, accidental deletion of an Active Directory object, and so forth.

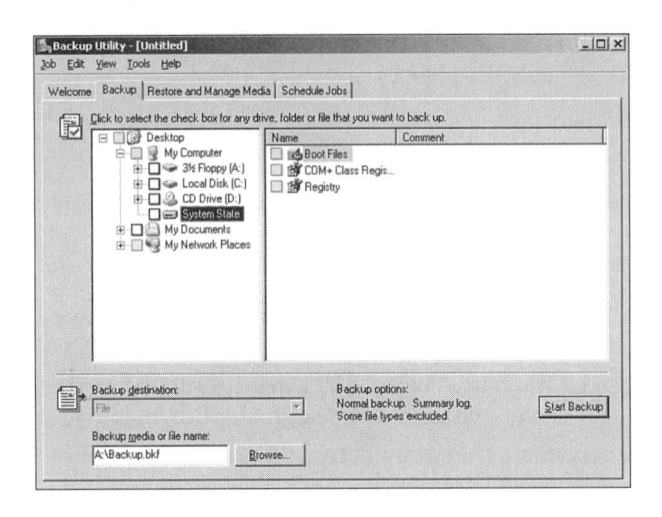

Figure 14.10 Windows Backup provides entry-level backup and restore capabilities.

Popular alternatives to Windows Backup include Veritas's BackupExec (www.veritas.com) and Computer Associates' BrightStor (www.ca.com). Both provide support for managing backups on multiple servers, utilizing robotic tape drives that hold multiple backup tapes, support for magneto-optical backup devices, and so forth. Windows Backup, on the other hand, supports only directly attached single-tape devices or backups to a file. Windows Backup supports only backing up the local server or network file shares; you cannot back up the all-important system state of a remote server.

For a quick tutorial on Windows Backup, visit www.samspublishing.com and enter this book's ISBN number (no hyphens or parentheses) in the Search field; then click the book's cover image to access the book details page. Click the Web Resources link in the More Information section, and locate article ID# **A011401**.

One important feature that's unique to Windows Backup is Automated System Recovery, Windows's built-in last-resort recovery system.

Automated System Recovery

There's a bit of confusion between ASR and System Restore, another feature of Windows XP. System Restore periodically makes *checkpoints* of the system state, including driver files. System Restore allows you to *roll back* to a previous checkpoint, effectively restoring the computer to a known-good condition. Windows Server 2003 does not include System Restore, which was designed primarily as a means of enhancing the reliability of client computers, which often have devices added and removed by end users. As a server operating system, Windows Server 2003 should be managed by experienced administrators (such as yourself), who can manually create backups prior to adding or changing hardware devices.

ASR is a feature of both Windows Server 2003 and Windows XP and is designed as a last-ditch means of returning a computer to operation. Essentially, ASR repeats the operating system setup and then overlays that setup with your last-known system state, services, and other baseline information. Prior to using ASR to restore a server, you should try restarting in Safe Mode, using the Last Known Good configuration and the other recovery tools you've become accustomed to in Windows 2000.

ASR Backup

ASR consists of two parts: the ASR backup set and the ASR restore process. You create an ASR backup set by using Windows Backup. The backup set contains the system state data, system services, and disk signatures. This backup enables the ASR restore process to reinstall Windows Server 2003, your system state, disk signatures, and system services in one operation.

To create an ASR backup set, simply launch Windows Backup. The Backup or Restore Wizard includes an option to create an ASR set: Select **All Information on This Computer** when the wizard asks you the following: What do you want to back up? You can also use Windows Backup's Advanced mode: Simply select **ASR Wizard** from the **Tools** menu, and follow the instructions on the screen.

Caution | Be sure that you're creating regular backups of any files or application data on your server. Restoring an ASR set wipes out all files and application data, so you'll need to have a recent backup in order to recover that information.

ASR Restore

Restoring a system by using ASR is straightforward. You'll need your ASR backup set, the backup media containing your files and application data, and the Windows Server 2003 installation CD. You'll also need a floppy disk containing drivers for your mass storage devices, if those drivers aren't included with Windows Server 2003.

Simply start your computer by booting with the Windows Server 2003 installation CD. During installation, press **F2** to enter ASR restore mode. You'll be prompted to provide your ASR backup set. After the ASR restore is complete, you can restore your files and application data.

Chapter 14 Maintenance

Note | ASR won't reinstall any applications that aren't included with Windows Server 2003. Be sure you have the installation media, installation keys, and any other necessary components to reinstall Microsoft or third-party applications prior to starting an ASR restore.

Keep in mind that ASR restores your system files to the state contained on the installation media. Unless you have an install CD with the most recent service pack integrated, you'll need to reinstall the latest service pack after ASR completes its restore. Also, you'll need to review your hotfix and security update situation to ensure that the server is brought up-to-date after the ASR restore completes. Tools such as Hfnetchk and SUS, both discussed earlier in this chapter, can help identify and apply recent updates.

15

64-BIT WINDOWS

In This Chapter

- Understanding 64-bit architecture, **page 255**.
- Running 32-bit applications, **page 258**.
- Comparing 64-bit and 32-bit Windows **page 259**.

What's New

If any modern technology has earned the term *venerable*, it's Intel's 32-bit processor architecture. Even today's newest Pentium computers have an architecture deeply rooted in the 286 and 386 processors of more than a decade ago. The 32-bit architecture has served us well, acting as the primary hardware platform for every version of Windows NT, but it's definitely time for something new: Intel's 64-bit Itanium processor family.

Servers based on these 64-bit processors are already available, and Intel is hard at work on new editions of the Itanium processor that run faster and provide additional features. Microsoft provided Windows Advanced Server Limited Edition—essentially a pre-release, production-ready version of 64-bit Windows Server 2003—to give 64-bit servers a network operating system, and of course Windows Server 2003 offers two 64-bit editions. But there's a great deal more to 64-bit computing than a new processor and operating system. Itanium servers include a new memory architecture, new peripheral bus, new disk-handling mechanisms, and much, much more. This chapter provides you with an overview of the world of 64-bit computing, introduces you to the 64-bit hardware platform, and shows you how 64-bit Windows differs from its 32-bit cousin. It also explains how Windows Server 2003's 64-bit editions provide compatibility for your existing 32-bit applications, so that you're not left to scramble for new versions of your software.

64-bit Overview

Both Microsoft and Intel are pushing 64-bit servers like there's no tomorrow. Many of the touted advantages are perfectly real, such as the truly enormous memory support included in the 64-bit architecture. 64-bit servers are perfect for memory-hungry database and data warehousing servers, and the 64-bit architecture offers throughput that makes it perfect for file serving, Internet content caching, and more.

Intel's 64-bit architecture is based around its Itanium processor family. The Itanium is not only a 64-bit processor, but also includes a number of general enhancements over Intel's latest Pentium processors. One major new feature is EPIC, Intel's Explicitly Parallel Instruction Computing architecture. EPIC provides far superior parallel computing, prediction capabilities, and other features that allow Itanium processors to effectively process more instructions at one time. Even though the initial Itanium processors had a clock speed less than half of the then-current Pentium processors, Itaniums were still faster due to their capability to process more instructions in parallel, rather than in sequence.

> **What About the Competition?**
>
> Many folks—including myself—have become accustomed to the competition between AMD and Intel processors. Every time Intel released a new Pentium, AMD wasn't far behind with a new, comparable processor. If you've enjoyed the lower prices created by this competition, you'll be pleased to know that AMD is countering Intel's Itanium with its own 64-bit chip code-named Hammer.
>
> You can get more details on Hammer at www.amd.com. Hammer's architecture isn't intended to be a straight clone of Itanium, although I would expect 64-bit Windows to run on Hammer when it is released.

Note   The Pentium family of processors has always had an ever-growing capability for parallel instruction processing. Unfortunately, many of those capabilities require special efforts on the part of software developers and compilers, so the Pentium processors weren't always working at their best.

Because Itanium represents a whole new line of processors, everyone is starting from scratch. Software developers and compilers will be able to take better advantage of Itanium right from the start.

Itanium 2's system bus runs at a blazing 400MHz, almost triple the speed of the fastest Pentium system busses (and faster than the original Itanium's 266MHz bus). Itanium also includes enterprise-class reliability features, such as enhanced error detection and correction capabilities and an integrated error reporting mechanism—all features that can exist because Itanium isn't based on what came before but is instead a radically new architecture. Obviously, the capability to support up to 256 processors in a single system presents exciting new ideas for some amazingly powerful (and expensive) servers.

As you'll read later in this chapter, Itaniums can fully emulate a Pentium processor, enabling Windows to more easily support 32-bit applications under a 64-bit environment. This backward-compatibility is a good sign for Itanium's longevity in the marketplace because businesses won't have to immediately scrap all their 32-bit software to implement 64-bit computers.

64-bit Architecture

64-bit's "big gun" is memory support. Although the Pentium's 4GB memory limit was impressive several years ago, 4GB doesn't go very far with today's high-end server applications. Itanium processors' memory support depends on their accompanying support chipset: Original Itanium computers supported 16GB of RAM per processor, whereas newer Itanium 2 computers support up to 64GB of RAM per processor—with up to 256 processors. That's a lot of RAM and should be enough for quite a few years. Itanium 2 processors also have three levels of cache memory, running at extremely high speeds. These caches help reduce the processor's need to access main memory by storing frequently used information within the caches. Sun Microsystems offers an interesting analogy that puts 64-bit memory capabilities into perspective: A 32-bit computer has enough addressing space to store the name and address of every person who has lived in the United States since 1997. A 64-bit computer can address enough memory to store the name and address of everyone who has ever lived on Earth.

Itanium 2 computers will also include support for Infiniband, the replacement for the PCI peripheral bus architecture you're already familiar with. PCI, as you know, supports the use of *busmastering* devices that can directly access main memory, removing some processing burden from the computer's main processor. Infiniband, however, uses a completely switched architecture, giving every device direct access to main memory and the processors. This architecture is analogous to a switched network environment, in which every network device has dedicated bandwidth, rather than having to share that bandwidth with other devices. Infiniband is faster, too, with bandwidths of up to 6Gbps. That's hundreds of times faster than even the fastest PCI bus.

Partition Management

Itanium machines use a radically new change to disk partitioning. Your 32-bit servers rely on a master boot record (MBR), which identifies the partitions on a disk by their cylinders, sectors, and head locations. The MBR also includes the partition's type, which can include primary, non-DOS, extended, and so forth. The MBR tracks which partition is active (bootable), as well. Unfortunately, the MBR scheme was designed decades ago when nobody could imagine hard disks so large that more than four partitions would be needed, so the MBR supports a maximum of four partitions. Itanium machines are built for the future, though, and use a much more flexible scheme called the GUID Partition Table (GPT).

Each GPT-based disk assigns two globally unique identifiers (GUIDs) to each partition on the disk. One GUID identifies the partition, whereas the other represents a partition type. Partition types include

- **EFI System Partition (ESP)**—This partition holds the operating system-specific boot loaders for the operating systems on your server. I'll discuss these in more detail in the next section, "Boot Architecture." Each server has only one ESP, which is at least 100MB in size and no larger than 1GB. The ESP is usually sized at 1% of the disk's total size. The ESP doesn't show up in Windows at all and is accessible only from the server's EFI command processor.
- **Microsoft Reserved partitions (MSRs)**—This special type of partition stores information for dynamic disks. I explain MSRs in more detail in the sidebar titled "Understanding MSRs."
- **Microsoft Data partitions**—These are regular partitions created in Explorer or the Disk Manager console, and they can be accessed by other operating systems installed on your server, unless of course you protect them by using NTFS permissions.
- **OEM partitions**—These are created by some server vendors and include special diagnostic utilities, setup utilities, and so forth. Vendors' utilities access the partition by its GUID because these partitions don't appear in Explorer. You can access them in the Disk Management console.

Itanium machines' partition management is extensible and much more flexible than the partition management system on 32-bit machines (which dates back to IBM's original PC computer from 1980).

Understanding MSRs

Understanding these is easier if you think about how 32-bit Windows treats disks. Remember that a standard MBR-based disk is treated by Windows as a basic disk. However, you can convert basic disks to dynamic disks. When you do, the partition information is transferred from the MBR to a Logical Disk Manager (LDM) database. Each dynamic disk stores an identical copy of the LDM database, which is located on a hidden partition located on the last cylinder of the disk (or the last 1MB, whichever is smaller).

64-bit Windows calls a GPT-based disk a basic disk and lets the server's firmware manage the partitions using the GPT. Converting a basic disk to dynamic moves the GPT information into the LDM database—essentially the same as in a 32-bit server, so far. However, GPT doesn't support the fancy partitioning Windows uses to hide the LDM database on a 32-bit machine. Instead, 64-bit Windows creates an MSR partition to store the database. Windows actually creates the MSR even if the disk is left as a basic disk, so the MSR is there if the disk is ever converted to dynamic.

MSRs are sized based on the physical disk size. The MSR is 32MB on a disk of up to 16GB and is 128MB on larger disks. MSRs are formatted as FAT16, which can be natively read by Itanium machines' EFI command processors. MSR partitions can't be seen in Explorer, but you can see them in the Windows Disk Management console.

Boot Architecture

One of the most noticeable changes in the Itanium architecture is its completely new boot architecture, which bears a closer resemblance to RISC-based computers (such as the Alpha) than to the traditional PC boot process, which is more than 20 years old. To quickly review, PCs use their BIOS settings to determine from which device—CD-ROM, floppy, hard disk, or network—to boot. The BIOS then looks for a boot sector on the appropriate device and loads it into memory. The boot sector contains code that looks for an operating system loader, such as Windows 2000's Ntldr. The operating system loader is responsible for getting the operating system up and running. In Windows's case, that includes running Ntdetect.com to find out what basic hardware is present, loading a SCSI driver (Ntbootdd.sys) if necessary, and so forth. Special provisions abound, including the El Torito bootable CD-ROM specification, which is supported by most servers. All this complexity makes it very difficult to create machines that can boot to different operating systems, troubleshoot missing or corrupted boot sectors, and so on.

Itanium machines work completely differently: They store boot information in a special non-volatile memory called *firmware*. Intel has developed an interface called Extensible Firmware Interface (EFI), which controls the settings in the firmware. Itanium machines also store their boot sector code right in the firmware, and not on disk. As a result, Itanium machines don't need Ntldr or a Boot.ini file. Itanium machines also use a secondary boot loader stored on disk, named Ia64ldr.efi. Note the .efi file extension, which indicates a file that can be executed by the EFI firmware. The EFI itself contains a command processor that is accessible from a boot menu and lists all the partitions available to it. You can execute the command processor's Map command to redisplay the list if necessary. The list includes

- **A GUID for each partition**—This is a long ID number, such as FD47389-87D4-116B-9488 849B7298A657.
- **A sequence number**—Indicates the partition's location on the disk. These are listed as blk0, blk1, and so forth.
- **An alias**—If a partition is formatted with a file system that EFI can read (which currently includes FAT, FAT32, and Joliet CD-ROMs), the partition is assigned an alias, such as fs0 or fs1.

Within the command processor, you can type a block name followed by a colon to access a particular partition. For example, entering **blk1:** and pressing Enter takes you to the second partition (the first partition is blk0). If the partition's file system is readable by EFI, you can use a standard Dir command to display a directory listing. For partitions with an alias, such as fs0:, you can also enter the alias name to access the partition: Type **fs0:** and press **Enter**.

Another important change is that EFI doesn't support El Torito bootable CD-ROMs, so you can't just pop a Windows Server 2003 CD in the drive and restart the computer to launch Setup. However, EFI does natively recognize the Joliet CD-ROM file system, so you can access the contents of the CD-ROM from within the command processor and launch Setup that way.

For example, if your Windows Server 2003 CD-ROM is assigned the partition alias fs2:, you can load the command processor, type **fs2:**, press Enter, and simply execute the Setup bootloader (Setupldr.efi). All 64-bit-compatible operating systems include an EFI-compatible Setup loader, which you can execute from the command processor.

The firmware's boot menu is essentially a macro system, allowing a single menu option to switch to a specified partition and execute a particular EFI secondary boot loader. This architecture enables you to easily set up multiboot computers without having to remember complex ARC naming paths (such as Boot.ini uses), troubleshoot the multifile 32-bit Windows boot system (Ntldr, boot.ini, Ntdetect.com, and so forth), or deal with master boot sectors and other disk-based boot schemes.

The new boot architecture takes some getting used to, though. You can think of it as a kind of mini-Recovery Console and boot menu, built right into the server hardware itself. After you're accustomed to using the new architecture, you'll find that it's more flexible and powerful than the decades-old system 32-bit servers use.

32-bit Windows Compatibility

Neither Microsoft nor Intel planned to leave its 32-bit users in the dust. Both 64-bit Windows and the Itanium architecture provide ample backward-compatibility with the 32-bit world, making it easier to implement these new products in your environment. The next two sections cover the software compatibility provided by Windows and the hardware compatibility provided by Intel's architecture.

Software Compatibility

Ever since the first version of Windows NT, administrators have become familiar with WOW, the Windows On Windows subsystem. Essentially, WOW emulates 16-bit Windows, allowing Windows NT to run 16-bit Windows applications for backward-compatibility. Although WOW was more commonly used on clients than on servers, where native 32-bit applications reign supreme, WOW is making a fresh appearance in 64-bit Windows. All editions of 64-bit Windows include WOW64, a 32-bit Windows subsystem that hosts 32-bit Windows applications. These applications run in what is basically an emulated 32-bit Windows environment, so they tend to be a bit slower than if they were running on 32-bit hardware in a 32-bit operating environment. Also, 64-bit Windows doesn't include the original WOW, making it tougher to run any 16-bit applications you still have laying around. Certain 16-bit applications will still run, perhaps most notably certain 16-bit Setup utilities used to distribute some older 32-bit applications.

So, by and large, any application written for 32-bit Windows will work fine (albeit a bit more slowly) with 64-bit Windows. You won't be running the 32-bit edition of SQL Server on 64-bit Windows, but you can certainly run 32-bit utilities and administrative tools. And, in case you're wondering, Microsoft will probably release a 64-bit edition of SQL Server around the same time as Windows Server 2003, and Microsoft is hard at work on 64-bit editions of its other popular .NET Enterprise Servers (such as SQL Server), Visual Studio, and more.

Speaking of Visual Studio, software developers don't need to wait for a 64-bit edition to start creating 64-bit applications. They can develop 64-bit applications on 32-bit Windows computers and compile them as native 64-bit applications; 64-bit Windows itself was, after all, written under 32-bit Windows. A Visual Studio 6 service pack has introduced a special 64-bit *thunking* layer, which enables developers to write 64-bit code on a 32-bit operating system.

Hardware Compatibility

64-bit Windows must boot from a GPT partition, but it allows you to use the older MBR scheme to partition other disks. This feature enables you to easily add existing MBR-based disks to your Itanium servers, primarily for migration and coexistence purposes. Because 32-bit Windows can't read GPT-based disks, MBR-based disks provide a convenient common ground for the two architectures. For example, removable drives such as Zip and Jaz drives can't be partitioned with GPT; the 64-bit architecture considers these to be *superfloppies* and supports only MBR-based partitioning. Other removable drives, including USB and IEEE-1394 (FireWire), must also be partitioned with MBR and can be easily transported between 64-bit and 32-bit machines.

> **Caution** Be very careful when using 32-bit disk management utilities in 64-bit Windows. These utilities won't be aware of the GPT partitioning scheme and might try to use MBR techniques instead, thus corrupting your GPT-based disks. You should use only 64-bit disk management utilities that are compatible with both MBR- and GPT-based disks.
>
> The GPT scheme includes a "dummy" MBR, which gives GPT-unaware applications something to work with that can't be hurt. However, you should still avoid using older disk management utilities to eliminate any possible risk of disk corruption.

As we've implied, most of your 32-bit peripheral equipment will work fine on 64-bit servers, especially external USB and IEEE-1394-based devices. Early Itanium servers still use PCI devices, as the new Infiniband hardware is just coming to market. SCSI and IDE disks work fine in Itanium machines, as do other IDE and SCSI peripherals such as CD-ROM and DVD-ROM drives.

Significant Differences

64-bit Windows doesn't include every bell and whistle of its 32-bit cousin. After all, both 64-bit Windows and Itanium-based server hardware are marketed (and priced) as enterprise solutions; you would no more configure an Itanium server to be a fax server than you would use a Ferrari to pick up the soccer team after practice. Some of the "missing features" between

32-bit and 64-bit Windows are simply features that an enterprise wouldn't use on 64-bit Windows. Other missing features reflect the intense amount of development that went into 64-bit Windows; not everything fit in under the deadline. Here are the major feature differences between 32-bit Windows Server 2003 and the equivalent 64-bit editions:

- **The .NET Framework isn't included with 64-bit Windows**—Expect that to change in the future; the whole point of the .NET Framework is that Microsoft (or someone) simply has to create a new common language runtime (CLR) in order to move the Framework to a different hardware platform. You'll see a 64-bit edition of the CLR in the future.

  ➤ For more information on the .NET Framework and the CLR, **see** "The .NET Framework," **p. 146**.

- **ASP.NET isn't available in 64-bit Windows**—This is because it's part and parcel of the .NET Framework. As soon as the Framework has a 64-bit CLR, ASP.NET should run just fine.

- **Obviously, the 32-bit editions of Windows Server 2003 don't take advantage of improvements in the Itanium architecture**—Windows Server 2003's 64-bit editions have additional features that leverage Itanium's native error logging mechanisms and much more. Although it's theoretically possible (according to Intel) to run 32-bit Windows on an Itanium, you wouldn't see much of an improvement in the operating system's performance, and you wouldn't see any additional features.

- **Only 64-bit editions of Windows include support for 64-bit software development via group policy**—New options in the user interface will enable you to specify whether 32-bit applications should be deployed to 64-bit computers, as well. This feature will provide interoperability in a mixed 32-bit and 64-bit environment.

- **Windows Installer on 64-bit editions of Windows also includes specific 64-bit application support**—This enables packages to include both 32-bit and 64-bit components. This capability allows a single installer package to support both 32-bit and 64-bit computers, reducing administrative overhead and software maintenance.

- **64-bit Windows includes printing support for 32-bit clients**—This enables administrators and users to manage and connect to printers that are hosted by a 64-bit edition of Windows from their 32-bit client operating systems.

- **64-bit editions of Windows include new driver installer routines**—These can choose available 64-bit drivers over 32-bit drivers, if both are provided during an installation. INF files, which list the drivers needed by a particular device, can include 64-bit-specific lists in addition to 32-bit driver lists.

- **64-bit Windows doesn't include, at least for now, Product Activation**—Microsoft doesn't feel that piracy, the reason Product Activation exists, will be an issue in the 64-bit world for the time being.

> For more information on Product Activation in 32-bit Windows, **see** "Activating Windows," **p. 13**.

- **64-bit Windows lacks some common media applications**—These include NetMeeting and Windows Media Player. This lack isn't critical in a server operating system, but you'll see 64-bit versions of these applications made available as free downloads and targeted at the 64-bit edition of Windows XP.
- **64-bit Windows doesn't support power management**—With no 64-bit portable computers on the near horizon, you probably won't miss this feature anyway. Another common portable computer feature, infrared communications, isn't supported in 64-bit Windows, either.
- **64-bit Windows does not include Remote Assistance**—Windows Server 2003 does include Terminal Services, so the underpinnings of Remote Assistance are available, but the actual feature isn't implemented.
- **Native CD burning isn't included in 64-bit Windows**—There's nothing stopping a third-party manufacturer from writing a CD burning application, however, and those will no doubt become available after 64-bit operating systems have enough market penetration.

Some other, minor features are not included in 64-bit Windows, but these mainly affect the client operating system—Windows XP. Speech recognition, for example, isn't included in Windows XP 64-bit. Altogether, Microsoft claims a 99% feature parity between 32-bit and 64-bit editions. As mentioned, some of the parts missing from 64-bit today, such as the .NET Framework, will undoubtedly be released in a future update.

Index

SYMBOLS

!SAC (!special administration console), 224-225

/S parameters (command-line tools), 225, 229

/Windows system root folders, security templates, 216

NUMBERS

32-bit Windows, 64-bit Windows compatibility, 258-261

64-bit operating systems, support, 85

64-bit Windows
  32-bit Windows compatibility, 258-261
  architectures, 255
  disk partitioning, 255
  EPIC (explicitly parallel instruction computing) architecture (Intel), 254
  Itanium computers, 256-257

2048-bit encryption, 166

A

ABOs (Administration Base Objects), 108

access permissions, 193

accessing resource properties (clusters), 206

account policies (security), 50

activation keys (Windows Product Activation), 25

Active Directory, 65
  AD/AM (Active Directory Application Mode), 77
  administrative tools, 69-70, 73

Active Directory

ADMT (Active Directory Migration Tool) 2.0, 68
architectural tools, 74-75
computer encryption certificates, mapping, 165
cross-forest trusts, 76-77
domain functional levels, 66-67, 78
forest functional levels, 66-67
functional levels, 66
GPMC (Group Policy Management Console), 68
integrated zones (DNS), 129-130
remote office logons, 78
replication from media feature, 78

active-active clusters, 200

active-passive clusters, 200-202

AD/AM (Active Directory Application Mode), 77

Add/Remove Programs (Remote Desktop for Administration), 181

Add/Remove Windows Components (Remote Desktop for Administration), 181

adding
configured assemblies, 151
resources (clusters), 204-205

addresses
anycast addresses, 162
APIPA (Automatic Private IP Addressing) addresses, 162
dynamic addresses, 165
global unicast addresses, 163
IP addresses
APIPA (Automatic Private IP Addressing), 128-129
clusters, 203
compressed IP addresses, 161
customizing, RRAS (Routing and Remote Access Service), 172
IPv4 addresses, 161-162
IPv6 addresses, 161-162
IPv6 protocols versus IPv4 protocols, 160
loopback address (IPv6 protocol), 162
NLB (Network Load Balancing) clusters, 209
unspecified address (IPv6 protocol), 162
IPv4 addresses, 161-162
IPv6 addresses, 161-162
link-local unicast addresses, 162
multicast addresses, 161-162
site-local unicast addresses, 162
unicast addresses, 161-163

administrative scripts, VBScript, 246-249

Administrative Templates\Network Components section (Computer Configuration policies), 97-98

Administrative Templates\Shared Folders section (New User Configuration policies), 99

Administrative Templates\System Components section (Computer Configuration policies), 95-97

Administrative Templates\System section (New User Configuration policies), 99

Administrative Templates\Windows Components section (Computer Configuration policies), 95

Administrative Templates\Windows Components section (New User Configuration policies), 98

administrative tools (Active Directory)
   domain controllers, 73
   domains, renaming, 73
   dragging/dropping, 69
   inheritance parents, showing, 69
   multiple objects, selecting, 70
   permissions, showing, 69
   RSoP (Resultant Set of Policy) feature, 70
   Saved Queries feature, 70

Administrator accounts (Remote Desktop for Administration), permissions, 183

ADMT 2.0 (Active Directory Migration Tool), 68

adprep command-line tool, 227

Advanced Settings dialog box (ICF), 169-170

Affinity setting property (port ranges), 212

All Programs menu (Start menu), 41

Allow Time Zone Redirection setting (Terminal Services client/server data redirection policy settings), 188

analyzing security databases, 52-53

anycast addresses (IPv6 protocols), 162

APIPA (Automatic Private IP Addressing)
   DHCP (Dynamic Host Configuration Protocol), 128-129
   IPv4 protocols, 162
   Registry key, 129

Application Compatibility settings (Computer Configuration policy sections), 95

Application Compatibility settings (New User Configuration policy sections), 98

application partitions (Active Directory architectural tools), 74

Application Pool dialog box, 110-112

application pools, configuring, 104-112

Application Server Mode (Remote Desktop for Administration), 181

application servers, 103

applications
   adding, 154
   assigning, 85
   binding policies, 152
   COM+ applications (Web services), 157
   custom configurations, 154
   dependencies, viewing, 154
   Manage Your Server application (RRAS), 171
   managing, 150, 154

How can we make this index more useful? Email us at indexes@samspublishing.com

applications

modifying, 154
network settings, changing, 175
remoting services, managing, 154
repairing, 154
software applications, creating, 146

Approval Log (SUS), 242

approving SUS (Software Update Services) updates, 237-238

architectural tools (Active Directory), 74-75

architectures

64-bit architectures, 254-255
IIS (Internet Information Services) console, 104-107
Itanium computers (64-bit Windows) boot architectures, 257

ASP (Active Server Pages), 156

ASP.NET (Active Server Pages.NET), 157

ASR (Automated System Recovery), 17, 250-252

assemblies

Assembly Cache, managing, 149-151
binding policies, 152
codebases, 152
configured assemblies
　adding, 151
　managing, 149-152
lists, 150-151
network-accessible assemblies, 152
versions, binding policies, 152

Assembly Cache, managing, 149-151

assigning applications, Install This Application at Logon option (Group Policy), 85

asymmetric key encryption, 141

audio CDs, burning, 36-37

auditing security, 62

automated backups, 128

automatic network configuration, 176

Automatic Partner Configuration (WINS), 127

Automatic Reconnection setting (Terminal Services Group Policy settings), 187

automatic replication, domain-based DFS (distributed file system), 138

Automatic Updates, 239-242

AWE (Address Windows Extensions), 7

B

BackupExec (Veritas), 250

backups

automated backups, 128
BackupExec (Veritas), 250
BrightStor (Computer Associates), 250
GPOs (Group Policy Objects), 93
manual backups, 128
System Restore, 250
Windows Backup, 249-252

backward compatibility, managing, 152

basic disks, 256

binding policies, 152

bone broadcasts, 60

boot architectures, 257

bootcfg command-line tool, 227

BrightStor (Computer Associates), 250

browsing security principal policies, RSoP feature (Active Directory administrative tools), 71

building clusters, 201

burning audio/data CDs, 34-37

C

CALs (client access licenses), 11

CD burners, 34-37

CD Writing Wizard, 36

CD-based installation (Windows Server 2003), 16-19

CDs, burning, 34-37

certificates, computer encryption certificates, 165

changing network settings, 175

choice command-line tool, 227

CIDR (Classless Interdomain Routing), 161

Class C property (port ranges), 212

client/server data redirection policies (Terminal Services), 188

clip command-line tool, 227

CLR (Common Language Runtime), 148-149, 152-153

Cluster Administrator, 204-207

Cluster Service. *See also* **NLB (Network Load Balancing)**

active-active clusters, 200

active-passive clusters, 200-202

clusters, creating, 203-204

Datacenter Edition, 8

DFS (distributed file system), 213

DHCP (Dynamic Host Configuration Protocol) Service, 213

Distributed Transaction Coordinator, 213

failovers, 202

file shares, 213

IIS (Internet Information Services), 213

majority node set clusters, building, 201

message queuing, 213

printer spools, 213

single node clusters, building, 201

single quorum device clusters, building, 201

Volume Shadow Copy Service tasks, 213

WINS (Windows Internet Naming Service), 213

clustering

terminal servers, 194-195

Windows (Enterprise Edition), 7

clusters

active-active clusters, 200

active-passive clusters, 200-202

How can we make this index more useful? Email us at indexes@samspublishing.com

clusters

creating, 203-204
DFS (distributed file system), 213
DHCP (Dynamic Host Configuration Protocol) Service, 213
Distributed Transaction Coordinator, 213
file shares, 213
IIS (Internet Information Services), 213
IP addresses, 203
majority node set clusters, building, 201
managing, Cluster Administrator, 204-207
message queuing, 213
naming, 203
NLB (Network Load Balancing) clusters, 208-212
preconfigured cluster packages, 201
printer spools, 213
resources, 202-206
single node clusters, building, 201
single quorum device clusters, building, 201
TCP/IP (Transfer Control Protocol/Internet Protocol), 203
Volume Shadow Copy Service tasks, 213
WINS (Windows Internet Naming Service), 213

code groups, 152-153

codebases, 152

codes
native codes, 146
permission sets, 152-153

COM+ applications (Web services), 157

command-line interface tools (WMIC), 226, 229

command-line tools, 218, 225-229

compatibility
backward compatibility, managing, 152
IIS (Internet Information Services) console, 107

compatibility addresses (IPv4 protocol), 162

compatibility addresses (IPv6 protocol), 162

compatws template, 49

compatws.inf security template, 217

compressed folders
Compressed Folders feature (Windows Server 2003), 33-34
NTFS folder compression, 32-33

Compressed Folders feature (Windows Server 2003), 33-34

compressed IP addresses, 161

Computer Configuration policy sections (Group Policy), 94-98

computer encryption certificates, mapping, 165

Computer Management console, 136

configuring
application pools (IIS console), 109-112
assemblies, 151
Automatic Updates, 239-240

control key functions (Remote Desktop client), 185
fax devices, 132-133
file/folder access, 62
Group Policy policies (RSoP console), 88
networks, automatic network configuration, 176
port range affinity (NLB clusters), 211
port rules (NLB clusters), 211
RIS (Remote Installation Services), 27
RRAS (Routing and Remote Access Service), 171
security databases, 53-55
Security Templates snap-in, 49-50
servers (IIS console), 108
Session Directory for terminal servers, 196
SUS (Software Update Services) synchronization schedule, 235-236
Terminal Services, 186-189
Web Services extensions (IIS console), 112-114
Web sites (IIS console), 108-109

Connect to Console check box (Remote Desktops MMC client), 183

connecting to terminal servers, 193

Connection bar (Remote Desktop client), 185

consoles
Computer Management console, 136
Disk Management console, 140
DNS (domain name system) console, 131-132
Fax Administration console, 132

Fax Console (fax service), 134
Fax Service Management console, 133
GPMC (Group Policy Management Console), 68, 92-93, 215
IIS (Internet Information Services) console, 101-103
   ABOs (Administration Base Objects), 108
   architecture, 104-107
   auditing log files, 61-62
   clusters, 213
   compatibility, 107
   configuring application pools, 109-112
   configuring servers, 108
   configuring Web sites, 108-109
   editing metabases, 119
   installing, 103
   POP3 services, 120-122
   rapid fail protection, 107
   security, 117
   SMTP (Simple Mail Transport Protocol) services, 120-122
   upgrading, 118-119
   Web Services extensions, 112-114
   Web-based administration, 114-115
MMC (Microsoft Management Console), 218
.NET Framework Configuration Console (.NET server)
   adding applications, 154
   custom application configurations, 154
   managing application remote services, 154

How can we make this index more useful? Email us at indexes@samspublishing.com

270 consoles

    managing applications, 150, 154

    managing Assembly Cache, 149-151

    managing code access security policies, 149, 152-153

    managing configured assemblies, 149-152

    modifying applications, 154

    repairing applications, 154

    viewing application dependencies, 154

  remoting services, managing, 149, 154

  RSoP (Resultant Set of Policy) console, 88-91

  SAC (Special Administration Console), 224

control keys (Remote Desktop client), configuring, 185

Control panel (Start menu), 41

cross-forest trusts (Active Directory)

  Group Policies, 83

  IAS (Internet Authentication Service), 76-77

Ctrl+Alt+Del settings (New User Configuration policy sections), 99

custom security templates, creating, 51

Custom topology (DFS replication), 138

customizing

  application configurations, 154

  desktops, 32, 40

  IP addresses (RRAS), 172

  RSoP (Resultant Set of Policy) feature (Active Directory administrative tools), 71

  Start menu, 42

D

DACL (discretionary access control list), modifying, 188

data CDs, burning, 34-36

data encryption, EFS (Encrypting File System), 56-57

data partitioning, Itanium computers (64-bit Windows), 256

data storage, 139-140

database backups, 128

Datacenter Edition, 9

  Cluster Service, 8

  IPSec/L2TP tunnels, NLB (Network Load Balancing) support, 165

  Terminal Server Session Directory, 194-195

  updates, 9

DC security template, 49

DC security.inf security template, 217

DDNS (Dynamic DNS), 58

DDNS (Dynamic DNS) tab (DHCP), 128-129

deactivating schemas (Active Directory architectural tools), 74

Debug Logging tab (DNS console), 132

Default Utilities (Start menu), 41

definition settings (Security Templates snap-in), 51

defrag command-line tool, 227

demand-dial connections (RRAS), 173

deploying software
    DFS (distributed file system), 137
    IntelliMirror, 220

desktop
    customizing, 40
    Remote Assistance, enabling, 38-40
    Remote Desktop, 37
    screensavers, 32
    themes, 32
    wallpapers, 32

device drivers, installing, 16

DFS (distributed file system), 137-138, 213

DHCP (Dynamic Host Configuration Protocol), 58, 128-129, 213

DHCPv6, 164

dialog boxes
    Advanced Settings dialog box (ICF), 169-170
    Application Pool dialog box, 110-112
    System Properties dialog box, 182

Diffie-Hellman key exchange, 165

disaster recovery
    ASR (Automated System Recovery), 17
    CD-based installation (Windows Server 2003), 16-17
    shadow copies (file sharing), 136

disconnected sessions (terminal servers), 195

Disk Management console, 140

disk partitioning, 255-256

diskpart command-line tool, 227

displaying Group Policy policies (RSoP console), 88-91

Distributed Transaction Coordinator, 213

DNS (domain name system), 58, 62, 129-132

DNS (domain name system) Client settings (Computer Configuration policy sections), 97

Do Not Allow Local Administrators to Customize Permissions setting (Terminal Services Group Policy settings), 188

Do Not Allow Smart Card Device Redirection setting (Terminal Services client/server data redirection policy settings), 188

domain controllers
    AD (Active Directory) integrated zones (DNS), 129-130
    hisecdc.inf security templates, 217
    renaming, Active Directory administrative tools, 73
    replication from media feature (Active Directory), 78
    securedc.inf security templates, 217

domain events, auditing, 62

domain functional levels (Active Directory), 66-67, 78

How can we make this index more useful? Email us at indexes@samspublishing.com

domain-based DFS (distributed file system), 137-138

DomainDNSZones (AD-integrated zones), 130

domains
AD/AM (Active Directory Application Mode), 77
remote office logons (Active Directory), 78
renaming, Active Directory administrative tools, 73

downloading themes, 32

dragging/dropping Active Directory administrative tools, 69

drivers
device drivers, installing, 16
http.sys driver, 104-106
null drivers, 221
printer drivers, 191

dsadd command-line tool, 227

dsget command-line tool, 227

dsmod command-line tool, 227

dsmove command-line tool, 227

dsrm command-line tool, 227

dynamic addresses, IPSec (Internet Protocol Security) protocols, 165

E

editing
IIS (Internet Information Services) console metabase, 119
port settings (NLB clusters), 211

EFI (Extensible Firmware Interface), 257

EFS (Encrypting File System), 56-57, 141

email, creating mailboxes, 120-122

EMS (Emergency Management Services), 20, 223-225. *See also* **headless servers**

Enable Result Caching option (WINS), 126

Enable TS per NIC setting (Terminal Services settings), 189

enabling
ICF (Internet Connection Firewall), 169
Remote Assistance, 38-40
Remote Desktop for Administration, 182
shadow copies (file sharing), 135

encrypted files, storing remote servers, 141-142

encryption
2048-bit encryption, 166
asymmetric key encryption, 141
EFS (Encrypting File System), 56-57, 141
symmetric key encryption, 141
terminal servers, 193

encryption keys, 165

Enterprise license agreements, 26

Enterprise Edition, 165

Enterprise Edition, 7, 156, 194

EPIC (Explicitly Parallel Instruction Computing) architecture (Intel), 254

Error Reporting settings (Computer Configuration policy sections), 97

ESP (EFI System Partitions), 256

event log policies (security), 50

event viewer snap-ins (DNS console servers), 131

eventcreate command-line tool, 227

eventquery command-line tool, 227

Exchange Server (Cluster Services), 200

extensions
- AWE (Address Windows Extensions), 7
- Security Settings extension (Group Policy), 48, 55
- Web Services extensions, 112-114

F

failback policies (cluster resources), 206-207

failover policies (cluster resources), 206

failovers, 202

farms, 194-195

Fax Administration console, 132

Fax Console (fax service), 134

Fax Monitor (fax service), 134

fax service, 132-134

Fax Service Management console, 133

faxes, 132-134

File and Folder Tasks (Windows Explorer), 136

file permissions (security databases), 54

File Share wizard, 137

file sharing
- clusters, 213
- Computer Management console, 136
- DFS (distributed file system), 137-138
- File Share wizard, 137
- NAS (Network Attached Storage), 139-140
- shadow copies, 135-136
- WebDAV (Web Distributed Authoring and Versioning), 142

file system policies (security), 50

files
- access, configuring, 62
- encrypted files, storing on remote servers, 141-142

filtering, GPO (Group Policy Object) Editor, 86-87

finding WINS (Windows Internet Naming Service) records, 126

firewalls, 169-170

firmware, 257

folders
- access, configuring, 62
- compressed folders, 32-34
- Security/Templates subfolder, 216
- system root folders, 216

forest functional levels (Active Directory), 66-67

ForestDNSZones (AD-integrated zones), 130

How can we make this index more useful? Email us at indexes@samspublishing.com

forests
    cross-forest trusts (Active Directory), 76-77
    domains, renaming, 73
    Group Policies, 83

formatting partitions (CD-based Windows Server 2003 installation), 17

forwarders (DNS), 131

freedisk command-line tool, 228

fresh installs versus upgrades, 30

fsutil command-line tool, 228

Full Mesh topology (DFS replication), 138

Full Screen mode (Remote Desktop client), 185

Full Security Permission Compatibility setting (Terminal Services settings), 189

functional levels (Active Directory), 66-67, 78

G

GC servers, remote office logons (Active Directory), 78

getmac command-line tool, 228

global unicast addresses (IPv6 protocols), 163

glue records (DNS), 130-131

GPMC (Group Policy Management Console), 68, 92-93, 215

GPOs (Group Policy Objects), 92-93, 220

GPO (Group Policy Object) Editor, 86-87

gpresult command-line tool, 228

GPTs (GUID partition tables), 256

Group Policies, 81
    Automatic Updates, configuring, 240-242
    Computer Configuration policy sections, 94-98
    cross-forest support, 83
    GPOs (Group Policy Objects), 92-93, 220
    Include OLE Class and Product Information option, 85
    Install This Application at Logon option, 85
    IntelliMirror, 220
    Join Session Directory setting (Terminal Servers Session Directory), 196
    managing
        GPMC (Group Policy Management Console), 92-93
        GPO (Group Policy Object) Editor, 86-87
    Network Configuration Operators Group, 175
    New User Configuration policy sections, 98-99
    policies, configuring/displaying, 88-91
    RPC Security Policy\Secure Server (Require Security) Group Policy, 193

RSoP (Resultant Set of Policy), 88-91
Security Settings extension, 48, 55
security templates, 216
Session Directory Cluster Name setting (Terminal Servers Session Directory), 196
Session Directory Server setting (Terminal Servers Session Directory), 196
Set Client Connection Encryption Level Group Policy, 193
setup security.inf security template, 216
Software Installation section, 84-85
Software Restriction Group Policy, 194
software restriction policies, 219-220
Terminal Server IP Address Redirection setting (Terminal Servers Session Directory), 197
Terminal Services Group Policies, 187-188, 193-194
troubleshooting, RSoP (Resultant Set of Policy) console, 87-88
WMI filters, 82

GUIDs (globally unique identifiers), 256

H

Hammer processors (AMD), 254

hardware
headless server hardware, 221-223
OOB (out of bandwidth) hardware, 222-224

headless servers, 215, 220-224. *See also* EMS (Emergency Management Services)

Health tab (Application Pool dialog box), 111

Help and Support Center, 38-40, 98

hfnetchk.exe, 48, 56, 243-245

hisecdc template, 50

hisecdc.inf security template, 217

hisecws template, 50

hisecws.inf security template, 217

hot-add memory, 7

hotfixes (security maintenance), 63, 232. *See also* updates

http.sys driver, 104-106

Hub and Spoke topology (DFS replication), 138

I

IAS (Internet Authentication Service), 76

ICF (Internet Connection Firewall), 169-170

ICS (Internet Connection Sharing), 168

Identity tab (Application Pool dialog box), 112

IEEE-1394 networking support, 175-176

IIL log file rotation (VBScript), 247-249

How can we make this index more useful? Email us at indexes@samspublishing.com

276   IIS

IIS (Internet Information Services) console, 101-102
   ABOs (Administration Base Objects), 108
   application pools, configuring, 109-112
   architecture, 104-107
   clusters, 213
   compatibility, 107
   installing, 103
   log files, auditing, 61-62
   metabases, editing, 119
   POP3 services, 120-122
   rapid fail protection, 107
   security, 117
   servers, configuring, 108
   SMTP (Simple Mail Transport Protocol) services, 120-122
   upgrading, 118-119
   Web Services extensions, 112-114
   Web sites, configuring, 108-109
   Web-based administration, 114-115

Iisback command-line tool, 228

Iiscnfg command-line tool, 228

Iisftp command-line tool, 228

Iisftpdr command-line tool, 228

Iisvdir command-line tool, 228

Iisweb command-line tool, 228

IKE (Internet Key Exchange), 166

IL (Intermediate Language), 148

images, Windows 2003 Server installation, 23

implementing EFS (Encryption File System), 141

importing security templates into security databases, 52

in-process applications, 106

Include OLE Class and Product Information option (Group Policy), 85

Infiniband, 255

inheritance, showing parents (Active Directory administrative tools), 69

insecure password warnings, 18

Install This Application at Logon option (Group Policy), 85

installing
   device drivers, 16
   Emergency Management Services, 20
   fax printers, 132
   fax service, 133
   IIS (Internet Information Services) console, 103
   Remote Desktop Connection client (Remote Desktop for Administration), 184
   Remote Desktop for Administration, 181
   RIS (Remote Installation Services), 26-27
   Session Directory servers, 196
   SUS (Software Update Services), 234
   Windows Server 2003
      CD-based installation, 16-19
      network-based installation, 19-20

RIS (Remote Installation Services), 26-27

third-party imaging software installation, 23

unattended installations, 20-22

WindowsProduct Activation, 23-25

IntelliMirror, 220

inuse command-line tool, 228

inventorying updates, 243-245

IP addresses

APIPA (Automatic Private IP Addressing), 128-129

clusters, 203

compressed IP addresses, 161

customizing (RRAS), 172

IPv4 addresses, 161

IPv6 addresses, 161

IPv6 versus IPv4 protocols, 160

NLB (Network Load Balancing) clusters, 209

IP Security Policies snap-in, 165

IPSec (Internet Protocol Security) protocol, 164-166

IPSec Monitor snap-ins, 166

IPSec/L2TP tunnels, 165

IPv4 protocols, 106-162

IPv6 protocols, 160-164

IPv6 stacks, 163-164

Itanium 2 processors (Intel), 254-255

Itanium computers (64-bit Windows), 256-257

Itanium processors (Intel), 254

J – K

JIT (just in time) compilation, 148

Join Session Directory setting (Terminal Servers Session Directory Group Policies), 196

Keep-Alive Connections setting (Terminal Services Group Policy settings), 187

Kerberos protocol, 58

keys

activation keys (Windows Product Activation), 25

encryption keys, 165

license keys (Windows Product Activation), 23-26

Registry keys (APIPA), 129

volume license keys (Windows Product Activation), 23

L

languages

IL (Intermediate Language), 148

.NET languages, 148

WSDL (Web Services Description Language), 155

LAR (Large Account Resellers), Select License agreements, 13

last logon timestamp attribute (Active Directory), domain functional levels, 78

How can we make this index more useful? Email us at indexes@samspublishing.com

Launch Nslookup option (DNS console), 132

legacy COM+ applications (Web services), 157

license agreements, 17, 23-26

license keys (Windows Product Activation), 23-26

License Server Security Group setting (Terminal Services licensing policy settings), 189

licenses, 11-14

licensing policies (Terminal Services), 189

Limit Maximum Color Depth setting (Terminal Services Group Policy settings), 188

link-local unicast addresses (IPv6 protocols), 162

load balancing (terminal servers), 194-195

loading packages (Include OLE Class and Product Information option), 85

local policies (security), 50

Local Security Policy snap-in, 48

Logging mode (RSoP), 88-91

Logman command-line tool, 228

logons
    auditing, 62
    remote office logons (Active Directory), 78

loopback addresses (IPv6 protocol), 162

low-bandwidth connections, RDP (Remote Desktop Protocol) 5.1, 191-192

M

mailboxes, creating, 120-122

maintenance
    administrative scripts (VBScript), 246-249
    automatic updates, 239-242
    backups, 249-252
    hotfixes, 232
    security, 63-64, 232
    service packs, 232-233
    SUS (Software Update Services), 233
        Approval Log, 242
        approving updates, 237-238
        Automatic Updates, 239-240
        configuring synchronization schedule, 235-236
        installing, 234
        Monitor Server page, 242
    updates, inventorying, 243-245
    Windows Backup, 250
    Windows Update, 233-234

majority node set clusters, building, 201

Manage Your Server application (RRAS), 171

Manage Your Server Wizard, 19

managing
  application remote services, 154
  Assembly Cache, 149-151
  backward compatibility, 152
  clusters (Cluster Administrator), 204-207
  DNS (domain name system) server permissions, 132
  GPOs (Group Policy Objects), 92-93
  Group Policy
    GPMC (Group Policy Management Console), 92-93
    GPO (Group Policy Object) Editor, 86-87
  SANs (Storage Area Networks), 140
  servers
    GPMC (Group Policy Management Console) servers, 215
    security templates, 216-218
    software restriction policies, 218-220
  shadow copies (file sharing), 135

manual backups, 128

manual replication, domain-based DFS (distributed file system), 138

manual security database configuration, 53

mapped addresses (IPv6 protocol), 162

mapping computer encryption certificates, 165

mass upgrades, 30

MBR (master boot record), 255

member servers, securews.inf security templates, 217

memory
  64-bit Windows, 255
  hot-add memory, 7

message queuing (clusters), 213

Microsoft Data partitions, 256

Microsoft security philosophy, 46-47

Microsoft Security Web site, 104

MMC (Microsoft Management Console), 218

MMS (Microsoft Metadirectory Services), 6-7

modifying
  applications, 154
  DACL (discretionary access control list), 188
  Support Information URL (Group Policy), 84-85

Monitor Server page (SUS), 242

monitoring active IPSec (Internet Protocol Security) polices, 166

MSIL. *See* IL

MSMQ (Microsoft Message Queue Service), 157

MSRs (Microsoft Reserved partitions), 256

multicast addresses (IPv6 protocols), 161-162

multipath failover (SAN), 140

multiple objects, selecting (Active Directory administrative tools), 70

How can we make this index more useful? Email us at indexes@samspublishing.com

N

naming clusters, 203

NAS (Network Access Server), 139-140

NAT/Basic Firewall interface (RRAS), 172

native codes, 146

.NET Framework, 145-147
ASP.NET, 156
CLR (Common Language Runtime), 148-149, 152-153
IL (Intermediate Language), 148
.NET languages, 148
security, 157

.NET Framework Configuration Console (Windows Server 2003)
application remote services, managing, 154
applications
adding, 154
custom configurations, 154
managing, 150, 154
modifying, 154
repairing, 154
viewing dependencies, 154
Assembly Cache, managing, 149-151
code access security policies, managing, 149, 152-153
configured assemblies, managing, 149-152
remoting services, managing, 149, 154

.NET languages (.NET Framework), 148

Net Logon settings (Computer Configuration policy sections), 96

NetBIOS (network basic input/output system) protocol, 126, 177

NetMon (Network Monitor), 59-61

netsh command, 128

netsh interface IPv6 command, 164

Netstat tool, 176

Network Configuration Operators Group, 175

Network Connections settings (Computer Configuration policy sections), 97

network-accessible assemblies (codebases), 152

network-based installation (Windows Server 2003), 19-20

networking
automatic network configuration, 176
IEEE-1394 networking support, 175-176
IPv6 protocol, 160-164
IPv6 stacks, 163-164
Netstat tool, 176
PPPoE support, 175
wireless networking, 177
xDSL, 177

Networking tab (Windows Task Manager), 174

networks
bridging, 174-175
changing settings, 175

New User Configuration policy sections (Group Policy), 98-99

NIC for Session Directory to Use for Redirection setting (Terminal Services settings), 189

NLB (Network Load Balancing), 157, 200, 207. *See also* Cluster Service
  clusters, 208-212
  DFS (distributed file system), 213
  file shares, 213
  IIS (Internet Information Services), 213
  IPSec/L2TP tunnel support, 165
  NLB (Network Load Balancing) Manager, 212
  print spools, 213
  WINS (Windows Internet Naming Service), 213

NLB (Network Load Balancing) command-line tool, 228

NLB (Network Load Balancing) Manager, 212

nodes (cluster resources)
  specifying, 205
  transferring resources, 206

None property (port ranges), 212

Notepad (VBScript), 246

notssid.inf security template, 217

NTFS folder compression, 32-33

null drivers, 221

NUMA (non-uniform memory access), 7

O

object-oriented programming, 146

objects
  ABOs (Administration Base Objects), 108
  GPOs (Group Policy Objects), 92-93, 220
  multiple objects, selecting (Active Directory administrative tools), 70

OEM partitions, 256

OOB (out of bandwidth) hardware, 222-225

Open Business program (Open License program), 12

Open license agreements, 26

Open License programs, 11-12

Open Volume program (Open License program), 12

openfiles command-line tool, 228

operating system upgrades, 27-30

options
  Enable Result Caching option (WINS), 126
  Include OLE Class and Product Information option (Group Policy), 85
  Install This Application at Logon option (Group Policy), 85
  Launch Nslookup option (DNS console), 132
  restore option (DHCP), 128
  View Previous Versions option (File and Folder Tasks), 136

How can we make this index more useful? Email us at indexes@samspublishing.com

packages

P

packages, loading (Include OLE Class and Product Information option), 85

pagefileconfig command-line tool, 228

partitioning Active Directory architectural tools, 74

partitions
- application partitions (Active Directory architectural tools), 74
- ESP (EFI System Partitions), 256
- formatting (CD-based Windows Server 2003 installation), 17
- GUIDs (globally unique identifiers), 256
- MBR (master boot record), 255
- Microsoft Data partitions, 256
- MSRs (Microsoft Reserved Partitions), 256
- OEM partitions, 256

passport authentication (IIS console), 108

passwords
- insecure password warnings, 18
- security databases, 55
- Setup Manager Wizard, 22
- terminal servers, 193

paths, upgrade paths (Windows Server 2003), 28-30

per-client licensing (CAL), 11

per-seat licensing (CAL), 11

perfmon command-line tool, 228

Performance tab (Application Pool dialog box), 111

permanent virtual circuit encapsulation (xDSL), 177

permission sets, 152-153

permissions
- Administration accounts (Remote Desktop for Administration), 183
- file permissions (security databases), 54
- root permissions (rootsec.inf security templates), 217
- showing (Active Directory administrative tools), 69
- terminal server access permissions, 193

personalizing CD-based Windows Server 2003 installation, 18

PFE (Programmer's File Editor), 246

Pinned Programs (Start menu), 41

Planning mode (RSoP), 89-91

policies
- active IPSec (Internet Protocol Security) policies, monitoring, 166
- failback policies (cluster resources), 206-207
- failover policies (cluster resources), 206
- Group Policies, 216, 219-220
- RSoP (Resultant Set of Policy) feature (Active Directory administrative tools), 70
- software restriction policies, 218-220
- Terminal Services client/server data redirection policies, 188
- Terminal Services Group Policies, 187-188, 193-194
- Terminal Services licensing policies, 189

POP3 (Post Office Protocol 3) services (IIS consoles), 120-122

port range properties, 212

ports
serial ports, 222
TCP ports (NLB clusters), 211
UDP ports (NLB clusters), 211

Power Management settings (New User Configuration policy sections), 99

PPPoE (Point-to-Point Protocol over Ethernet), networking support, 175

Precedence tab (RSoP), 88

preconfigured cluster packages, 201

Prevent License Upgrade setting (Terminal Services licensing policy settings), 189

printer drivers, 191

printer spools, 213

printers, installing, 132

prncnfg command-line tool, 228

prndrvr command-line tool, 228

prnjobs command-line tool, 228

prnmngr command-line tool, 228

prnport command-line tool, 228

prnqctl command-line tool, 228

product activation (software), 13-14

product ID, 14

program codes, 146

properties
cluster resources, accessing, 206
port range properties, 212

protocol property (port ranges), 212

protocols
DHCP (Dynamic Host Configuration Protocol), 58, 128-129
IPSec (Internet Protocol Security) protocol, 164-166
IPv4, 160-162
IPv6, 160-164
Kerberos protocol, 58
NetBIOS (network basic input/output system), 177
POP3 (Post Office Protocol 3) services (IIS consoles), 120-122
PPPoE (Point-to-Point Protocol over Ethernet), networking support, 175
RDP (Remote Desktop Protocol), 180
RDP (Remote Desktop Protocol) 5.1, 180, 183-184, 190-194
SMTP (Simple Mail Transport Protocol), 120-122
SOAP (Simple Object Access Protocol) protocol, 155-157

Publish tab (Computer Management console), 136

Q – R

QFE (quick-fix engineering). *See* **hotfixes**

QoS Packet Scheduler settings (Computer Configuration policy sections), 97

How can we make this index more useful? Email us at indexes@samspublishing.com

queries
  DNS (domain name system) queries, forwarders, 131
  Saved Queries feature (Active Directory administrative tools), 70
  VBScript, 246

raising functional levels (Active Directory), 67

rapid fail protection (IIS console), 107

RDP (Remote Desktop Protocol), 180

RDP (Remote Desktop Protocol) 5.1, 180, 183-184, 190-194

Recently Used Programs (Start menu), 41

recursion (DNS), 131

Recycling tab (Application Pool dialog box), 110

redirecting sound cards, 191

registries (UDDI), 155

Registry key (APIPA), 129

Registry policies (security), 50

Relaxed Security Permission Compatibility setting (Terminal Services settings), 189

relaying SMTP (Simple Mail Transport Protocol), 120

relog command-line tool, 228

remote administration, 220-225

Remote Administration Mode (Remote Desktop for Administration), 181

Remote Assistance, 37-40

Remote Assistance settings (Computer Configuration policy sections), 96

Remote Desktop, 37

Remote Desktop client, 185

Remote Desktop Connection application, 179-180, 183-184, 190-194

Remote Desktop Connection client (Remote Desktop for Administration), 183-184

Remote Desktop for Administration, 179-180
  Administration accounts, permissions, 183
  Application Server Mode, 181
  enabling, 182
  installing, 181
  Remote Administration Mode, 181
  Remote Desktop Connection client, 183-184
  Remote Desktop MMC client, 183-184
  Remote Desktop Web client, 185-186
  security, 182
  Select Remote Users button, granting Administration account permissions, 183

Remote Desktop MMC client (Remote Desktop for Administration), 183-184

Remote Desktop Web client (Remote Desktop for Administration), 185-186

remote file sharing (WebDAV), 142

remote office logons (Active Directory), 78

Remote Procedure Call settings (Computer Configuration policy sections), 97

remote servers, storing encrypted files, 141-142

Remote tab (System Properties dialog box), 182

remotely administered servers. *See* headless servers

remoting services, 149, 154

Remove Disconnect Option from Shut Down Dialog setting (Terminal Services Group Policy settings), 188

Remove Windows Security Item from Start Menu setting (Terminal Services Group Policy settings), 188

renaming domains and domain controllers, 73

repairing applications, 154

replication, 75, 137-138

replication exclusion lists (DFS), 138

replication from media feature (Active Directory), 78

resources (clusters), 202-203
  adding (Cluster Administrator), 204-205
  failback policies, 206-207
  failover policies, 206
  nodes, specifying (Cluster Administrator), 205
  properties, accessing, 206
  specifying (Cluster Administrator), 205
  transferring (Cluster Administrator), 206

restore option (DHCP), manual database backups, 128

restoring GPOs (Group Policy Objects), 93

Restrict Terminal Services Users to a Single Remote Session setting (Terminal Services Group Policy settings), 188

restricted Group Policies (security), 50

Ring topology (DFS replication), 138

RIS (Remote Installation Services), 26-27

root permissions, rootsec.inf security templates, 217

root trusts, 83

roots, creating (DFS), 138

rootsec.inf security template, 217

routing faxes, 134

RPC Security Policy\Secure Server (Require Security) Group Policy (Terminal Services), 193

RRAS (Routing and Remote Access Service) snap-in, 170-173

RSoP (Resultant Set of Policy) console, 88-91

RSoP (Resultant Set of Policy) feature (Active Directory administrative tools), 70

rss command-line tool, 228

How can we make this index more useful? Email us at indexes@samspublishing.com

S

SAC (Special Administration Console), 224

SAK (Server Appliance Kit), 221

SANs (Storage Area Networks), 139-140

Saprep.exe utility, 221

Saved Queries feature (Active Directory administrative tools), 70

saving
Security Templates snap-in changes, 51
updates (SUS), 234

sc command-line tool, 228

SCA (Security Configuration and Analysis) snap-in, 48-49, 52

scheduling shadow copies (file sharing), 135

schemas, deactivating (Active Directory architectural tools), 74

schtasks command-line tool, 229

screensavers, 32

scripts, administrative scripts (VBScript), 246-249

Scripts settings (Computer Configuration policy sections), 96

Scripts settings (New User Configuration policy sections), 99

Secedit tool, setup security.inf security template, 216

Secedit.exe command-line tool, 48, 55, 218

securedc template, 50

securedc.inf security template, 217

securews template, 50

securews.inf security template, 217

security, 45-46
account policies, 50
auditing, 62
code access security policies, managing, 149, 152-153
cross-forest trusts (Active Directory), 76-77
data encryption (EFS), 56-57
DDNS (Dynamic DNS), 58
DHCP (Dynamic Host Configuration Protocol), 58
DNS (domain name system), 58
EFS (Encrypting File System), 141
encrypted files, storing on remote servers, 141-142
encryption
2048-bit encryption, 166
EFS (Encrypting File System), 141
terminal servers, 193
event log policies, 50
file system policies, 50
firewalls, 169-170
hfnetchk.exe, 48, 56
IIS (Internet Information Services) console, 61-62, 103, 117
insecure password warnings, 18
IPSec (Internet Protocol Security) protocol, 164-165
local policies, 50
Local Security Policy snap-in, 48

maintenance, 63-64
Microsoft security philosophy, 46-47
Microsoft Security Web site, 104
.NET Framework, 157
NetMon (Network Monitor), 59-61
passwords (terminal servers), 193
Registry policies, 50
Remote Desktop for Administration, 182
restricted Group Policies, 50
SCA (Security Configuration and Analysis) snap-in, 48-49, 52
secedit.exe, 48, 55
Security Configuration Manager
    hfnetchk.exe, 48, 56
    Local Security Policy snap-in, 48
    SCA (Security Configuration and Analysis) snap-in, 48-49, 52
    secedit.exe, 48, 55
    Security Settings extension (Group Policy), 48, 55
    Security Templates snap-in, 48-51
security databases, SCA (Security Configuration and Analysis) snap-in, 52
security holes, 57
    DHCP (Dynamic Host Configuration Protocol), 58
    DNS (domain name system), 58
    IIS (Internet Information System), 61
    NetMon (Network Monitor), 59-61
Security Settings extension (Group Policy), 48, 55
security templates, 48-51
Security Templates snap-in, 48-51

smart cards (terminal servers), 194
system service policies, 50
terminal servers, 193-194
Terminal Services, 189
WebDAV (Web Distributed Authoring and Versioning), 142

Security Configuration and Analysis snap-in (MMC), 218

Security Configuration Manager, 48-52, 55-56

security databases, 52-54

security hotfixes. *See* **security updates**

security policies, 152

security principal policies, browsing (RSoP), 71

Security Settings extension (Group Policy), 48, 55

security templates, 52-53, 216-218

Security Templates snap-in, 48-51

security updates (security maintenance), 63-64, 232

Security/Templates subfolder (security templates), 216

Select License agreements, 12-13, 26

select program license keys (Windows Product Activation), 26

Select Remote Users button (Remote Desktop for Administration), 183

selecting multiple objects (Active Directory administrative tools), 70

serial ports, 222

How can we make this index more useful? Email us at indexes@samspublishing.com

server appliances. *See* **headless servers**

server management, 215-220

server-based DFS (distributed file system), 137

servers

application servers, 103

configuring (IIS console), 108

Datacenter Edition

Cluster Service, 8

NLB (Network Load Balancing) support of IPSec/L2TP tunnels, 165

Terminal Server Session Directory, 194-195

updates, 9

DNS (domain name system) servers, 130-132

Enterprise Edition, 7, 165, 194-195

Exchange Server (Cluster Services), 200

GC servers, remote office logons (Active Directory), 78

headless servers, 215, 220-224

licenses, 11

member servers, securews.inf security templates, 217

NAS (Network Access Server), 139

remote servers, storing encrypted files, 141-142

SANs (Storage Area Networks), 139-140

Session Directory servers, 195-196

SQL Servers (Cluster Services), 200

Standard Edition, 6-7

Terminal Server SIDs (Security Identifiers), 217

terminal servers, access permissions, 193

passwords, 193-195

VPN servers (RRAS), 173

Web servers, 10, 200

WINS (Windows Internet Naming Service) server, 126-127

service packs (security maintenance), 63, 232-233

Session Directory, configuring terminal servers, 196

Session Directory Cluster Name setting (Terminal Servers Session Directory Group Policies), 196

Session Directory Server setting (Terminal Servers Session Directory Group Policies), 196

Session Directory servers, 195-196

Set Client Connection Encryption Level Group Policy (Terminal Services), 193

Setup Manager Wizard, 21-22

setup security.inf security template, 216

Setup Wizard, 27-28

setx command-line tool, 229

shadow copies (file sharing), 135-136

Shadow Copies tab, 135

shutdown command-line tool, 229

single node clusters, building, 201

Single property (port ranges), 212

single quorum device clusters, building, 201

single-host addresses. *See* unicast addresses

site-local unicast addresses (IPv6 protocols), 162

smart cards (terminal servers), 194

SMS (Systems Management Server), 233

SMTP (Simple Mail Transport Protocol), 120-122

snap-ins
   IP Security Policies snap-in, 165
   IPSec Monitor snap-in, 166
   Local Security Policy snap-in, 48
   Remote Desktops MMC client (Remote Desktop for Administration), 184
   RRAS (Routing and Remote Access Service) snap-in, 170-173
   SCA (Security Configuration and Analysis) snap-in, 48-49, 52
   Security Templates snap-in, 48-51
   Terminal Services Configuration snap-in, 186
   Terminal Services Manager snap-in, 186

SNMP settings (Computer Configuration policy sections), 98

SOAP (Simple Object Access Protocol) protocol, 155

software
   applications, creating, 146
   deploying
      DFS (distributed file system), 137
      IntelliMirror, 220
   developing, 145-147

headless server software, 223-224

product activation, 13-14

upgrades, Software Assurance program, 13

Software Assurance program, 13

Software Installation section (Group Policy), 84-85

Software Restriction Group Policy (Terminal Services), 194

software restriction policies, 218-220

Software Restriction settings (Computer Configuration policy sections), 94

sound cards, redirecting, 191

SQL Servers (Cluster Services), 200

Standard Folders (Start menu), 41

Standard Edition, 6-7

Start menu, 41-42

storing encrypted files on remote servers, 141-142

stub zones (DNS), 130

subnet masks, 161

superfloppies, 259

Support Information URL, modifying, 84-85

supported upgrade paths (Windows Server 2003), 28-30

SUS (Software Update Services), 233
   Approval Log, 242
   Automatic Updates, 239-240
   installing, 234

How can we make this index more useful? Email us at indexes@samspublishing.com

Monitor Server page, 242
synchronization schedule, configuring, 235-236
updates, approving, 237-238
symmetric key encryption, 141
System Properties dialog box, 182
System Restore, 250
System Restore settings (Computer Configuration policy sections), 96
system root folders, 216
system service policies (security), 50
systeminfo command-line tool, 229

T

tabs
Alternate Configuration tab (DHCP), 128-129
DDNS (Dynamic DNS) tab (DHCP), 128
Debug Logging tab (DNS console), 132
Health tab (Application Pool dialog box), 111
ICMP (Internet Control Message Protocol) tab (ICF Advanced Settings dialog box), 170
Identity tab (Application Pool dialog box), 112
Networking tab (Windows Task Manager), 174
Performance tab (Application Pool dialog box), 111
Precedence tab (RSoP), 88
Publish tab (Computer Management console), 136
Recycling tab (Application Pool dialog box), 110
Remote tab (System Properties dialog box), 182
Security Logging tab (ICF Advanced Settings dialog box), 170
Services tab (ICF Advanced Settings dialog box), 169
Shadow Copies tab, 135
takeown command-line tool, 229
taskkill command-line tool, 229
tasklist command-line tool, 229
TCP ports, 211
TCP/IP, clusters, 203
templates, 48-53, 216-218
Terminal Server IP Address Redirection setting (Terminal Servers Session Directory Group Policies), 197
Terminal Server Session Directory, 180, 194
Terminal Server SIDs (Security Identifiers), 217
terminal servers, 182, 193-196
Terminal Servers Session Directory, 195-197
Terminal Services, 180
client/server data redirection policy settings, 188
configuring, 186-189
Group Policy settings, 187-188

licensing policy settings, 189

RDP (Remote Desktop Protocol) 5.1, 190-194

remote administration (headless servers), 220-224

RPC Security Policy/Secure Server (Require Security) Group Policy, 193

Set Client Encryption Level Group Policy, 193

settings, 189

Software Restriction Group Policy, 194

terminal services client component. See Remote Desktop Connection application

Terminal Services Configuration snap-in, 186

Terminal Services Manager snap-in, 186

Terminal Services settings (Computer Configuration policy sections), 95

Terminal Services settings (New User Configuration policy sections), 98

themes, 32

third-party imaging software installation (Windows Server 2003), 23

tokens, 197

tools

administrative tools (Active Directory), 69-70, 73

architectural tools (Active Directory), 74-75

command-line interface tools, 226, 229

command-line tools, 218, 225-229

Netstat tool, 176

topologies (DFS replication), 138

transferring resources (clusters), 206

troubleshooting Group Policy (RSoP console), 87-88

trusted forests (Group Policies), 83

trusts (Active Directory), 76-77

tutorials

IPv6 protocols, 161-163

MMC (Microsoft Management Console) tutorial Web site, 218

Secedit.exe command-line tool tutorial Web site, 218

typeperf command-line tool, 229

U

UDDI (Universal Description Discover and Integration) registries, 155

UDP ports (NLB clusters), 211

unattended installations, 20-22

unicast addresses, 161-163

unsecure code, 46

unspecified addresses (IPv6 protocol), 162

updates, 232. See also hotfixes

Automatic Updates, 239-242

Datacenter Edition updates, 9

inventorying, hfnetchk.exe, 243-245

SUS (Software Update Services)

approving, 237-238

saving, 234

How can we make this index more useful? Email us at indexes@samspublishing.com

upgrade paths (Windows Server 2003), 28-30

upgrade setups. *See* **winnt32.exe**

upgrades
  IIS (Internet Information Services) consoles, 118-119
  mass upgrades, 30
  operating system upgrades, 27-30
  Software Assurance program, 13
  versus fresh installs, 30

UPnP (Universal Plug and Play), 168

URLs (uniform resource locators), modifying, 84-85

user interface themes, 32

User Profile settings (Computer Configuration policy sections), 96

User Profile settings (New User Configuration policy sections), 99

utilities, Saprep.exe, 221

V

VBScript, 246-249

VDS (Virtual Disk Services), 140

versioning shadow copies (file sharing), 135

View Previous Versions option (File and Folder Tasks), 136

viewing
  application dependencies, 154
  shadow copies (file sharing), 136
  View Previous Versions option (File and Folder Tasks), 136

virtual machines (CLR), 148

viruses, 46

volume license agreements, 14

volume license keys, 14, 23

Volume Shadow Copy Service tasks (clusters), 213

VPN (virtual private network) servers (RRAS), 173

VPN (virtual private network) Web sites, 173

W

waitfor command-line tool, 229

wallpapers, 32

Web development (.NET Framework), 145-147

Web farms, 107

Web gardens, 107

Web servers, 10, 200

Web services, 154
  extensions, creating/configuring (IIS console), 112-114
  legacy COM+ applications, 157
  SOAP (Simple Object Access Protocol) protocol, 155
  WSDL (Web Services Description Language), 155

Web sites
  BackupExec (Veritas), 250
  BrightStor (Computer Associates), 250
  configuring (IIS console), 108-109

IPv6 protocols, 160, 163
Microsoft Security Web site, 104
MMC (Microsoft Management Console) tutorial Web site, 218
remote administration, 221
RRAS (Routing and Remote Access Service), 171
Secedit.exe command-line tool tutorial Web site, 218
UPnP (Universal Plug and Play), 168
VPN, 173

Web-based administration (IIS console), 114-115

WebDAV (Web Distributed Authoring and Versioning), 142

whoamii command-line tool, 229

Windows Backup, 249-252

Windows Clustering (Enterprise Edition), 7

Windows Compatibility Reports, 28

Windows Media Player, burning CDs, 36-37

Windows Media Player settings (New User Configuration policy sections), 98

Windows Messenger settings (Computer Configuration policy sections), 95

Windows Messenger settings (New User Configuration policy sections), 98

Windows Product Activation, 23-26

Windows Server 2003, 149-157
Compressed Folders feature, 33-34
domain functional level (Active Directory), 66
forest functional level (Active Directory), 66
installing
   CD-based installation, 16-19
   network-based installation, 19-20
   third-party imaging software installation, 23
   Windows Product Activation, 23-25
RIS (Remote Installation Services), 26-27

Windows Settings\Security Settings section (Computer Configuration policies), 94

Windows Task Manager, 174

Windows Time Service settings (Computer Configuration policy sections), 97

Windows Update, 233-234

Windows Update settings (Computer Configuration policy sections), 95

Windows Update settings (New User Configuration policy sections), 98

winnt.exe, installing Windows Server 2003, 19

winnt32.exe
operating system upgrades, 27
Windows Server 2003, installing, 20

WINS (Windows Internet Naming Service) server, 126-127, 213

How can we make this index more useful? Email us at indexes@samspublishing.com

Wireless Network (IEEE 802.11) settings (Computer Configuration policy sections), 94

wireless networking, 177

wizards
    CD Writing Wizard, 36
    File Share wizard, 137
    Manage Your Server Wizard, 19
    Setup Manager Wizard, unattended installations, 21-22
    Setup Wizard, operating system upgrades, 27-28

WMI (Windows Management Instrumentation), 246

WMI (Windows Management Instrumentation) command-line tool, 225-227

WMI (Windows Management Instrumentation) filters, 82

WMIC command-line interface tool, 226, 229

worker processes (IIS console), 104

WOW (Windows on Windows) subsystem, 258-259

WSDL (Web Services Description Language), 155

WWW Service Administrator and Monitoring component (IIS console), 106

X – Z

xDSL, 177

zipped folders. *See* **Compressed Folders feature (Windows Server 2003)**

Wouldn't it be great

if the world's leading technical publishers joined forces to deliver their best tech books in a common digital reference platform?

They have. Introducing **InformIT Online Books powered by Safari.**

POWERED BY Safari

- **Specific answers to specific questions.**
  InformIT Online Books' powerful search engine gives you relevance-ranked results in a matter of seconds.

- **Immediate results.**
  With InformIt Online Books, you can select the book you want and view the chapter or section you need immediately.

- **Cut, paste, and annotate.**
  Paste code to save time and eliminate typographical errors. Make notes on the material you find useful and choose whether or not to share them with your workgroup.

- **Customized for your enterprise.**
  Customize a library for you, your department, or your entire organization. You pay only for what you need.

Get your first 14 days **FREE!**

InformIT Online Books is offering its members a 10-book subscription risk free for 14 days. Visit **http://www.informit.com/onlinebooks** for details.

informit.com/onlinebooks

informIT Online Books

Your Guide to Computer Technology

informIT

www.informit.com

Sams has partnered with **InformIT.com** to bring technical information to your desktop. Drawing on Sams authors and reviewers to provide additional information on topics you're interested in, **InformIT.com** has free, in-depth information you won't find anywhere else.

ARTICLES

Keep your edge with thousands of free articles, in-depth features, interviews, and information technology reference recommendations—all written by experts you know and trust.

ONLINE BOOKS

POWERED BY Safari

Answers in an instant from **InformIT Online Books'** 600+ fully searchable online books. Sign up now and get your first 14 days **free**.

CATALOG

Review online sample chapters and author biographies to choose exactly the right book from a selection of more than 5,000 titles.

SAMS www.samspublishing.com